Lita

A Less Traveled R.O.A.D.–

The Reality of Amy Dumas

Lita

A Less Traveled R.O.A.D.–
The Reality of Amy Dumas

Amy Dumas
with Michael Krugman

POCKET BOOKS

New York   London   Toronto   Sydney   Singapore

I dedicate this book to Cody.
Our ten short years together have provided me with a lifetime
of joyful thoughts and invaluable life lessons.
I will always love and cherish you, for my journey,
I believe it would have been different had we not become friends.

INTRODUCTION

BY MATT HARDY

In the world of sports entertainment, it is often hard for an outsider to distinguish the difference between reality and fiction. The boundaries of genuine events and staged acts have become so intermingled and blurred over the years that you never truly know what is actually real. There is one woman that brilliantly emerges out of this hazy subculture just as true as she entered. Her name is Amy Dumas, better known to her multitude of fans as Lita, and she is the living definition of the word *real.*

"What you see is what you get" has never been more appropriate than when speaking about Amy. When she steps into the ring as the bad-ass, never-say-die, alluring punk girl, she's not playing a role, she's just called something different. The WWE named her Lita, but she's just being Amy. I think this is the reason she is one of the most popular female wrestlers of all time—because she's real.

Lita is the girl who's cool enough to hang with anybody. She's the girl who isn't afraid to say or do what she truly believes. She's the girl that all the guys can't stop looking at and they don't even know why. She doesn't imply that she's better than anyone. She suggests that she's just like everyone else. Her authenticity makes her more beautiful than any model or voluptuous diva. Amy has all the qualities that most people wish they had, and that's why they relate so well to her. That's why every night arenas full of fans chant, *"Lita! Lita! Lita!"*

On a personal level, Amy is an incredible person that I am very lucky to know. When I first spent time with her, I quickly saw how unique and special and different she is. It doesn't take long to realize that Amy has unparalleled heart, compassion, and courage. There is never a time when she is afraid to be herself or state what she feels within her soul. She is unprecedented—a role model for both young women and men, as she epitomizes what *independence* really means.

Amy is coming off one of the most difficult battles she has ever fought—returning to the ring after suffering a severely broken neck. No woman in sports entertainment history has ever returned from this serious an injury. She will be the first. Now, nothing can stop her from fulfilling her destiny as one of the top WWE female performers of all time, possibly even the greatest. Nothing can change Amy's aura or presence, not even a career-threatening broken neck. She will always absorb people's emotions and draw them to her.

As you learn about the inspiring journey of Amy Dumas, I'm sure that you will be motivated to live life to the fullest and achieve success against all odds. In order to accomplish those goals, Amy would probably want you to remember these words: Don't try to be something you're not. Forget about patterning yourself after someone else. Be true to yourself. Stay real.

CHAPTER I

Every year, on the morning of April 14, my mom calls at 10:36 to wish me "Happy Birthday."

My parents—Christie and Mike Dumas—got married right out of college. My dad started out as a schoolteacher, but after a few years, he went to work for a company in Fort Lauderdale, Florida, that did wall coverings for various hotels and businesses. When I was little, he would bring home books of wallpaper samples. I really enjoyed looking at the different colors and designs—it was like reading through a book without a story. I would always go and show him which ones I liked best.

Me and my mom.

We moved around a lot because my dad's position in the company kept changing. Every time he moved up, we'd have to relocate. It was all in the same region, but still far enough away to where it was like starting a new life each time.

When I was two, my family moved from Fort Lauderdale to Jacksonville. One of my earliest memories is of riding to the Magic Market on the back of my mom's bicycle. She had a brown ten-speed and I had a yellow bike seat on the back.

From Jacksonville we moved to Winter Park, right outside of Orlando. That's where my brother Billy was born.

Billy is almost five years younger than me—he was born New Year's Eve 1979. To be honest, we were never that close. I was a good-natured easygoing kid, but Billy was always just totally evil tempered. He was a real terror. None of my friends wanted to come to my house to hang out; Billy was that bad.

As a baby, he just cried and cried. My mom would hold him under his arms and say, "I'll make you do a little dance if you don't stop crying." She'd tiptoe him with his little feet touching the table, but he wouldn't stop screaming. His face would be totally purple, bawling at the top of his lungs.

No question about it, Billy was a handful. Even when he got older, he had an incredibly short fuse. I'd be watching TV and Billy would say, "Give me the remote control, stupid." I would be in the middle of a show, so I'd say, "No," then he'd start beating me up. I had to run away so I wouldn't get in trouble—my parents always told me that I was the older sister and I should've known better than to provoke him. I'd go into my room and lock the door and he'd kick the door open. All the locks on every door in the house were broken because of Billy's temper.

Billy and me.

I think moving around so much was what made me such a loner as an adult.

One day when I was seven, we were in the car with my mom, running errands. Billy was whining and crying because he swallowed his gum, so my mom gave him another piece.

"I want another piece of gum, too," I said.

"You don't need another piece," Mom replied. "Now wait in the car, I'll be right back."

That was the last straw. I had had enough. So when we got back home I decided to run away. I went to my room and packed up the TWA Airlines bag my grandfather had given to me. I packed socks, underwear, and a Ziploc bag full of peanuts. Then I wrote my mother a note: *"Mommy, I'm running away because it's not fair that when Billy chews his gum and swallows it and starts crying he gets another piece but if I ask for another piece of gum you say, 'No, you already have one.'"*

My mom was in the shower getting ready for one of the little cocktail parties my parents used to throw. I took my bag and walked to the end of the first block of the cul de sac where we lived, which was as far as I was allowed to ride my bike without supervision. I got brave and walked another block, to the intersection of the main street, which was a pretty big four-lane street. When I got there I just stood on the corner for a few minutes. *I don't know where I'm going,* I thought, *so I probably should go back before I get in trouble.*

When I got home, my mom was getting dressed and I told her that I ran away. I wasn't even gone long enough for her to notice! My note was still sitting right there where I'd left it. Of course, my mom felt really bad. We sat and talked for a good while. My mom still has the note.

Because of my dad's job, I kept getting uprooted from my schools and my friends. I think moving around so much was what made me such a loner as an adult. I was never miserable about moving, I just accepted it.

I loved hearing her stories.
I always thought that was
a great way to deal with life—she had
a good time early in
life which she enjoyed
to the fullest.

This is how it is, I thought. *You have to take care of yourself because you never know if your friends are going be there the next day.*

I was in second grade when we moved from Winter Park to Deerfield Beach, in South Florida. Deerfield Beach is like the not-so-rich town in between all the rich towns around there, like the multimillion-dollar mansions in Boca Raton a couple miles south.

I was pretty much okay with it at first, but then reality hit. I realized that everything I was used to was not going be there anymore. I said to my mom, "Could we at least take our house with us?" I'd seen trailers on the highways, and thought we could just move the house.

We were in Deerfield for a pretty long time, all the way though sixth grade. That house is where I have my best childhood memories. It wasn't a big house, but it was nice. My father was doing pretty well at work, so it wasn't a real stressful time for us, financially speaking. We got a hot tub and my mom got a new convertible.

Those were good times. My parents were getting along really well in those days. My parents were both big tennis nuts, so we'd go to the swim and tennis clubs and to keep me busy I'd be at the pool while they would play tennis. That's how I got into being on the swim team.

My favorite Grandma, my dad's mother, had a condo in Pompano, which is just south of Deerfield Beach. We called her "Maga." That came from one of my older cousins. When he first started learning how to talk, all his words came out kind of backwards. So instead of "Grandma," he said "Maga." And it stuck.

When my parents went on little weekend trips, playing in tennis tournaments, Maga would come stay with us. I just loved hanging around her.

Maga was just a really neat lady. She would tell me stories, drinking her Schaeffer beer and smoking her long brown More cigarettes. She talked

My dad's mom, "Maga."

about what a good guy my grandfather was. Like my dad, his role in the family was to discipline the kids and bring home the money. He came from a fairly affluent family. He was in the military and was killed in the Korean War.

That was Maga's heyday. She had a good husband from a well-respected family, she had good kids, she went to fancy parties. Her life was relatively perfect. But after my grandfather died, she had to become the fighting single mom. It was a hard life, raising kids on her own without much money. She pinched pennies and always did the best she could.

In a lot of ways, she lived through her memories of the good old days. I loved hearing her stories. I always thought that was a great way to deal with life—she had a good time early in life which she enjoyed to the fullest. She accepted that those days had ended. Maga rolled with the punches and made the most of her situation at the time, whatever it was. She never acted depressed, at least she never did in front of me.

She had a great attitude towards life, she was very open-minded and always supportive. She would never put me down or say that any idea I had was stupid. Parents have to question you—"Are you sure you don't want to go to college?"—but because she was my grandmother, she didn't have to.

I always enjoyed spending time with Maga. When my parents would go away for the weekend, Billy and I would either stay with her or she'd come stay with us. Maga had an old car and for some reason, there was no backseat. It was just carpet and the wheel wells. My brother and I would be back there and when Maga would flick her cigarettes out the window, they'd always come back in through the back window. "Quit doing that, Maga," I'd say. "You're burning me!"

"No, I'm not," she'd reply. "I threw it out the window."

But every time she flicked her cigarette, it would always come right back in.

Eventually my mom gave her our old family car. We were doing pretty well and when Mom bought a '84 Mustang GT convertible, she gave Maga our Impala. She wanted to make sure that we had seatbelts on when Maga carted us around.

In seventh grade, my family moved to Atlanta, which really broke Maga's heart. My parents made me tell her the news over Thanksgiving dinner. I guess they knew she wouldn't be happy about it and they wanted me to tell her in order to soften the blow. They told me to say, "The good news is my dad got a promotion, but now we have to move to Atlanta."

Of course I didn't say it like they told me to. I said, "Guess what, Maga. Dad got a promotion."

"Oh that's great," she said. "Congratulations, Michael, I'm real proud of you." She was so happy, and then I said, "But we have to move to Atlanta," and Maga started crying. It was real sad.

We moved to Marietta, Georgia, which is maybe twenty-five minutes north of Atlanta. We lived in a little development called Chimney Lakes. Our house there was pretty big. That's when we started running into financial problems. I think my parents were a little overzealous when they bought it.

It was pretty nice. Chimney Lakes had a neighborhood pool and of course I was on the swim team. That was the one constant in my childhood—no matter where we went, I was on the swim team.

Because I started swimming at an early age, I was always pretty good. But it wasn't until I got to Atlanta that I started swimming year-round. The team I was on was called Swim Atlanta and they were very serious people—the guys would shave their whole bodies, and some people were training for the Olympics.

I would go there after school and swim, sometimes four nights a week. Once a month, the team would participate in a swim meet. They were mostly in the same region, but sometimes we'd travel three or four hours away from Atlanta. They were big events, two or three days long, especially compared to the neighborhood meets, which would usually take all of two hours.

I played other sports in addition to swimming, like soccer and softball, but swimming was definitely what I was best at. I was never the top swimmer on any team, but I was good. My stroke was the butterfly, which a lot of swimmers hate doing, so therefore I was a valuable asset, especially on relay races which start off with the butterfly.

The coach would try to get me excited—"Amy, we really need you to get us started, you're the lead swimmer going into the race and the team needs you!"—but those type of talks never really hyped me up. *I'll swim the butterfly as best I can*, I thought. *Obviously I can't do it any better than I can do it, so why are you telling me this? I'm not going to try any harder because you gave me this pep talk.*

I was always really into my times. For example, 32.4 seconds was a good time for a 50-yard race. I didn't care if I got first place, but if I did 32.6, I'd be really mad at myself. The truth is, I've always been more in competition with myself than anyone else. I was much more interested in my personal best than how the team did. I think that's one of the things that led me to wrestling—it's very much a sport for loners.

Finding that "special pink rock."

My Most Vivid Memories of Childhood

1. *Catching lightning bugs at my grandparents' house in St. Louis. I'd put them in mayonnaise jars with holes in the lid that I made with an ice pick.*

2. *Collecting little snails after it rained in Winter Park. I named them all "Shirley."*

3. *Walking along the railroad tracks with my dad and finding "special pink rocks" to bring back home.*

4. *I had an imaginary friend named "Makey." We drew together with crayons on the hardwood floor under my bed—which my mom discovered when we moved from Jacksonville to Winter Park.*

5. *My parents had a dinner party the night before my brother and I were having our portrait photographed. I got bored and went into my parents' room and cut off a big chunk of hair with my mom's sewing scissors. The next day, I had a cute little bowl cut for the pictures!*

6. *Spending weekends with my grandmother. I loved sitting in her parrot chair, which I thought was just the coolest.*

7. *I was ten-years-old when* **Pee Wee's Big Adventure** *came out. I decided to imitate the bicycle scene and ended up the same way Pee Wee did—scraped hands and knees! If you don't know what I'm talking about, put this book down and go rent the movie. It's my all-time favorite!*

8. *Hanging from the top of my swing set, falling, and knocking my tooth out on the swing below.*

9. *They put up a new jungle gym in the kindergarten playground. I got pushed off and cracked my head on the concrete ring at the base of the fireman's pole. That was the only time I ever got stitches . . . until I got to WWE!*

10. *I was supposed to clean my room on weekend chore days, but I'd always procrastinate and play until I heard my mom coming in her "mad shoes"—she wore flip-flops while doing chores, so I could always hear her coming towards my room to bust me!*

CHAPTER 2

My relationship with my father wasn't a very close one. In a way, I never felt like I really knew my dad. He was just *there*.

We had a rare heart-to-heart when I was thirteen and he explained that he was being a dad in the way that his dad taught him. "The man of the family's role," he said, "as far as his involvement with the children, is to discipline them and to bring home the money. I'll shoot hoops with you, and show you how to change the oil on your car, but other than that. . . ."

A little father and daughter bonding.

That one sentence told me so much about his personality. Not that it makes it right, but it showed me where his head was. His attitude was very old school, "I just worked all day and now I'm going to watch the game or mow the lawn or whatever." Spending time with his kids was not one of his top priorities.

One time I was waiting for my mom to pick me up after swim practice. I stood there, waiting and waiting, and nobody showed up to get me. Finally I got a quarter and called home, "Mom, are you not going to come and get me?"

She said, "I'm cooking dinner, so I sent your father."

"Well, he hasn't shown up," I said. "I'm the only kid here."

As we talked, my dad walked in the door. "Michael," my mom said. "Where's Amy?"

"I drove by," he said, "and she wasn't there. I just figured she got a ride home with someone else."

He just drove by the swim practice, and when he didn't see me, he just kept going. He didn't even put on the brakes. For some guys, being a dad is second nature, and for other guys, it just isn't. I think my dad didn't entirely have the fatherhood instinct. He just didn't get it.

Even though I had no trouble making friends, I was always a bit of a loner. Before we moved to Georgia, I attended sixth grade at Deerfield Beach Middle School. It was the coolest school—the student body there was the most mixed of any school I went to.

I felt very comfortable there. There was a feeling that everybody got along. It didn't feel cliquey at all and I hung out with all types of people. At lunch there would be people doing the double Dutch jump ropes, there would be one ghetto blaster playing rap and then across the yard there'd be another one playing metal. I was always a floater, hanging out

with the metalheads, then walking over to the other group, asking, "Hey, what are you listening to?"

I basically hung out with whoever I felt like hanging out with. At that point I didn't have an established group of my own, but even later, when I mostly hung out with the punk rockers and the skaters, I was still a floater.

After we moved to Atlanta, I did seventh grade at Mayberry Middle School. That place was very different from what I was used to. Instead of homerooms, we had *pods*. It was the craziest thing—"Okay, Amy, you're going to be in Pod A."

Pods? What the hell is a pod?

Seventh grade turned out to be a very transitional year for me. I spent a lot of time trying to fit in, and not feeling like I did. It wasn't like I was some horrible outcast, but I'd never had to try to make friends before. I was blatantly trying to be friends with the popular kids, doing things like trying out for cheerleading. It's not that I had aspirations of being a cheerleader or even thought it was cool but it seemed to be what people were doing, so I thought, *Well, I just moved here so I'll go with it, give it a shot.*

Of course, by the end of the tryouts, I was so glad that I didn't get picked. The girl standing next to me was so super-nervous. She stood there with her arms straight and this glued-on Vaseline smile. I laughed at her, saying, "Chill out, man!" *If that's what they want,* I thought, *I hope they don't pick me because that girl looks pretty miserable right there.*

It wasn't that I was looking to find the right clique. It was more like I was searching for my own identity through other people, which is never the way to go.

Then I met Kerry Burke and just like that, I found my place in the universe.

Kerry was a year ahead of me, so I didn't interact with her much at school. She lived in my neighborhood, so we both rode the bus home together. I thought Kerry was so cool—her hair was frosted black and white, all spiky like a peacock on top.

She must've seen something in me, because we started chatting. One day we were on the bus and she gave me some tapes. "Here's a bunch of music I listen to," she said. "Listen to it."

Before Kerry, I pretty much just listened to what was on the radio. The first concert I ever went to was Julian Lennon—his "Live In '85" tour. I went with my mom. We had fun, but it didn't exactly change my life.

Now, all of a sudden, a whole new world of music that I didn't even know existed opened up to me. Kerry was big into the Cure—that was her favorite band, but she also knew a lot about hardcore punk rock and bands like the Circle Jerks, the Dead Kennedys, D.I., Black Flag, and 7 Seconds. *Whoa!* I thought. *I've never heard anything like this before and it's really freaking cool!*

Before I met Kerry, I was just your basic normal kid. I dressed the same as all the other kids. These days, kids dress just like adults, which is *so* disturbing. You see eight year olds wearing little belly shirts and hip-hugger pants. It's kind of funny—Terri Runnels comes in to work wearing all these cute outfits. The girls in the locker room ask her about her clothes and she says, "Oh I got it in the children's department!"

Terri's so small, and of course those clothes look a lot different with her boobs hanging out of them, but still! If I had a daughter, I wouldn't want her dressing like that.

Anyway, it wasn't long before my wardrobe began reflecting my interest in punk rock. I started wearing things like guys' white V-neck T-shirts and Doc Marten boots. I didn't do the retro thing, the stereotypical old-time punk rock with the spikes and the leather. It was more of a skater look—ripped-up baggy clothes and flannel shirts. Of course, it was still a look that would throw off your more conservative, suburban parents.

My last year of middle school, Kerry took me to my very first punk rock show—7 Seconds and the Circle Jerks. It was one of the last shows ever held at the Metroplex in Atlanta, which was a legendary venue for punk shows.

It was the summer before eighth grade. I was still so young, and even though it was an early show and we would be home by midnight, I still had to beg for my mom's permission, "Please, please, please, I really want to go!"

My mom was always cool. Her attitude was *Make sure you get good grades and I'll give you the freedom to explore*—just as long as the cops didn't bring me home. We always had a very open line of communication. Looking back, I don't know how intentional it was, but she always made me feel comfortable around her. If I needed to ask her a personal question or go to her about something private, I always could.

It was an all-ages show, which was cool because I was only thirteen. The whole experience was incredible. We stood in line, waiting for the doors to open, and when we got in there, I was blown away. It was that same feeling like when I realized I wanted to be a wrestler, like, *Holy shit, this is cool!*

Everything about it was amazing—the people, the music, the atmosphere. The Metroplex was small and super-dark, there were no seats. It was like a congregation of all these freaks, but freaks *in a good way.*

It was the first time I ever encountered slam dancing and I thought that was just so cool. Back then, slam dancing was very much about community.

It was like punk rock was our secret, and no one could ever know what it was like unless you were there.

It was a place where you could feel like you were part of something, as well as let out any and all of your aggressions.

It was such a positive vibe. There I was, this little girl, in the middle of the pit and I felt completely safe. I "doubled" with this other girl, which is where you lock arms—like square dancing—and go into the pit together. Then you just run around and bump into each other and have fun. If you went down, somebody picked you up. You would barely hit the ground before somebody picked you back up. You might end up with a couple of bruises on your feet from people stepping on them, but other than that, the pit was totally harmless.

People you'd never met would launch you up on top of the crowd, hold you there, then let you back down, safe and sound. Ten minutes later, you'd bump into them in the pit and say, "Thanks, man." You didn't know their names or anything, but they had your back for that hour and a half. Everybody was family when they were in the pit and then when the show was over, we all went back into anonymity again.

The whole thing was kind of magical. There was a feeling of *We're so lucky because we know about the show and nobody else does.* It was like punk rock was our secret, and no one could ever know what it was like unless you were there.

That night was an epiphany for me. For the first time in my life I knew, *This is where I belong.*

CHAPTER 3

The hardcore punk community was like a family. The group that I hung out with was comprised of all different types. There were skinheads, there were skaters, there were straight edge punk rockers. Basically, they all hung out together because they were different. They weren't jocks or preps or nerds. A lot of them were real screw-ups, some of them were real mean and wanted to drop out of school and drink and do drugs. I didn't do any of that but yet I still was drawn to them. I was drawn to the lifestyle and the look, even though I had little in common with any of those people.

I got into bands like Big Drill Car and Samiam, plus big-time Berkeley bands like Schlong. I really loved all the bands on Lookout Records, like Operation Ivy—whose members later formed Rancid. And of course, I really loved the Dead Kennedys.

All these bands had their addresses on the back of their seven inches. I'd write to them and occasionally I'd get letters back. For every three letters I'd write, I'd get one back, but I always got a kick out of that. It wouldn't be much more than three sentences: *"Dear Amy, Thanks for writing. We'll be in Atlanta on these dates . . ."*

Looking back, most of these bands were really just a bunch of kids in a garage, but to me, they were a legitimate big-time band because they had a record out.

JAWBREAKER

with: **saltmaker**

when: june 11. $5
where: SOMBER REPTILE 9:

Some of my flyers did manage to escape my dad.

My mom was a little freaked out. "Why are these people writing you? Why are they calling you?" She knew I wasn't doing drugs or drinking or anything, but at the same time, I think she thought my involvement in the punk scene had the potential to get me into trouble. To be fair, though, she was mostly pretty cool with it. My friends coming over with pierced noses and dyed hair, all my punk clothes, none of that ever threw her.

My dad, on the other hand, just didn't get it at all. He would ask why I was wearing a specific shirt and what did it mean? He definitely would've preferred if I dressed in the preppy clothes that he wore.

Another example of my father not getting me—my room was completely covered, floor to ceiling, with punk rock fliers. My dad hated it, probably because it wasn't wallpaper.

One of my favorite local bands at the time was called Something. They had a decent following, they'd get two or three hundred people at their shows. I was going to paint one of the walls in my room green, then a friend of mine was going to do their logo with a Sharpie. I took down all my fliers so that I could rearrange them around this big Something logo. Those fliers were so important, they meant everything in the world to me, so I stacked them in a very neat pile on my floor.

Fifteen

AUG. 28

NINE P.M.
@ BLUE CHAIR
1625 E. 7TH AVE.
YBOR CITY
(813) 247-1300

PAUL CAGLIONI 7/6/95

Well, it turned out that that same day was trash day. My dad went around the house, emptying all the trash cans, and when he went in my room to get my trash, he picked up all my fliers and threw them away.

I was devastated, to say the least. Those fliers were my life! I was crushed to the point that I hated him. I wanted to kill him! I thought he was the most evil person alive! It took a lot to rile me up; that broke me. "I hate you Dad," I said through my tears. "I'll never forgive you!"

If he had said, "I'm your father, don't talk to me like that," and then apologized, it would have been one thing, but he just didn't get it. "What's the big deal?" he said. "It was thirty pieces of paper, who cares?"

That made me even angrier and more upset with him. I didn't speak to him for weeks, which aggravated him to no end. He simply didn't get me.

I can understand him being the macho dad, thinking, *I'm not going to back down to my fifteen year old.* But he could've said, "I really don't get why you're so angry, because to me those fliers were just crinkled-up pieces of paper. But I can see that it upset you, so I'm sorry."

To this day, thinking about that makes me sick. I've never been much of a pack rat, but I really wish I still had those fliers.

Of all the punk bands I listened to, the one I was most drawn to was 7 Seconds. There was something about them that stuck out immediately. They had it all—catchy melodies, sing-along choruses, and a powerful message of positivity that instantly struck a chord in me. The average person would probally hear a 7 Seconds song and say, "This is nothing but screaming and yelling—I can't understand one word of this!" But I studied those lyric sheets and sang along with every word.

7 Seconds just had this very positive force—that was actually the name of their label, "Positive Force." They showed me that you could be straight and clean and a good person and still be cool. I was never a serious straight-edger—the punk philosophy that Ian Mackaye of Minor Threat

FRIDAY · FEB. 10

7 SECONDS

ALL AGES

WITH

AFTER WORDS

WRECK

EARLY SHOW

and Fugazi summed up with the lyric, *"Don't drink/Don't smoke/Don't f***"*—but I definitely felt a real connection to that attitude. Some people referred to positive force punks as "green punks," because while we were punk rockers, we were like hippies in terms of our "Can't we all just get along?" attitude. Instead of breaking someone's window if you don't like what they do, why not go up and introduce yourself and say, "Hey man, I think it's kind of uncool what you're doing. It's just my opinion, it's food for thought." That was the whole mentality.

The attitude was, "I don't hate you for anything you do, just as long as you're not harming another human being. You don't have to be exactly like me for me to like you." That is my philosophy to this day and I attribute that back to 7 Seconds.

I wonder how much of that was in me to start with. There's no question that they really affected me, but as I got older, I realized I was probably drawn to them because I already felt the same way.

I have so many great memories of 7 Seconds shows. One night they played at the Masquerade in Atlanta, and Kevin Seconds was squatting down, doing one of his monologues. I was in the front row, and as he talked, Kevin reached out and held my hand. It was probably only for five seconds, but it seemed like a minute and a half. I was just so filled with love for him—not like I wanted to have sex with him, it wasn't that kind of feeling. It was like, he is so cool and smart and honest. It's a cliché, but Kevin spoke the things I felt inside. At the same time, it was like I didn't know I was feeling these things until he spoke them. You know? That's how cool he was.

Another thing that made 7 Seconds stand out was that they weren't just for boys. Whenever I saw them, there were always girls in the pit.

Punk was a big boys club in a lot of ways. Basically, there were punk rock guys and new wave girls and they all hung out together. But I was a punk rock girl! I dressed like a punk rock guy—I wore eight-hole Doc Martens oxbloods with double-stripe knee socks, cutoff shorts, and a band shirt with a flannel over it. In the summer I'd take the flannel off and tie it around my waist. Mostly my T-shirts were 7 Seconds shirts—I must've had eight different 7 Seconds shirts—but I also occasionally wore other bands, like Fugazi.

That's pretty much what I wore all through high school. I was the only person that dressed like that. My punk rock girlfriends wore little skirts with fishnets and boots, but that look wasn't for me.

From what I gathered, 7 Seconds were also pretty cool people. There's nothing worse than when you idolize somebody and when you meet them, they're dicks. That's such a crusher.

One of the great things about punk rock was that the barrier between rock star and the fans crumbled. The bands would actually speak to the people in their audience. Everyone would get together after the show and hang around the van and talk all night.

The first time I met any of the band was at the Wreck Room, maybe six months after that first show at the Metroplex. I met the drummer, Troy Mowat, after their set. I knew that it wasn't cool to be starstruck, so I just said, "Hey, great show tonight. Drive safe, see you next time."

My friend Eric Snoddy—we called him Noodlehead, because he had long cool-ass dreads—knew everybody on the Atlanta punk scene. He was maybe thirty years old when I was fifteen—it's hard to tell how old people are at that age—but he was just one of those people that was always there. He bounced at every club in town, he managed a bunch of local bands and knew all the touring bands. Ask any scenester in Atlanta, "Do you know Eric Snoddy?" and they'll say "Oh yeah!"

Eric was always really nice to me. When bands I liked would play eighteen-and-over shows, he would always get me in. One night after a 7 Seconds show, Eric came over to me and said, "C'mon, I'll bring you back and you can meet the band."

I was introduced to Kevin Seconds, and then I started talking to Troy. I was so psyched—I was wearing a 7 Seconds shirt, boxers with long underwear, knee socks, and my boots. When I got to the back, Troy was wearing his 7 Seconds shirt and boxers—we were basically wearing the same outfit!

Troy told me that the band had the next day off and that the Travel Lodge they were staying at was offering free coupons to the Six Flags Over Atlanta amusement park.

"We're all thinking about going there," he said. "Do you want to come with us?"

Of course I did! But I played it cool. "Yeah," I said. "Sure. Just call me, here's my number."

I didn't think they'd really call. I went home and got into my bed and at 3:33 A.M.—I'll never forget that—the phone rang.

Oh shit! I thought and picked up the phone. "Hello?"

"Is Amy there?"

"This is Amy . . ."

All of a sudden, my mom picked up the phone. "Amy, who's calling so late?"

I just kept talking, like she wasn't on the line. "Oh, hey Troy. What's going on?"

My mom started getting louder, "Amy, get off the phone!"

"I'm sorry," Troy said, "I didn't know you still lived at home."

"Don't worry about it," I said, still playing it cool. I kept talking, trying to ignore her, but my mom was getting angrier and angrier. "Amy, I am serious! Get off the phone now!"

I sat there thinking, *This is not happening!* Finally she hung up. "Sorry about that," I said. "So are you going to go to Six Flags?"

As I was talking, I heard footsteps walking down the hall—boom, boom, boom! My door opened up and my mom was pissed!

"Um, can you just hold on one second?"

I put the phone to my chest. "Mom! It's the drummer from 7 Seconds! Please!"

"I don't care who it is! You hang up that phone right now."

I put the phone back to my ear and Troy totally understood what was going on. "Do you want me to call you tomorrow?"

"Yeah, that'd be great," I said. "Talk to you later."

Oh my God, that was so embarrassing! My mom was just being protective. She didn't want guys in bands calling her fifteen-year-old daughter, especially at three-thirty in the morning.

Troy was a good guy. He called back and asked me to drive a bunch of them to Six Flags. But I was only fifteen—I didn't have a car yet! My one friend who was old enough to drive, she had already left for summer school. This was back before cell phones, so I couldn't call her and say, "Forget school. We're going to Six Flags with 7 Seconds."

I really didn't want to have to admit that I was fifteen, so I lied to Troy, "Sorry, man, but my car won't start."

That was a big disappointment. Years later, I met Troy again at the Black Cat in Washington, DC.

"I'm sure you won't remember this," I said, and told him the story.

He was pretty amused. "Wow, I think I *do* remember that!"

At the time I was sure he was just being nice and didn't really remember, but when I became a WWE wrestler, I discovered that you do remember cute stories about your experiences with the fans.

Especially when they're a little ridiculous or embarrassing.

CHAPTER 4

Not long after I discovered punk rock was when I first began going out with boys. I'd always hung out with boys, but not in any romantic dating kind of way.

My first official date was in eighth grade—his name was Mike Terrebeki, and he was one of the skate kids that hung out in Kerry Burke's basement. We went to see *Bill & Ted's Excellent Adventure* at the local movie theater. After the movie, his mom drove us home. We were in the back seat and Mike whispered something to his mom as we pulled into the cul de sac towards where I lived. We got to my house and Mike said, "I'll walk you to the door."

"No, it's cool," I said. "See you later."

"Really, I'll walk you."

We got to my door and he kissed me. I was so surprised! It hadn't even occurred to me. I knew we were going on a date, but I didn't even think in terms of doing anything like kissing.

Mike later told me that he had whispered to his mom that she should drive around the cul de sac while he made his move! All I remember was worrying that my mom would see us through the window. I was so majorly embarrassed!

My first real boyfriend was Jake Harvey. He also lived in Chimney Lakes and was part of my little clique of friends. We began dating the summer before I started at Lassiter High School.

Jake was also a skater boy. He was really cute—he had blond hair, which he wore in a total skater cut, with just a little hair over his eyes. He was kind of clean-cut. He'd wear baggy jeans with a plaid shirt instead of a ripped up punk rock T-shirt.

He was fifteen—almost two years older than me—and he had a scooter, which was very cool, because Chimney Lakes was pretty big, probably two miles from one side of the neighborhood to the other. Jake would come pick me up on his scooter, then we'd go back to his house on the other side of the neighborhood.

Amy Klug, my best friend all through high school, went out with Jake's best friend, Mark Thompson, so the four of us double-dated all the time. We went to the movies, we went to concerts, we pretty much hung out together constantly.

Our main hangout was Mark's basement. The main reason we didn't spend a lot of time at my house was my crazy brother Billy. He actually had a heel catchphrase that he'd yell over and over as he hit me: "You're stupid and you're ugly and you have no friends!"

I'd be watching TV and he'd come into the room, yelling, "Give me the remote control!"

"After the show I'm watching."

"You're stupid and you're ugly and you have no friends!"

He'd go crazy and start beating me up. I'd shove him off and run away into my room. But once he was riled up, there was no calming him down. *"You're stupid and you're ugly and you have no friends!"*

He would yell at the top of his lungs, his face would turn as red as can be.

Billy would get so mad at me for the slightest reason. On the rare occasions that my friends would be all over, he'd come jumping out from the hallway with a plastic bat or his toy metal detector and hit me over the head as hard as he could.

My friends would try to do something to stop him, but I'd say, "Leave him alone, we'll get in trouble!"

"But he's hitting you!"

"I know," I'd say. "I'm older and I'm supposed to know better than to provoke him."

That confused my friends to no end. "But he's hitting you! That's crazy!"

I never lifted a finger to prevent Billy from beating on me. I actually believed what my mom had said, that I was somehow inciting him. I'd shout, *"Ow!* Stop it, Billy!"

"Shut up!" he'd scream. *"You're stupid, you're ugly and you have no friends!"*

Billy's mellowed out over the years—he attends Marquette University and is doing pretty well. But we weren't close as kids and we're not close as adults. It's kind of sad, I guess, but what can you do?

Anyway, Jake and Mark had a little band, called Wrong Answer Zoo Breath. The two of them were like Frick and Frack, and Mark was definitely the crazier of the two. Jake was actually a little more conservative than even I was. He was afraid to get in trouble, not that we ever really did anything all that wrong. We never did anything that was bad or dangerous, but occasionally we would lie to my mom about where we were going, things like that. Jake would always be the one to say, "We probably shouldn't be doing this."

When the four of us went out, Jake was always the best behaved member of the group. If we went to the movies and threw popcorn at the screen, Jake would be the one to say, "*Shhhh!* The attendant is going to get mad!" He was like the voice of reason, which isn't a bad thing for a bunch of kids to have around.

Jake was my first real boyfriend, my first do-everything boyfriend. We went out for a year and a half. All things considered, that's pretty long for a high school relationship.

One day when I was a freshman, a girlfriend and I were browsing at the pet store in the shopping center right next to my neighborhood. It was around Easter, and they were selling little baby ducks. I guess the idea was you would give them to your kid for Easter, they could play with them for the day, then throw them into the pond.

I just thought they were so cute! They were these puffs of tiny little blonde fuzzy fur! We decided to pool our money and buy a couple of the baby ducks.

The deal was, I'd name one and my friend would name the other. I immediately named mine "Kevin," after the singer in 7 Seconds. My friend tried to name hers after some poet. It was a long, unwieldy name, so I said, "Forget that—his name is Troy," after the drummer in 7 Seconds.

At first we kept them in a laundry basket in my house, but as they got bigger, we brought them outside. I got a baby pool and they would swim in there. They were kind of clumsy and they'd just flop around in the water.

They weren't fully grown ducks by this time. They had just started growing their adult feathers, so they weren't babies either—they were teenagers. They'd sleep outside my window and every morning when I woke up, I'd make duck noises and they'd respond, "Quack, quack, quack."

Jake had turned sixteen and gotten his license, so he'd pick me up for school everyday. Before he showed up, I'd go out and feed the ducks. Then I'd turn the garden hose on them and watch them play in the water. When Jake got there, I'd walk up my driveway and Kevin and Troy would follow me, just like I was their mama. When I got in the car, they'd turn around and walk back down to the backyard.

My neighbors' dog was always after the ducks. One time it got Kevin by the leg. I chased the dog away, but Kevin's leg was broken, It was so sad, he had a little limp and couldn't get in the baby pool by himself anymore.

The dog kept getting over the fence to hassle the ducks. One day I was inside my room and I could hear them outside quacking. It sounded like trouble so I ran out there—Kevin was in the dog's mouth, and Troy was pecking at the dog's paw, trying to stick up for his brother. Fortunately, I got out there just in time to make the dog spit Kevin out. His wing had a little puncture on it, but he was still alive.

I went next door and said, "I've got these ducks on my property. Can you make sure your dog stays on your side of the fence?"

"My dog never leaves our backyard," my neighbor said. "It must be a wolf or a fox or something that's been attacking your ducks."

"Look," I said, "I can see your dog in your backyard and I'm telling you I saw that same dog's mouth attached to my duck's leg. Please try to keep him locked up, okay?"

Well, one morning I did my usual "Quack quack" out the window, but there was no response. I was running late—as I always was—so I didn't think too much about it, I just got in the shower. When I got to the kitchen to get my breakfast, my mom had a sad look on her face. "I'm sorry, honey," she said, "but the dog got the ducks."

She said it looked like the dog broke their necks. They weren't too badly beaten up and their little bodies were right next to each other.

I was so upset! My mom was being real sweet, saying things like, "They were good ducks."

Then she told me that my father wanted to wake me up when he found them. Not because he knew it was going to upset me—he wanted me to clean up all the feathers so the yard wasn't a mess. That was his mentality—he just wasn't an especially sensitive father.

My mom put Kevin and Troy in a plastic garbage bag, and I had to bury them. I was so crushed, I couldn't lift the bag knowing they were in there. It freaked me out. I just couldn't do it. So I dug a hole and then Jake picked up the bag and put them in. It was just awful.

Not long after that, I decided to get replacement ducks. I named them Jeff and Aaron—after Jeff Ott and Aaron Cometbus, the singer and drummer of one of my other favorite bands, Crimpshine. Unfortunately, Jeff and Aaron—the ducks, that is—weren't nearly as cool as Kevin and Troy were. They were more like wild animals. They didn't come to me, they didn't like being picked up. They were just ducks.

Also, I think the novelty of the whole duck thing had worn off for me. I probably didn't pay as much attention to them as I had to Kevin and Troy. Maybe I didn't give Jeff and Aaron a fighting chance. I was like, "Come on, do your duck tricks," and when they didn't do anything, I said "Oh, screw you, then," and put them in the pond.

CHAPTER 5

School was always easy for me. I always had good grades, mostly Bs, even though I rarely opened a book. I'd start papers the night before, and get them done five minutes before the bus came to pick me up. If I'd studied for more than half a second, I would've easily gotten all As.

My main extracurricular activity in high school was the swim team. I didn't take it too seriously. The only reason I was on the swim team was because it was something I'd done my whole life. It was fun, but it wasn't as big a deal for me as it was for the rest of the kids on the team. I'd go to swim practice after school three times a week, but on the other days I'd meet up with my friends and skate in the Kroger's parking lot until we got kicked out.

The truth is, I coasted through high school. The thing that I was most interested in was seeing bands, which I did all the time. As time went on, my musical spectrum got much wider. I started getting into bands like the Descendents and Fugazi and Dag Nasty.

It's the same for most kids that are really into music—you start out listening to the first bands you're introduced to, and from there you figure out how to find more bands that are cool. *Maximumrocknroll* magazine was my bible. I'd scour the record reviews to see who was supposed to be any good, then I'd order their record.

Until I got into wrestling, I was a major band geek. I was the kid who'd know things like, "This guy played guitar on one song with this band and then he started a new band and they put out a split single on this obscure label . . ."

I loved going to gigs and seeing bands. Going to punk clubs was very different from most people's understanding of a rock concert—the gigs were dark little spaces, with no rows of seats, no fancy lighting setups. In fact, sometimes there wasn't even a stage! It was essentially a bunch of people hanging out with a band. Punk gigs were a very interactive experience. The bands and the audience would often talk back and forth between songs. It was really intimate and exciting.

One memorable night was when I saw Green Day at the Existentialist Church in Atlanta, just outside of the Little Five Points section of town. There were maybe forty or fifty people there—no one knew who Green Day were yet, they had released a couple of 7-inches on Lookout! and were out on their very first tour. They were good guys—they were just a year older than me, telling fart jokes and doing stupid shit. They fit right in with my whole group of friends.

One of Green Day's roadies was a guy named Lucky, who's since died of a heroin overdose. In addition to being a roadie, Lucky was the guy who tattooed people with the Fifteen Dot—it was one dot of ink, dotted into the skin fifteen times, representing the Lookout! band, Fifteen. Everybody in Fifteen had one, everybody in Operation Ivy and Green Day had one, along with various people around the country who were invited to be part of the circle. When Lucky asked me if I'd like a Fifteen Dot, I said "Hell, yeah!"—I definitely wanted to be included in that community. He broke out his metal lunch box, took out some needles, some rubbing alcohol, and some india ink and gave me my very first tattoo—it basically looks like a blue mole on my left forearm.

Of course I would've loved to have gotten a real tattoo, but you had to

He broke out his metal lunch box, took out some needles, some rubbing alcohol, and some india ink and gave me my very first tattoo—it basically looks like a blue mole on my left forearm.

be eighteen to do that. The next best thing was getting pierced, so I got two in my tongue and two in my nose. It was just to be punk rock and to do something different.

My mom didn't like them but I had friends that had piercings and she'd always been cool about it. She made me take them out when we went to see my grandma, but other than that she didn't care.

My parents got divorced when I was seventeen. It was in my junior year of high school. My mom took me to lunch at Subway. We had just ordered our sandwiches and she said, "I brought you here so I could talk to you by yourself and tell you your father and I have decided to get a divorce."

It was pretty upsetting. I started crying and my mom said, "Oh I'm sorry, I should've let you finish your sandwich before I told you."

At the time, I didn't really see it coming. There was never any fighting, though at the same time, they were never especially affectionate towards one another. They coexisted and that's what I was used to seeing.

Looking back, it's pretty obvious that they were unhappy, but at the time, it totally threw me for a loop.

My relationships with my mom and my dad were always very separate. We didn't do a whole lot as a family. We didn't have an Annual Dumas Family Trip to the Beach or anything like that. So when they divorced, it wasn't as if our strong family bond was breaking and my life was going be ruined because of it. I felt bad for my brother, though. He was just starting adolescence and was already an angry kid.

At first, my mom moved into the guest room. She stayed there until we sold the house, and then we moved into a two-bedroom apartment in Norcross, Georgia. Billy had one bedroom and me and my mom shared the other one.

Norcross was in a different school district, so in order for me not to spend my senior year at a new high school, I was given a car. It was a used Chevrolet Spectrum, a little hatchback. It was real cute.

Sharing a room with my mom at that age kind of sucked. My mom's attitude was, "Well I figured you'd be moving out after you were done with high school, so it wasn't worth spending more money to bump up to a three-bedroom apartment."

That pretty much was my plan, but it was still hard for the six months that I lived there. Fortunately, I had my car so at least I was mobile.

Since most of my clique of friends were two years older than me, they all graduated when I was in tenth grade. School lost a lot of its luster for me that year. Dropping out wasn't an option, but I hated school so much at that point that I really started to drag my feet. I would show up late everyday. I barely studied. I was pretty miserable.

I realized that I had to get out of there as fast as I possibly could. In order to graduate you had to have between fifteen and eighteen credits—if you never failed a class in your entire time in high school, you'd have eighteen credits. So in my senior year, I doubled up on a couple of classes and in December of '92, graduated with the bare minimum of fifteen credits.

The first thing I did after graduating was to start looking for an apartment.

CHAPTER 6

There were two things I wanted in an apartment: that it would allow dogs and be really cheap. The one I found was in this great little house on Myrtle Street, right by Piedmont Park. It was divided into three apartments, the owner lived on the top floor, a family lived in the front apartment, and there was another little apartment in the back which was just perfect.

There was one minor problem—literally! It was February 1993, so I was still seventeen and wasn't able to legally rent on my own until my birthday in April. I explained my circumstances to the landlord and, fortunately, he was totally cool with waiting a couple of months to sign the

lease. I moved in just before I started classes at Georgia State University.

At that time, my goal was to teach middle school, so I majored in education. I did that for three semesters, but the fact is, going to college felt like I was still in high school. The only difference was that I was able to pick my own direction.

Bre

The Myrtle Street apartment was a tiny space, just a small bedroom, a living area and a kitchen, which became known as "the Skate Ramp," because the floor sagged right in the middle. But it was a very cute place, with hardwood floors and high ceilings. Plus it was cheap—just $375 a month.

Once I found a place to live, the next thing on my list of things to do was get a dog. From the time I was little, I had always wanted a dog, but my parents were dead set against it.

After I moved into Myrtle Street, my friend Bre Johnson and I went to Atlanta Animal Control to get a dog. We went to Animal Control because with all the overpopulation, it's always better to rescue an animal. The only thing I knew was that I wanted a big watchdog, maybe a Doberman. I was moving into an apartment by myself and wanted something that would look halfway intimidating. Also, I wanted a dog that I could wrestle around with, as opposed to paint its toenails.

Bre and I walked into Animal Control, and there was this gorgeous red Doberman, just a year old. He completely fit the bill as far as what I was looking for. When I saw him in the shelter, he had his "Please take me home" face on. There was something goofy about him, too. He was kind of quirky, which I loved right away.

I filled out all the paperwork for him to get his shots and get neutered, and two days later I brought him home. Bre had a rottweiler named Drew and we decided to try and get the two dogs socialized right away, so that they'd be able to pal around together. I was outside, waiting for her to bring her dog out, when Cody bolted. He went running towards Piedmont Avenue, which is a pretty busy four-lane street. I started running after him, yelling, "Cody, stop!" But of course he didn't know his name yet—he'd just got it four hours ago!

He ran into the street and WHAM! an SUV smacked right into him. I started screaming, thinking, *Oh my God, my dog got killed on the day I got him home! I'm a horrible person!*

I dropped to my knees, not really knowing what to do. I looked up, and there's Cody, staring at me, like, "What's the problem?" He was completely fine.

The girl who hit him was pretty freaked out. Cody had dented the front fender of her SUV—it was like she had hit a deer! Fortunately, she was cool and didn't ask me for any money to fix her SUV. She was more concerned about Cody, which was nice.

I immediately took Cody to have him checked out by Dr. B, my boss at the Montrose Animal Hospital, where Bre and I worked as kennel attendants. I was worried that maybe he'd broken something, or had some kind of internal injuries. But Dr. B said he was fine. "He'll probably be a little sore," he said, "but there's nothing wrong with him."

I was so relieved! It would've been so awful if Cody had been badly hurt before we'd even had a chance to get to know each other.

The next day, Cody and I were on my couch, and I tried to pet him on the belly. But he still wasn't ready to trust me and he snapped at me. I think that established the tone for the rest of our lives together—we respected each other's boundaries. We had to feel each other out and establish our relationship. It took us a while to fully click. It wasn't love-at-first-sight, which makes sense, because I've never been a love at first sight kind of gal. It's simply not my nature.

Later that week, Cody tried to bite me again. I was giving him a bath and touched his feet, which he didn't like one bit. It was in our first week together and he didn't trust me yet. All of a sudden, my excitement turned to nervousness—*What did I just get myself into?*

That's been the pattern of my life. I decide what I want without thinking about what it actually entails. I do it, then think, *What did I get myself into?*

But I always manage to pull an amazing experience out of it.

My Top Ten Favorite Dog Breeds

1. *Mutts*
2. *Doberman*
3. *Pit bull*
4. *Labrador*
5. *Border collie*
6. *Great Dane*
7. *English bullmastiff*
8. *Cavalier King Charles spaniel*
9. *Boston terrier*
10. *Greyhound*

CHAPTER 7

My friend Bre is one of the few people from high school that I'm still very close with today. The two of us did pretty much everything at the Montrose Animal Hospital—we were the shit workers that ran the place and got no credit for it.

As animal hospitals go, Montrose was pretty posh. So posh that there were certain dogs that I wasn't allowed to bring to the front because the owners couldn't handle the thought of their little pug associating with somebody with two nose rings. No, seriously!

When your job is shoveling shit, your whole day revolves around your breaks.

I thought working there was going to be horrible and it wound up being one of the best jobs I've ever had. The staff at Montrose was a classic motley crew—they paid you nothing and treated you like total garbage, so you had to be a little bit off to work there.

Tammy was the manager and her best friend was Karen, our groomer. They were both really Southern, with heavy Georgia accents. Everything they said was prefaced with "They God!" which is basically a Southern way of saying "Oh my gosh, you guys aren't going to believe this!" There was also an older lady working there named June, but we called her "June Bug." It sounded cute, but we really said it because she was a little creepy, like a june bug.

The kennel workers were the lowest rung on the hospital staff ladder. No matter if we'd done everything we were supposed to, they would come up with something else, like cleaning the baseboards in the lobby with a toothbrush or something equally ridiculous. So we made a little hiding place in one of the kennels. We kept it filled with towels, and we'd lay down in there so no one could see us.

When your job is shoveling shit, your whole day revolves around your breaks. We'd try and schedule our breaks around TV shows—talk shows and soap operas, mostly.

One afternoon, Bre and I were sitting in the break room and Karen came running in from the groom shop. We didn't listen to the radio in the back because the dogs were always barking, but Karen just had her quiet little poodles that she was grooming. She came in, all shocked, and said, "They God! That Kurt Cobain done shot himself in the head y'all!"

Both Bre and I were big Nirvana fans, but we just had to bust out laughing. It was just the craziest delivery of bad news I've ever heard! To this day, when I see Bre, we always have to hit that line—*"They God! That Kurt Cobain done shot himself in the head y'all!"*

CHAPTER 8

I didn't really date anybody during the years I lived on Myrtle Street. I hooked up occasionally, but for the most part I was just having fun, hanging out with Cody and working at Montrose. In a way, that whole rock 'n' roll life was my boyfriend—going to shows, meeting new people, making these nice little connections. That's all I needed at that point. It was a great time.

I was making minimum wage at Montrose, so $375 a month rent was all I could afford. There were times when I'd carry a flashlight and not turn any lights on in the house as not to waste electricity.

I had a $40-a-month food allowance, which I nailed every time. I was a vegetarian back then, so once a month I'd buy pasta and rice, and every week I'd get some vegetables and tofu and stir-fry them together.

It's funny—Cody's dog food probably cost me $30 a month. I probably could have gotten him the cheap stuff and saved a few dollars, but I made sure he always got the primo shit.

I lived on Myrtle Street for a little more than a year. Even though it was a very small apartment, I'd always let bands crash there. If a band was passing though town and didn't have a place to stay, I always volunteered. "My place is the shits, but you're more than welcome to sleep there." So many bands slept on my floor—Tilt, Fifteen, a million others.

Among the musicians who crashed at my apartment was a hardcore punk band from Richmond, Virginia, called Avail. The night they played in town I was wearing one of my countless thrift store shirts—a red T-shirt that said "The Godless Red Hoard" on it. I didn't know what it meant. It was probably a community baseball team somewhere, but it only cost a quarter at the thrift store and that's what mattered.

One of the members of Avail was named Beau. He wasn't technically a musician—he was the band's "dancer," which meant that he jumped around on stage like a wild maniac. I thought Beau had a cool look to him, weird hair and lots of tattoos. Sometime that night I walked by him and he said, " 'Godless Red Hoard,' what's that?"

If a band was passing though town and didn't have a place to stay, I always volunteered.

"I don't know, I bought it at a thrift store," I said, and kept walking. I wasn't being rude. That was the answer to the question. I didn't think, *This guy is starting a conversation with me.* He asked a question, I gave him the answer, end of story.

After the show, we all went to the Waffle House, and Beau and I ended up hitting it off. By the end of the night, we'd exchanged numbers, and after Avail left Atlanta, we talked on the phone all the time. Pretty soon, I started driving up to Richmond to spend time with him.

It was an eight-hour drive. I'd head up there after work on Friday, then leave at midnight on Sunday, drive all night and go straight to work on Monday morning. It was a pretty intense relationship, even though Beau and I would only see each other two or three times a month.

After a few months of driving back and forth between Atlanta and Richmond, Beau and I made plans for me to move up there. I'd already dropped out of college, the lease on Myrtle Street was up, and I really didn't have any reason to stick around in Atlanta, so I decided, "Why not?"

I found an apartment with a friend and then, two days before I was going to drive up and cosign the lease, Beau told me that he changed his mind. He was really harsh. "Obviously I can't prevent you from moving up here to Richmond," he said, "but I don't want to hang out anymore."

I was shocked. I totally didn't see it coming. "Well, if you're apprehensive about me moving up there, don't worry about it so much," I said. "I won't smother you. I'll give you space. Believe me, I can find stuff to do."

"I'm serious," Beau said. "I just don't want to hang out."

"Okay," I said, taking a deep breath. I was really angry, but kept my cool. The question was, what the hell did I do now?

After Beau dumped me, I literally had no idea what to do with my life. I decided to put off any long-term decisions and hit the road with my friends in the band, Fifteen. They were on tour and invited me to come along for the ride. It was perfect timing, because it gave me a chance to chill out for a bit and think about what I wanted to do next.

I traveled up and down the East Coast with Fifteen for a couple of weeks, then made my way back to Atlanta. Since my lease had ended, I stayed with June, who I worked with at Montrose. That wasn't a particularly great situation, because she had two big dogs and Cody really doesn't play well with others.

I felt like my life in Atlanta had gotten a little stagnant. It wasn't horrible, but I definitely felt a little "been there, done that."

I was talking to a friend of a friend and I told him my story: "I was supposed to move to Richmond to live with my boyfriend and the son of a bitch broke up with me two days before I was supposed to move."

"Oh, man," he said. "That sucks. If you want, a bunch of us are getting a group house in DC. We're still looking for people to live in the house, so you're welcome to move in with us."

I thanked him, but wasn't sure that was what I wanted to do. Since I had to get out of June's, I started looking for a new apartment. Once again, I had to find something cheap that allowed dogs, but couldn't find one that suited my needs. I decided, "What the hell?" I called my friend and said, "Do you have that guy's number?"

I gave him a call and asked, "Were you serious about letting me move in with you guys?"

"Absolutely," he said.

Two weeks later, I packed up my stuff and Cody and I headed for Washington, DC.

CHAPTER 9

The group house was in Hyattsville, Maryland, which is just outside of DC near the University of Maryland. It was a cool house. Four people could've lived there very comfortably. For ten of us, it was a little crowded. It was nine guys and me.

One of the guys—Ken Olden, from the band Damnation—had a studio in the basement where he did all his recording. He had some expensive equipment in there, a high-quality 16-track setup, so other bands were coming by all the time to record.

Our space in DC.

Ken and I shared the basement. He got the real bedroom and I lived in the laundry room. There was a bathroom down there, which was cool, because it was only the two of us sharing it. All in all, it was a good deal for $80 a month rent.

I slept right next to the washer and dryer. People would just come in when I was sleeping and do their laundry. I had a mattress which I put up on milk cartons, because the floor would get flooded from the washing machine.

I had to be very efficient with space because all I had was my bed and a tiny little closet. I fit all my things in there—my clothes, my stereo, my records.

Sometimes bands would come by to record and all their equipment would be shoved into the laundry room. I would open the door and it would be so packed I couldn't even slide in there.

Ken was a good guy. One of our usual evening activities was to jam in the basement, and Ken taught me how to play bass. He also let me sing on some of his stuff, which I really enjoyed.

With ten people in the house, things got pretty messy. As you'd imagine, with that many people living in a small space, eventually people started to not get along with each other.

It suited me for the time being, but I was actually still a little freaked out. Beau was the first guy I'd really been into since Jake Harvey, and getting blown off like that was definitely upsetting. I'll admit it—I was flat out hung up on him.

I was pretty bummed out. I'd sleep all day and stay up all night. I loved roaming around the city at hours when nobody else was awake.

I didn't mind living in such a small space, but it was definitely rough on Cody. He spent all day in there when I went to work, just sitting on the bed. The other guys in the house didn't like Cody all that much, and didn't really help me out with taking care of him when I needed a hand.

It wasn't easy being the only girl in the house. Although I'd made this big move to DC, I wasn't really doing anything progressive with my life. The owner of Montrose Animal Hospital owned a kennel in Rockville, Maryland, so I worked there for a while, which was fine but paid the same minimum wage I was getting at Montrose. I never seemed to have very much money, so I started dumpster diving, which really isn't as bad as it sounds. There was a Dunkin' Donuts right near the house and there would always be muffins and donuts in the dumpster. The grossest thing that would ever be in there was coffee grounds, which in the grand scheme of things, is no big deal.

I still had my car—I didn't have insurance or anything, so I always drove with my fingers crossed—and I'd go and dumpster dive down in Georgetown, which is a pretty posh neighborhood in DC. One night I was dumpstering behind this very expensive fancy restaurant and the cooks caught me. They were cool though—they brought me into the kitchen and made me some real food, which was nice.

Mostly though, my general motivation was for the feeling of exploring, of being alone in the middle of the night, just kind of wandering around and seeing what was out there, what happened during those hours that nobody else knew about.

CHAPTER 10

One day in DC, the two nose rings that had prevented me from bringing dogs to the front at Montrose once again worked to my disadvantage. I was wrestling on the ground with Cody and his canine tooth got caught on both rings. I immediately yanked back and screamed, which made Cody yank the other way.

Blood flew everywhere but the rings weren't entirely ripped out. They were just hanging there. I didn't know what to do! It didn't warrant a trip to the emergency room, but it hurt a lot and I couldn't just leave those two pieces of metal dangling from my bloody left nostril. Fortunately, Ken was home and he rescued me with a pair of wire cutters.

Since I was now eighteen, I decided it was high time to get the tattoo I'd always dreamed of—the Fifteen Dot just wasn't enough. Conveniently enough, one of my housemates was an aspiring tattoo artist, so I let him experiment on me. First he did one on my heel, which came out in all of a week, so he did another one on my arm. It wasn't very big, a little half circle on my shoulder, but I really didn't like it very much. It was four tribal symbols—three symbols for my name and then a fourth one representing independence.

Next he did the word "punk" inside my lip. It also came out within a week, but we did it again and it stuck. After that, I decided I wanted a serious tattoo—no more messing around.

I went to a place called Tornado Tattoo in Atlanta and talked to their ink artist, a guy named Whirlwind Walt. I chose to get the word "iconoclast," written in Russian characters on the back of my neck. I had it done in Russian because I wanted it in another language. I definitely didn't want Japanese, because everybody gets Asian characters, so I found a Russian dictionary and used the Cyrillic alphabet.

There was a conscious punk band called Iconoclast that I liked. They weren't my favorite band by any means, but I thought "iconoclast" was an amazing and powerful word. The dictionary definition is *"someone who tries to destroy traditional ideas or institutions,"* which is how I've always tried to live my life. Not so much destroying, but *questioning.* Doing things because I want to, not because I'm supposed to.

I met so many great people in DC. I spent a lot of time at a place called the Beehive Community Space and Infoshop. It was a small collective where punks and poets, artists and activists could get together and exchange ideas. There was always something going on there—live music and political meetings and performances of all kinds. It was a very cool and interesting scene, a place that really got my creative juices flowing. I was really lucky to be invited into that world.

Through the Beehive, I became close with a lot of bands on the DC scene. Eventually I started playing bass in a band with my friend, Nick Pimintel. We had become friends when I first moved up to DC. I was still very hung up on Beau at that point, and Nick and I became really close. We did everything together that a boyfriend and girlfriend would do, though we were never intimate at all.

Our band was called Mary Lou Rotten. We were definitely influenced by the East Bay punk rock sound. I played bass, Nick played drums, and two of our friends—both named Chris—played guitar. The two Chrises

That's one of the great things about wrestling—it's like being a rock star for people who don't smoke cigarettes.

each had a nickname—one was Model, because he had a real *GQ* look, and the other was Parent, because he was the level-headed voice of reason in the band. We never played a show—we mostly jammed in the Damnation basement studio—but it was a lot of fun.

I also played bass in a few other projects, mostly in a friend's practice space. One of the bands was with Guy Picciotto from Fugazi on drums and Christina Billote from Slant 6 on guitar and vocals. We played a grand total of once, at the Cooler in New York City. We weren't awful, either—we were doing a cool lo-fi garage thing, similar to the Strokes, who of course didn't even exist at the time.

I also played a little bit with Chris Bald from Ignition, and in another side band with Christina and Gregg Foreman from Delta 72. Gregg and I were hanging out quite a bit, so we'd get together and play a lot. When Christina came around, we'd have "official" practices.

We played our only set at a club called Planet Fred. It was a going-away party for a friend of ours named Jessica. She was an awesome girl, this super-butch lesbian that everybody in the scene was friends with. She was moving to Alaska to work in the canneries.

We tried to think up a name so that we could announce ourselves at Jessica's party. Gregg and I came up with the name Three Card Trick, but Christina totally hated it. We didn't think it was that bad, but she was super-adamant against it—"Absolutely not!"

"Geez," we said, "it's just for a party!"

I really loved playing rock 'n' roll. The only drawback for me was that everyone smoked cigarettes and I really hated that. That's one of the great things about wrestling—it's like being a rock star for people who don't smoke cigarettes.

CHAPTER II

In the beginning of 1995, I decided that I wanted to travel to Europe. Obviously that cost money, which I didn't have at the time. I was still working at the kennel and dumpster diving at night.

I'm not someone who plans things out in advance, but I made a budget for myself. I tried to figure out what my living expenses were and how much I'd need to save so that I could go to Europe by the summertime.

There was a food co-op at the University of Maryland where you could volunteer for food credit. I started working there, so between that and dumpster diving, I had zero food expenses. My rent

Too cool for the room: Christina, one of the musicians I played with in DC.

was $80 a month, and other than what I spent on gas and going to shows, every penny I made went into my Europe fund. I made this little chart so I could stay on track, but no matter what I did, I kept coming up short of my goal. I simply wasn't making enough money.

One of my roommates knew about my situation and he told me that a girl we knew, Shawna, was working as a stripper.

"Really?" I said. "I never would've guessed."

The next time I saw Shawna at a show, I asked her about what she was doing. She was cool. "Why don't you come down one night just to observe?" she said. "And if you think it's something that you could do, I'll let you borrow an outfit and have a try out."

A few nights later, I went down there. The strip club was called the Royal Palace. It was owned by a Vietnamese family and looked just like a Chinese restaurant, which is what the girls who worked there called it. People would ask what they did for a living, and they'd joke, "I work at a Chinese restaurant."

I watched Shawna do her thing and was really impressed. She was a punk girl like me, with really short spiky hair, but there she was onstage with a little bob wig, a pearl necklace, and high heels. She looked like a sexy 'twenties flapper.

I hate saying I'm going to do something and then not following through.

Afterwards, I thanked her for letting me come down and check it out. Shawna told to me think about it, and if I wanted, she'd set up an audition for me.

I talked about it with a few friends, but couldn't decide if it was really something I wanted to do. I sat on it and sat on it. It wasn't like, *Oh God, I could never take my clothes off in public,* or anything like that. I thought, *They'd never hire me. These women are professional strippers and I'm just me. I hang out at rock clubs and work at the dog kennel and eat donuts out of the dumpster.*

About a month later, someone asked me if I'd ever gone for the audition. That just hit my button. I hate saying I'm going to do something and then not following through. *Fine,* I thought. *I'm going to go down there, I'm going to have the audition, they're going to laugh at me and that'll be that. I'm not going to get hired, but at least I did it.*

Sitting there in the Royal Palace, I wasn't nervous, even though it was a completely alien experience. I'd never walked in a pair of heels in my life. I never wore makeup. I remember putting on a lot of red lipstick thinking, *Well, strippers wear a lot of red lipstick.* I didn't have a lot of information to go on. There was Julia Roberts in *Pretty Woman*—and she wasn't even playing a stripper, she was playing a prostitute.

I watched some of the other girls to see what they did. It's kind of the same idea with wrestling—if there's a move I've never done before, I can usually watch someone do it, then go mimic them and pull off a version of it, as long as I don't overanalyze what I'm trying to do.

The place was so low-rent that the girls had to dance to music playing on a jukebox—there were times when the dancers would be on stage, in the middle of a routine, and the song wouldn't change from one to the next. They had to yell to the bartender, "Hey Mary, can you kick the jukebox?"

Anyway, before I went on for my tryout, I looked at the jukebox so that I could find music that I was vaguely comfortable with. I picked "Justify My Love" by Madonna, Blondie's "Rapture," "Fell on Black Days" by Soundgarden, and a song by Prince.

When my time came, I got up there and did it. It was only a fifteen-minute set, but it felt like two hours. I was definitely awkward in the high heels—I held onto the poles the whole time, because if I didn't, I would've fallen over.

When I finished, the owner, Mr. Qui, hired me on the spot. He had a very thick accent, the kind of accent that you have to get used to in order to understand it. He was telling me the deal, saying "Anytime I call you, forty dollar, day or night. Anytime I call you, you come."

Well, I didn't know the first thing about the strip club business. I thought Mr. Qui was saying that anytime he called me, I had to have sex with him for forty dollars! Day or night!

I was pretty freaked out! I listened to him, nodding my head, thinking, *Okay, bye!* Mr. Qui just stood there smiling. I later asked Shawna, "What was he talking about?" She explained what Mr. Qui was really saying—I would get a shift pay of forty dollars on top of whatever tips I made. Also, I'd get a couple of dollars for every drink that I sold—they were glasses of cranberry juice that we called "champagne." Needless to say, I was pretty relieved.

The Royal Palace wasn't exactly your stereotypical "gentlemen's club." It was a strictly bare bones operation, a real dive. The floor was so rotten, it wasn't level anywhere, so they laid down this cheap office-grade carpet. But it didn't help much—we would constantly get our high heels stuck through the carpet into the rotten wood floor and trip. Most of us could barely walk in high heels to save our life anyway.

It was pretty seedy and kind of punk rock, which I liked. There was an incredible mix of girls working there. Every type of person from every walk of life were represented among the dancers that worked there. There were the beautiful just-barely-eighteen-year-old girls that got in a fight with their mom and somehow found their way in there. There were the girls that were working their way through school, stripping their way to their master's degrees. Punk rock chicks. A couple of ghetto girls. There were also two Vietnamese women, both in their mid-forties, that had been working there forever.

There was a political pecking order among the dancers, just like I found in the locker room when I started wrestling. For instance, the girls that had been working there for a long time made sure you knew that they had first dibs on the big spenders—"When that guy comes in, you'd better stay away because he's mine."

The family that owned the Royal Palace were nice people. They took good care of the people that worked there. A while after I started dancing, Mr. Qui developed health problems and had to have triple-bypass heart surgery. The family was so moved by it, they gave the dancers health care. So with the exception of when I lived with my parents, the only time

**I'd force a smile out for
the quarter of a second
that they actually were putting money in my
   garter, but other than that I was pretty
much in my own head.**

in my life that I've had health insurance was
when I was a stripper.

While the staff and management were pretty
decent, the clientele was God-awful. Basically,
the Royal Palace drew an eclectic mix of perverts
and weirdoes.

Friday and Saturday nights were the worst.
That was when we'd get the most mainstream
crowd, yuppies and fratboys, along with the
usual perverts and weirdoes. Those nights
were just mentally exhausting. The music was
twice as loud, the place was twice as smoky, and
there were twice as many guys hooting and hollering in there. It was just gross.

I could only handle one weekend night a
week, so I'd usually work two double shifts during
the week, then one weekend night. That way I
could make the most money in the shortest
amount of time.

Even though I didn't make as much money
working the day shifts, I still preferred them
because that way I had my nights to myself. We
had a regular lunch crowd, a little business
crowd that would bring take-out food in so they
could eat while they watched the girls. There
were all kinds of guys, from construction workers
to businessmen. A lot of politicians would also
come there, because they were less likely to be
spotted at this hole-in-the-wall dive bar than
they were at one of the more well-known gentlemen's clubs.

The dancers at the Royal Palace worked totally nude, but it was just on the stage. We didn't do lap dances. We would just dance onstage, and the customers would tip us by putting money into our garters. After our sets, we would walk around the bar and fraternize with the customers and try and get them to buy us "champagne." That was never one of my specialties.

The fact is, I was a horrible stripper. When I was dancing, I could shut my mind off or think about what I was going to do that weekend. I'd force a smile out for the quarter of a second that they actually were putting money in my garter, but other than that I was pretty much in my own head. One time a customer slipped a couple of singles into my garter and said, "It seems like your mind really isn't here." He was really sleazy, implying that if I wasn't thinking about dancing, I must be thinking about sex.

"As far as I'm concerned, I could be bagging groceries," I said, and that was the truth. It was just a job to me. All I did was get up there and do my thing. I was naked. What more do you want? If that wasn't good enough, too bad.

I could never bring myself to tell my mom that I was dancing. It wasn't a moral issue, I just didn't want her to worry about me. I hated it, because when we'd talk on the phone I'd have to lie when she'd ask things like, "How was work this week?"

Instead of being honest about what I was really doing, I told Mom that I worked at a restaurant across the street from the Royal Palace, a vegetarian place called Food for Thought. It was a little hangout spot where a bunch of my friends worked.

Since I was so rotten at schmoozing the customers, I'd dance my fifteen minute set, then change into my street clothes and walk across the street to the restaurant and hang out over there. It was so much nicer over there—it was sane and quiet and somehow the cigarette smoke over there didn't bother me quite so much. I'd zone out and play World Cup Soccer Pinball, which would always get me in a good mood. The replay was set pretty low, so it was easy to get a free game and that always cheered me up, like "Yes! I kicked ass in World Cup Soccer!" Then I'd go back across the street and work the pole.

The Royal Palace wasn't the worst place on earth, as these things go. Looking back, I have a lot of okay memories about working as a stripper, but at the time, I hated it. I think once you're past something, it's much easier to look at the good points than the bad.

CHAPTER 12

After six months at the club, I'd saved more than enough money to go to Europe. I left with one month left on my lease at the group, so that there was someone to watch Cody while I was away.

I decided that $1800 would cover my trip to Europe. I bought a $500 round-trip ticket on Icelandair and an unlimited Eurail pass. My plan was to go to one country one day, then sleep on the train, and go to another country the next day. That way I would save myself the price of a hotel room for the night.

"The Germans."

I brought some summer clothes along with one pair of long johns, one pair of cutoff Dickies, and one sweatshirt. It ended up being cold the whole month I was there, so that was pretty much all I wore.

I had one group of friends over there in Germany that I called—obviously—"The Germans." Damnation had toured in Europe and made friends with these guys, who then came over to visit America. I hung out with them in DC and we became pretty tight, so when I went to Europe, I ended up spending a couple of days with them in the town they lived in, just outside of Frankfurt.

I traveled most every night. Basically I'd just get into the train station, walk around and see the sights, then go back to the station and head on to my next destination. The train was my friend. I loved that I could just hop on the train and go somewhere and see different places. I loved the freedom of not having to do anything. I didn't go there with any specific purpose so all I had to do was have a good time.

I hit Italy, Belgium, Denmark, Prague. I flew into London, because flights were cheap. Unfortunately, I thought it sucked. It was like a colder, foggy New York.

From England, I took a ferry back over to the Continent and hit Amsterdam. That's where I got the tattoo on my shoulder. I had a friend that got tattooed there and he gave me the artist's number. I had never liked the tribal tattoo on my right shoulder, so I figured that I'd add to it to cover it up.

I thought a tattoo would make a great souvenir of my trip. People always ask me what it symbolizes and the truth is, it represents nothing other than my independence and spontaneity. Because I went over there and just did it.

Trying to sleep in a train station in Venice.

I don't think it's the coolest tattoo ever. It's not especially neat looking, I'm not really obsessed with three-eyed demons. What's important to me is that it's different. I like that I have a big tattoo on my arm, but that's about it. That actually means a lot to me, but it's hard to explain to people who would rather hear that it's a drawing of the Mayan god of protection.

Getting the tattoo was no big deal, but trying to heal it on the train was a bitch. It was very hard to sleep, because you're always leaning on the window and that really hurt. Plus, you need to keep a tattoo extremely clean in the first few days, but the trains are set up so that you have to pay to use the restroom—so I'd have to spend money that I barely had just so I could rinse my shoulder in the sink. They have a strict rule about no bathing in the sinks, and the restroom attendants would get so mad at me. They didn't speak much English, but they'd yell at me to get out of the sink. I'd explain, "I'm not taking a bath! I'm cleaning what more or less constitutes a wound!"

Europe was a great experience—I met interesting people and saw some incredible places. I had a good time while I was there, but after all was said and done, I had to go home and find a new place to live.

My lease at the group house had expired, and to be honest, that whole arrangement had pretty much run its course. I decided to get a place with my friend Luci, who I met when I first came up to Washington.

When I first met Luci, I thought, *I don't know if I can deal with this giggly chick. She's happy all the time!* Luci has a somewhat intentionally naïve outlook on life, which I thought would really aggravate me, but I ended up liking her a lot. We get along great, even though we're very different people. She's just an awesome person.

We found a one-bedroom place in a downtown DC neighborhood called Mount Pleasant. The apartment was in a row house, so we actually had a little backyard, which was very cool. There was also a little alley, where I parked my car. The rent was $680 a month, which was expensive, but I was making good money dancing.

Our yuppie neighbors hated us. The neighborhood was gentrifying and they didn't think we deserved to live next door to them. They also hated Cody, because he sat outside and barked. Every time he'd bark we'd bring him in and say, loud enough for the neighbors to hear, "Come on inside, buddy. We don't want the neighbors to get mad. God forbid that you act like a dog and bark in the backyard." They were real assholes.

Luci was a great roommate, especially as far as Cody was concerned. She loved him and treated him as if he were her own dog. That was something that helped me make the decision to go on the road with one of my favorite bands, Fifteen.

I was still dancing, saving as much money as I could, but otherwise didn't have much going on in my life. When my friends Fifteen asked if I'd like to join them on tour as a roadie, it sounded like just what the doctor ordered. My job was to get the equipment out of the van, help set up, sell the T-shirts, whatever needed to be done.

There were twelve of us in a fifteen-passenger van—Fifteen and another East Bay punk band called Busy Backson. Then there was me, my friend Mikey from Florida, and this guy named Gorman working as roadies. All the seats were taken out, and the equipment was stored underneath a loft that they'd built in the back.

I loved being on the road. I felt like I was part of this magical thing. We were like a little family—they had my back and I had theirs. I really enjoyed the dichotomy of all these different personalities. Even though we were living together in small spaces, there was always a good vibe, a good energy.

Every night was a new experience. Granted, it'd be the same basic elements, but I loved the way we'd unload the equipment, play the gig, then pack it all back into the van and go on to the next experience.

We would drive from city to city, often driving nonstop for ten or twelve hours at a time. Every now and then, road fever would break out and all of us would throw down in a huge wrestling match. One of the guys called it "the worms." The idea being, you were completely mentally deranged from sitting in the van for so long that "the worms" would take over your body and make you fight.

So you'd be sitting there, hanging out in the loft, listening to the radio, and all of a sudden someone would say, "Uh-oh, I can feel the worms . . ." Next thing you knew, they were pouncing on you from behind.

Everyone would start yelling and screaming and laughing, except for whoever was driving at the time. That was always funny. We'd all be

jumping around like monkeys, and whoever was driving would get totally aggravated.

The worms would get the worst when we were less than ten miles from the venue. By then we were aching to get out of the car so bad that we'd just go completely crazy.

Traveling with Fifteen was a great adventure. People would jump on and off the road with us. Jeff Ott—the lead singer—was always inviting people to come along—"Chris from No Idea fanzine is going to ride with us from Arkansas to Texas."

The rest of the band would get so aggravated, because there was so little room in the van to begin with. But Jeff loved the idea of being this tight-knit little gypsy community, picking up tagalongs as they traveled around America. I considered myself very lucky to have been one of those tagalongs.

Jeff was very passionate about his music and his politics, and if you're very passionate, you're inevitably going to piss people off. He could get pretty preachy during a Fifteen show. He had a tendency to ramble a lot between songs. But there were a number of issues that meant a lot to him and getting his message out was often more important to him than the music.

He got married a few years back and doesn't tour as much as he used to. The same thing happened to a lot of my punk heroes. They set out to change the world in a fifteen-passenger van, then the years passed and the world didn't change so they said, "Screw it. I'm going to change my own personal existence instead."

In a way, being on the road with Fifteen was a microcosm of my entire life, which was constantly moving to different towns but never really getting settled.

We were down in Florida when I got some bad news from home. I called Luci to check in and she told me how she'd come home from work that day and it looked like someone had been murdered. Cody was spewing out blood from his mouth, his ears, his nose. He was pissing out blood.

It didn't take long to figure out what had happened. The neighborhood had a bit of a rat problem and, when Luci and I moved in, the nasty neighbors told us that they wanted to have their exterminator put rat poison in the alley and our backyard. "Fine," I said. "Just tell me when you do it so I can keep Cody out of the yard."

A few weeks later, the rats were still around, so the neighbors had the exterminator lay down more poison. Only this time, they didn't tell us. Cody, of course, ate all the poison and it just tore his insides out.

I totally freaked out. I was planning to stick with Fifteen for a while and tour with them until they went back home to Berkeley, California. I was having so much fun, but I immediately returned to DC.

Luci had taken Cody to the animal hospital. The vet said he was very lucky, that most dogs don't make it through rat poisoning. They gave him a number of blood transfusions, but he wasn't out of the woods.

We brought Cody home, but he needed twenty-four-hour care. Luci and I arranged our work schedules so that if she was working a day shift, I would work the night shift. If I was working a day shift, she would work the night shift. We pretty much didn't see each other for a month.

The vet explained that after Cody's organs healed and regenerated he'd be as good as ever. We took care of him as best we could, but I just felt so helpless. We made a bed for him out of blankets from the Salvation Army and one of the couch cushions, which we covered in a garbage bag. Cody just laid there, he was so sad and pitiful. His breathing was shallow, he had zero bladder control, so he'd lay there pissing blood. He was completely messed up, but fortunately, after a very long recuperation, he pulled through.

I felt really guilty about what had happened. Not that I could've stopped him from eating the rat poison, but I still felt bad. There I was, kicking it on the road, with not a care in the world. Cody getting sick was like a wake-up call—"Okay, back to reality."

CHAPTER 13

I ended up stripping off and on for almost four years, all the way through the beginning of my wrestling career. When I started working on the indies, I'd dance three double shifts in a row in order to make enough money to afford to not get paid anything for wrestling and still have the lights on in my house.

I was pulling in great money. On an average shift, I'd leave there with $200 to $400. Probably the best night I ever had, I took home $900.

Cody in the yard in DC.

Still, it was definitely amateur hour at the Royal Palace. For the most part, the dancers had to do our own security. One night I was walking around with another girl, Danni, collecting tips. This drunk guy slipped a couple of bucks into Danni's garter, and then tried to grab himself a feel. Danni and I said, "Sweetheart, you can't do that. You know there's no touching."

"Okay," he said and went to tip me. Of course he tried to touch me, and I got pissed. "I told you you couldn't do that," I said, and I whacked him on the back of the head with my purse.

"Owww!"

He went down! He grabbed his cocktail napkin and held it on the back of his head and when he pulled it away, it was soaked with blood. I had busted his head open with the deodorant crystal I kept in my purse!

"Shit," I said, "what do we do?"

"Let's get him out of here," Danni said.

We called over one of the bouncers. "Hey Michael, I just busted this guy's head open," I said. "You've got to get this guy out of here, or else he's going to get me fired!"

Michael and I led the guy out the door. I was really scared that he'd come back and rat me out to the managers, but he was pretty wasted and we never saw him again. I tipped Michael an extra $20 that night for helping me out.

That kind of thing happened a few times. Us girls didn't take kindly to guys trying to touch us when we were dancing. I punched at least one guy square in the eye for grabbing at me during my routine. Another time I was dancing with my back to the crowd. Somebody touched me, so I turned around and jumped on the guy's back. I was pissed! I punched and clawed at his head, screaming for the bouncers. "Get over here! This bastard touched me!"

When those sort of incidents happened it was as if pure instinct took over, the need for self-preservation. I just couldn't help it.

One night I got into a thing with this pimp-type guy. He was making trouble for the girls, and I had words with him a few times over the course of the night. At the end of my shift, I walked outside to go to my car and there he was. He started running his mouth, calling me "baby girl."

I got hot and started screaming at him, "All you have in your life is power over women, power over people that are less strong than you! That's what gets you off! Well, you're not so tough!"

I really got in his face, which didn't go over too well. He got mad and started cursing me out, calling me every name in the book. One of the cocktail waitresses came out and tried to break it up, but I wasn't going to let it go so easily.

"No! He shouldn't talk to us like that," I shouted. I was as mad as I could possibly be. The guy was a total asshole, and I wasn't going to take any more shit from him.

"I could kill you right now," he finally said, getting into his Mercedes. "but I'm going to make your life such hell you're not going to want to live it."

A week later he came back to the club. He grabbed one of the girls. "You know Misty?" he said, referring to me by my stripper name. "Well, her real name is Amy Dumas. I've got her license plate, her home address, her birth date, her Social Security number. You tell her I'm going make her life hell."

All his information was accurate. Needless to say, I was scared. By this time, I'd begun seeing Beau again—we didn't speak for a long time after he blew me off, but eventually we got to a point where we were kind of friendly. Well, not exactly friendly, but I'd go see Avail if they were playing in the DC area.

We reconnected when Avail did some recording in Silver Spring, Maryland, just outside of DC. Their bass head blew up and Beau said, "I think Amy has an Ampeg Bass Head, maybe we can go borrow it."

He called me and said it was an emergency, and I ended up going to the studio. We hung out, just chatting, and it was actually pretty cool. We had always had a really strong attraction and it was still there. We talked on the phone a few times and pretty soon, we started dating again. It was a casual thing at first, because I was in DC and he was in Richmond, but we both felt good about it.

Beau and I got to a really good place. "I don't know how much longer I can do this long distance thing," he said, "because I really like being around you and I'm not around you as much as I want to be."

So when the pimp guy announced his plan to ruin my life, I decided to get out of Dodge. I decided to move to Richmond.

CHAPTER 14

When I moved from DC to Richmond, it was the first time I ever took any of my stuff with me. Beau came up with Avail's van and we packed up my bed and my couch, along with my clothes and my boxes of records.

I found a place in a little area in downtown Richmond, called Jackson Ward. It was an old split-level house, divided into two apartments, upstairs and downstairs. I rented the whole house, then sublet the bottom floor to friends.

Cody and Beau's dog Ford.

To me, wrestling was just a bunch of rednecks fake-punching each other. A lot of overweight guys in Speedos being really bad actors.

Right after I moved in, Avail went out on a long tour, which left me all alone in a new town. I knew a few people, but only because Beau had introduced me around, like, "Hey, this is my girlfriend, be nice to her out of obligation to me."

That's one reason why I continued dancing at the Royal Palace, even after I moved to Richmond. I'd drive up on Thursday and work double-shifts on Friday and Saturday. It was a good excuse to see my friends and keep making a good living.

When Beau was around, things between us were pretty good. He didn't officially move in, but he stayed over quite a bit. One Monday night, I was doing other things around the house and I heard him yelling at the TV. "What are you watching?" I asked.

"*WCW Nitro,*" he said.

"What the hell is *Nitro?*"

"Wrestling," he said. "I've loved it since I was a kid."

"What? How did I not know this about you?"

He tried to explain what was going on, and who all the characters were, but I just thought wrestling was silly. To me, wrestling was just a bunch of rednecks fake-punching each other. A lot of overweight guys in Speedos being really bad actors. It wasn't until I saw the *luchadors* on *Nitro* that my preconceived notion of wrestling began to change.

The *luchador* who really captured my attention was Rey Mysterio. He was like nothing I'd ever seen before. I was intrigued by so many things—his mysterious mask, his small size, his unbelievable athletic ability. He was doing such cool moves, this acrobatic high-flying style that was completely different than what I was used to seeing when I happened upon wrestling on TV. I found myself really getting into it. I couldn't help myself—I cared about what happened to this little guy in the mask.

I began watching *Nitro* every week. In the beginning, I just loved watching the *luchadors* wrestle, but it wasn't long before I found myself becoming more and more involved in the storylines. Before I knew it, I was hooked.

The more I watched, the more I thought about becoming a wrestler. I had no idea how one would go about doing such a thing, but I knew that I wanted to be part of that magical colorful world.

Of course, the role of women in wrestling was very different then. There were no serious female wrestlers. Women were managers or valets or some kind of eye candy. But that didn't matter to me. I didn't care if all I did was stand outside the ring or just be a pawn for the storyline. I wanted to learn how to wrestle.

During the summer of 1997, Beau went off on a six-week tour with Avail, so I decided to go down to Atlanta to visit my mom. A friend of mine lived in a duplex, and the other half of the place was vacant, so I just squatted there for the summer. I ran a power cord over there so I'd have some light, I used my friend's cordless phone, and I was good to go.

That was the only time I ever stripped at a club other than the Royal Palace. I figured dancing would be a good way to make some money while I was down there, so I *"rocked in Atlanta at TattleTails,"* just like Mötley Crüe sang about in "Girls Girls Girls." It was a totally different vibe than I was used to and after two weeks, I said, "Okay, that's enough money," and quit.

While I was down in Atlanta, I found out that WCW was running a TV taping in Macon. That wasn't all that far, so I bought two tickets. On the day of the show, the friend I was supposed to go with bailed at the last minute, so I drove down there by myself.

I was so excited! I was still pretty naïve—I didn't know there was such a thing as a wrestling groupie—so I got all dressed up in the hope that I'd stand out in the crowd and get noticed by somebody in the company. I needed to find out how I could be part of the business in some way. I didn't care if it was working with the lighting crew or helping to set up the ring, I wanted to be a part of it in some way, shape, or form.

During the show, the WCW crew guys kept flashing me with the little laser pens. One of the guys came over and stood by my seat. Finally he leaned down to me and pointed to the empty seat next to me, "Hey, is anyone sitting here?"

"No," I said. "I'm here by myself."

"I just wanted to make sure your boyfriend wasn't getting popcorn or something," he said. "I didn't want him to kick my ass for sitting here."

I was friendly, but I wasn't really paying attention. I was really engrossed in the match that was going on in the ring. He could tell that I was distracted and got up to leave. "Sorry to bother you," he said. "Maybe I'll see you later."

"Wait a second," I said. "You mean to tell me that you're going to distract me from the match and then I don't even get to go backstage?"

He laughed and gave me a pass. Then I went and hung out with the lighting guys and watched the show on one of the monitors. After a while I wandered off and just stood around backstage. The wrestlers were just walking around—I saw Van Hammer, Glacier, all those "big" WCW stars of the time.

As I was standing there checking out the scene, Debra came over to me and told me she liked my shoes. I was a fan of hers—I thought her "Queen of WCW" character was funny as hell—so I was really excited to meet her. I wanted to engage her in conversation, but there's not much you can say to "I like your shoes" except for "Thanks, I like yours, too."

A bunch of the wrestlers and Nitro Girls stood around the monitor with me, watching what was going on in the ring. Other than Debra, no one even acknowledged me, and in turn, I didn't approach anyone. As far as I was concerned, I was just a fly on the wall. I had spent enough time hanging out with bands to know when not to bother the performers standing around backstage.

After the show, the crew guys gave me one of the "WCW NO ACCESS" signs that was posted backstage so that I could get it autographed. That kind of thing never interested me, but I did save the sign and the backstage pass as souvenirs. I'm not very sentimental, but I had them both framed as a reminder of my first-ever live wrestling experience.

I knew that I wanted to get into the wrestling business but I still had no idea how to actually become a wrestler. A friend of mine in Richmond suggested that I try getting involved in kickboxing. That seemed like it could be a way of getting my foot in the door, so I went down to this little martial arts studio and tried it out.

I didn't love it. There were a lot of drills, you had to wear pads, the teacher was constantly correcting me on my form. I found it to be a very controlled environment, sterile almost.

I only did the kickboxing for a month or so, but it cost me $600 because when I joined, I had signed on for a year. It was one of those gym deals where they take the money straight out of your bank account and I couldn't get out of it. It was very frustrating.

It was an amazing period of self-discovery for me. I found out how much I enjoyed and craved a certain kind of intense physical activity.

Then my friend Acie brought me to the judo club at Virginia Commonwealth University, and that I liked right off the bat. Judo kicked your ass hard, which made me feel great. All the rolling around and fighting reminded me of when we got the worms in the Fifteen van—only here they taught you better ways to do it, where you actually got to take people down and make them pass out. It was awesome!

Judo is very much like submission wrestling. The main difference is that there are no knee or ankle submissions. It's just chokes and arm submissions. *Ne-waza* is the term for ground-work techniques, and *tachi-waza* is technique done from the standing position. *Tachi-waza* is a bit harder to do with a guy because of the weight difference—it's much easier for them to throw you down. With *ne-waza*, you're a little more equally balanced, though strength still plays a big role.

With the exception of a couple of different rules, *ne-waza* is very similar to amateur wrestling. Both use a point system—in judo, you win when you get to one point. If you do a sloppy throw, it's a quarter point. If you start from a standing position and you can get your opponent to land flat on their back, that's one point and they're done. The same applies to submissions—if you tap, you lose.

I was much stronger on the ground. As the guys threw me down, I'd use their momentum to flip all the way over onto my stomach, which was not points against you. That was easy for me, because I was pretty agile, and once we were on the ground, the odds evened up considerably.

I had a few really good submission moves in my arsenal. There was one chokehold that I was particularly good at. I'd lock my opponent in a regular choke using the *judo gui,* then throw my leg over. My legs were stronger than a guy's arm, so once I locked that hold on, it was all over. I got almost everybody in the VCU Judo Club to tap out with that.

I began getting so into judo that it actually sidetracked my goal of become a wrestler. I began competing in regional tournaments all around the Southeast—in Virginia, West Virginia, North Carolina, South Carolina.

The tournaments were categorized by weight and sex, though I also enjoyed fighting in open tournaments where I could go toe to toe with the guys. When you go up against the guys, your technique had better be good. Otherwise there's no way that you're going to get them off their feet or choke them out. If your skills aren't there, they're just going to out-muscle you down.

I always enjoyed working with the guys. Even though I knew that they could overpower me, and that, ultimately, it was only a matter of time before they made me tap, it was always fun to see how long I could go with them. And occasionally I'd get something on them, which felt great.

The physicality of judo was so exciting for me. I came out of pretty much every session with some kind of bruise. Nothing major, though—occasionally someone might break a toe, but for the most part, judo injuries consist of strained muscles, and rug burns.

It was an amazing period of self-discovery for me. I found out how much I enjoyed and craved a certain kind of intense physical activity.

Up until very recently, intensity was the main thing that was lacking in women's wrestling. Even though the matches are essentially scripted, a wrestler has to have a fierce go-get-'em attitude in the ring. Fighting in judo tournaments definitely brought out my aggressive side as well as my strong sense of competition, both of which really helped me develop my style and character as a wrestler.

Judo also taught me how to maintain my focus while staying intense. I learned not to be afraid of getting injured, to quickly shake the cobwebs out and regroup, to know that pain is no big deal and I could worry about it later.

I got better and better at judo with each passing week. Had I stuck it out, I bet I could've gone pretty far in the world of women's judo. Who knows? Maybe I could've made it all the way to the Olympics!

CHAPTER 15

"Why don't the Mexicans ever get to do interviews?" I asked Beau one night during *Nitro*.

"Well," he said, "I think most of them probably can't speak English."

"Really? You mean the Mexicans are really from Mexico?"

I was genuinely surprised. I honestly thought the Mexicans was just a gimmick for the smaller wrestlers, in the same way that Mortis wasn't really a monster. It had never even occurred to me that the Mexican wrestlers might actually be Mexican. A light bulb went off over my head, *Eureka! Maybe if I go down to Mexico I can meet other Mexicans who will teach me how to wrestle!*

I began studying up on *lucha libre*—the professional wrestling of Mexico. Then I called a travel agent to see what type of deal I could get on a flight. "I want to go to Mexico," I said.

"Mexico City?" the travel agent asked.

"Okay, sure." Honest to God, if she'd said "Acapulco," I would've said the same thing. I bought myself a round-trip ticket to Mexico City, with not the slightest clue as to what I was going to do once I got down there.

The one thing I did before leaving the States was buy a copy of *Let's Go Mexico.* I found myself a cheap hotel—$12 a night—and headed straight there as soon as I landed. I was the only American staying there, but there was a wannabe actor from Colombia with a similar goal to mine—he wanted to break into Mexican soap operas, which are pretty big throughout Latin America. We had both come to Mexico City with the same basic plan, to check into the cheapest hotel and see what we could accomplish in the amount of time it took for our money to run out. We had some good conversations, even though I knew nothing about the Mexican soap opera scene and he knew nothing about wrestling.

I had taken three years of high school Spanish, so my Spanish wasn't too bad. Of course, I hadn't used it since graduating high school, but it came right back to me. It was actually quite amazing. I surprised myself really with how quickly I was able to get comfortable speaking Spanish. It might not have sounded too pretty, but I had no problem communicating with people. Of course, it's not like I had much of a choice. For all intents and purposes, nobody in Mexico spoke English.

Once I'd settled in, I went to the hotel manager and explained to him how I had come to Mexico to check out *lucha libre.* "How do I find it?" I asked.

"I don't know," he said.

I was shocked! "What do you mean you don't know?"

"Sorry," he said, "but I just don't know where they would do anything like that."

I was so crushed! My plan was pretty simple—go to Mexico, check into a hotel, then ask the guy in the lobby how to find the *lucha libre.* I didn't really know what to do from there, so I started asking strangers in the street. Finally someone pointed me in the right direction—Arena Mexico.

Arena Mexico is the Madison Square Garden of Mexico City. I took a taxi there and bought a ticket off a scalper for eight dollars. There weren't a lot of people hanging around, but there were vendors selling *lucha* masks, so it was clearly the place.

I went inside and there were bleachers set up. There was dirt on the ground and these three rings in the middle of the place—and I don't mean wrestling rings. I went to my seat, wondering, "What's going on here?" All of a sudden, an elephant comes walking out. I had bought a ticket for the circus!

It turns out that I had shown up on one of the two weeks out of the year that *lucha libre* was preempted by the circus. I went to the ticket taker and said, "This isn't what I'm here for. I'm here to see wrestling."

"Oh, you want to go to the Arena Coliseo," he said. "That's all the way on the other side of town."

He began giving me very complicated directions for getting there by train. I didn't have much cash on me, so I asked, "Can I walk there?"

"Sure," he said, "but it's pretty far."

I started walking. And walking. And walking. It was pitch dark outside and I had no idea where I was going.

Forget this, I thought. *There will be other events. I'm going to call it a night.*

The next day I was determined to get to a *lucha* show. I took a cab to the Coliseo, which was a smart move because it was located in a really bad section of town. The second the taxi dropped me off, I knew for sure that I was in the right place. There were tons of peddlers selling programs, and everywhere I looked there were kids wearing *lucha* masks.

I went to the ticket booth to buy my ticket. As I got to the window, there must've been ten different scalpers grabbing at my sleeve, "Front row! I've got front row!" I took a chance and bought myself a front row seat for $10. I couldn't have been happier—front row for my first *lucha libre* show!

The setup at the Coliseo was very different from the way wrestling is done in the States. For one thing, there was no guard rail separating the audience and the action. There was the ring, then some wood on the floor, then fifteen or twenty rows of seats. It got pretty wild—the wrestlers would often get tossed out of the ring and land on the people sitting in the first few rows.

Above all that there were two other levels—the cheap seats. Those sections were surrounded with fencing, like cages. The idea being that the fans couldn't throw stuff at the wrestlers. The fans in Mexico take their *lucha libre* very seriously, and when they get mad, they're out for blood!

I took my seat—in the front row!—and right next to me was an old woman who I soon learned was the biggest *lucha libre* fan on Earth. Her name was Guille, and she hadn't missed a single show in thirty-five years. She was like everyone's favorite aunt—super-charismatic and full of life.

Guille told me everything I needed to know—who was a heel, who was a babyface. The promotion was called CMLL—*Consejo Mundial de Lucha Libre*. It's one of the biggest wrestling organizations in the world and the oldest running promotion in existence. The world's best *luchadors* were part of CMLL, including La Parka, Lizmark, Ultimo Guerrero, El Hijo del Santo, and many others. Also, a lot of famous North American wrestlers have worked there, including Chris Jericho and Chris Benoit, who was known as "the Pegasus Kid."

Of course, all the wrestlers knew Guille. She'd get out of her seat, walk right up to the ring and kiss the babyfaces on their hands. Then she'd pat their cheeks—she was so cute!

As I was chatting with Guille, a guy in a suit came over to us. "Hello," he said, in Spanish. "What are you doing here?"

"I'm just here to see the show," I replied. "I want to wrestle."

He must not have understood me. "Are you visiting family or friends here?"

"No," I said. "I don't know anybody here at all. I'm here because I want to wrestle."

He started speaking English and introduced himself as Enrique, CMLL's press director. He had noticed me sitting there and wanted to see who I was. I guess I kind of stood out, being the only *gringa* chick in the front row.

We talked a bit—I told him how I'd accidentally gone to the circus the night before—and he seemed nice enough. After a while, the show was about to start. "Come with me," Enrique said.

He brought me over to the announcers' booth, which was situated in the same place the *Raw* announce table is, back by the entrance ramp. As the show started, I heard them say that their "special friend from America is here with us."

I was so excited. They mentioned me on TV—I was famous! I sat there

for the first couple of matches, and then said to Enrique, "I don't mean to insult you, but I'd really like to see the rest of the show from my seat in the front row."

"Of course, of course," Enrique said. "No problem. I'll come and get you after the show and give you a ride back to your hotel."

"That's really not necessary," I said. "You can just give me directions on how to get back there on the subway."

"Please trust me," he said. "I really don't want you to take the subway."

He seemed like a good guy, so I said, "Okay." From that night on, Enrique picked me up and dropped me off after every *lucha libre* event. I'm sure he had an ulterior motive, but he was always a total gentleman.

Back in my front row seat, I began to truly understand what was involved in wrestling. Until that point, I hadn't seen any matches up close. I realized just how hard the wrestlers were hitting each other, and how much punishment their bodies take from hitting the mat or landing on the wood outside the ring.

As promised, Enrique gave me a ride back to my hotel after the show. An Anglo wrestler called Steele was staying not too far from where I was, so Enrique gave him a ride as well. I immediately hit it off with Steele— whose real name is Sean Morley, later to be known as Val Venis. He was a godsend—just a totally cool guy, a really fun person to hang out with.

Back in my front row seat, I began to truly understand what was involved in wrestling.

Over the next few weeks Sean and I hung out quite a bit. He had just signed with WWE and had already filmed those early Val Venis vignettes, though they hadn't aired yet. He was very excited about his character, he had big plans for what he was going to do once he got up there.

Sean was also very interested in my goal of becoming a wrestler. He was always very encouraging. It was fun for me to talk freely with somebody who was on his way to where I wanted to be.

I went to *lucha libre* three nights a week. It was a truly amazing experience. Once again, there was that special feeling of being in this secret world that most people don't know about.

It wasn't long before I knew all the various CMLL storylines and characters. Among the wrestlers working there were Fuerza Guerrera (Juventud's father), Shocker—1000% Guapo, and Emilio Charles Jr. There were also a lot of wrestlers there who weren't Mexican. Ultimo Dragon was there, Tajiri used to wrestle the second match every night.

One of my favorites was a guy called Mr. Aguila—later to be known in WWE as Papi Chulo and then, Essa Rios. Papi, as I called him, really stood out to me. His mannerisms were totally over the top and he wore a Marilyn Manson T-shirt and had the craziest masks—he actually reminded me slightly of Jeff Hardy's Willow the Whisp character. Most of the *luchadors* didn't have a lot of raw charisma. They ran more of a mysterious gimmick. But Mr. Aguila was really magnetic and always set off the crowd when he was in the ring.

The few female wrestlers in *lucha libre*—such as Diabolica and Lady Apache—were actually quite good. Stylistically, they were very similar to the men—a combination of Mexican and Japanese techniques, with some sex appeal thrown in for good measure. What's interesting is that at that time—1997—American women wrestlers weren't doing anything even remotely like that.

The people at CMLL treated me really well, but I could tell that no one took my interest in becoming a wrestler too seriously. Enrique understood that I wanted to be part of the business but didn't truly grasp the concept of my wanting to wrestle. He thought I could make a lot of money in Mexico working as one of the Corona models on their show.

"But I want to wrestle," I told him. "How about we work out a deal where I do modeling for your company and you train me as a wrestler on the side?"

That seemed like an equitable arrangement, so Paco Alonso—the Vince McMahon of CMLL—let me appear in a couple of vignettes promoting the big mask vs. mask match between Steele and Rayo de Jalisco Jr.

In one vignette, I was on a couch with Sean and another beer model. We were watching Steele's previous match with Rayo. "Look what I did to him," Sean laughed. "I totally humiliated him! I'm going to kill him next week!"

All of a sudden, Rayo and his gang of heels burst in. The other girl and I cowered on the couch as the two wrestlers exchanged words—"I'm going to get your mask!" "No, I'm going to get your mask!"

It was pretty cool, being on CMLL TV. My trip to Mexico couldn't have gone any better—I got close to the action and made any number of connections. No question about it, I was on the right track to a career in wrestling.

CHAPTER 16

While *lucha libre* was the focus of my Mexican trip, it wasn't the only thing I did while I was down there. A friend of mine in Richmond hooked me up with an acquaintance of hers named Penny.

I was feeling pretty defeated the morning after my aborted attempt at seeing a *lucha* show, so I gave Penny a call and introduced myself. She invited me to join her and a few friends for a drink. They turned out to be a small group of young American journalists who had come down to Mexico to gain experience as foreign correspondents.

I met them at this small open-air cantina where we had tacos and margaritas. From there we went to a tiny little karaoke bar where they hung out pretty regularly. The other customers could barely speak English, but they got up there and sang dreadful versions of American classic rock songs.

Now normally I'm not the type to ever sing karaoke, but I couldn't pass it up. I got up there with two of the other reporters and we sang 4 Non-Blondes' "What's Going On" and Kansas' "Dust in the Wind." We were God-awful, but it was definitely a blast. The journalist clique were all very cool people. Even though I hadn't been to a *lucha libre* show, I was having an amazing experience that was unlike anything I'd ever done before.

Two weeks after arriving in Mexico City, I left my hotel and moved into an apartment with one of my new friends, a reporter named Allison. She had a spare room in her three-bedroom apartment, so she invited me to stay with her. It was a great deal—I paid her a thousand pesos, which at the time was just a little more than a hundred dollars.

It was a really nice apartment. All I had was a little room with a sleeping bag on the floor, but it was so much better than the cheap hotel where I'd been staying. There was a phone with an answering machine, so people could leave messages for me. Plus they had an Internet hookup, and I was able to e-mail my friends back home in the States. For a hundred dollars, it really worked out great.

While the apartment itself was really nice, the building it was in was horrible. The hallways smelled like piss, and there was a wild dog that seemed to have the run of the place—I would always pet him with my foot because he was so nasty dirty!

Mexico City is the most crowded place I've ever been. Everywhere I looked there were people and cars and dogs and more people. The whole city was actually crawling with wild dogs. There was packs of them everywhere. There would be bumper-to-bumper traffic in the middle of a four-lane street and in the middle of it were fifteen wild dogs, just running free.

The streets were also filled with poor people. Everywhere I looked there was someone begging for money. There was one really old woman who looked exactly like Mother Teresa. I gave her money every time I saw her—not much, just one or two pesos, but I couldn't just walk past and ignore her.

In addition to poor people and wild dogs, Mexico City also has some of the worst air pollution in the world. Between that and the high altitude, my breathing was definitely affected. I was plagued by a scratchy throat and nosebleeds throughout the whole trip.

I ended up leading a triple life in Mexico City.

Nevertheless, I developed a nice life for myself there. Every day I'd wake up and walk across the street to get my breakfast at a little fruit stand. I always got the same thing—a yogurt and fruit parfait made with bananas, coconut, honey, wheat germ, and strawberry yogurt. Not only was it healthy and delicious, it was cheap—fifty cents for a big parfait. Yum!

From there I would walk over to the pool hall where Allison's boyfriend Jorge worked. I'd spend the afternoon hanging out there, shooting pool.

There was a great restaurant by the pool hall that served an all-you-can-eat Buddhist vegetarian buffet for only three dollars. When I went to Mexico, I had been a total vegetarian for about seven years, but I was fully prepared to make changes if necessary. I had no idea what I was going to find when I got there and I was ready to do whatever it took to make the most of it. As it turned out, it was easy to maintain my vegetarian lifestyle and eat really amazing food for very little money.

I ended up leading a triple life in Mexico City. I would spend three nights a weeks seeing *lucha libre,* two nights hanging out with my American friends, and two nights at a local judo club that my friend Ernesto from the VCU Judo Club hooked me up with.

Like just about everything else in Mexico City, it wasn't exactly what I was used to. It was in someone's garage and the mats were made of garbage bags filled with sawdust. But it was still really fun to be able to practice my judo in another country.

It was also quite hard. For one thing, the high altitude messed with my wind so bad. There I was, trying to concentrate on the sensei's instructions—which were in Spanish, obviously—and hoping that I wasn't going to die from lack of oxygen. On top of that, every time I took a bounce on the mat, sawdust would fly up into my face, making it even harder to breathe. It was wild!

Our sensei was a pilot for Mexican Airlines and I became very friendly with his son, Juan. He was training to become a pilot just like his father. Juan spoke excellent English, so it was nice to hang out with him. We had a very easy, very comfortable relationship.

Juan was a good guy, but the other guy I hooked up with in Mexico was definitely a bad boy. I met Carlos through my little clique of Americans. Penny had a little get together, and when I got there, she asked if I'd like something to drink. "Sure," I said. "I'll take some water."

"Sorry, but we don't have any water," Penny said. "We've got beer and tequila."

I didn't realize that water is pretty expensive in Mexico. Now, I had hardly ever done any serious drinking before—most of my friends back home were straight edge punks, so I'd probably only drank three or four times in my life at that point. Well, when in Rome, right? I took a beer, which I hated. I've never had a taste for the stuff—I could just about tolerate a Corona, but I'd only sip at it to keep my throat from getting dry.

There I was at this dinner party, with a dozen or so of my reporter acquaintances and a few of their Mexican friends. They were all sitting around, making conversation, holding CDs in their hands. I couldn't figure out what was going on, but then I noticed that these CDs all had big mountains of cocaine on them.

It was all very casual. People were just chatting, having a beer or a cocktail, enjoying their private pile of coke. I didn't do any—I never had any interest in drugs—but it didn't bother me, either. Everyone was very mellow, nonchalantly doing a line every now and again.

Now, I'm going to make an educated guess and say it was Carlos who "supplied" the cocaine. He had a big tattoo on his arm, so he was really intrigued by my tattoo. He turned out to be a cool guy—for an alleged coke dealer—and we ended up spending some time together when I wasn't at *lucha* events or taking judo classes. We would go to clubs together and drink tequila. The deal was that the clubs had a ten dollar cover charge which included all the tequila you could drink. Well, ten dollars was a lot of freaking money for me, so I was determined to get my money's worth. While I didn't ever develop a taste for beer, I definitely learned to enjoy tequila!

We ended up spending quite a bit of time together. Carlos knew all the hot spots, all the places that stayed open to six in the morning. He even took me to Acapulco, because I wanted to see one of Mexico's beaches.

Carlos was a great guide. He would always take me somewhere different, just checking the whole city out. It was all very casual—he had fun hanging out with me and I had fun hanging out with him. It was nice to have a local friend to show me the places that weren't mentioned in my *Let's Go Mexico.*

No question about it, I got the absolute most bang for my buck while in Mexico City. I went down there with no intention of pressuring myself. If I didn't like it, then I'd go home early. I'd told everybody I knew that I was going down there to learn how to become a professional wrestler, but honestly, all I expected to do was see some *lucha libre* and have some fun. I figured I'd come home with some good stories to tell, and that'd be that.

But that's not what happened. I loved the whole vibe of being in Mexico. If it weren't for Cody, I would've just gotten my stuff, turned around and gone right back.

Instead of feeling like I'd gotten wrestling out my system, I had the best six weeks of my life. I got back to Richmond with one goal—to save money and return to Mexico as soon as possible.

CHAPTER 17

The first thing I did once I got back to Richmond was start saving again. I spent the summer dancing at the Royal Palace, driving up to Washington every week, working double-shifts, trying to make as much money as fast as I possibly could. In September, I bought a plane ticket for Mexico. I hadn't saved as much money as I might've liked, so I only booked a three-week stay.

Since it was going to be a much shorter trip, I decided to totally immerse myself in the wrestling world. Instead of staying with Allison, I reserved a room at the Hotel Mont de Mar, which was where all the foreign wrestlers stayed. I wanted to come into contact with as many people that weren't from Mexico as possible. I wanted to learn how they got there, how they got booked.

I met a whole bunch of people at the hotel, including such WWE wrestlers as Ricky Santana, Kevin Quinn, and Miguel Perez from Los Boricuas, and the Headhunters—known to one and all as the Fat Boys. There were also a lot of North American indie workers there, like Canadian Tiger Mike Lozansky, Phil Lafon (who worked as one-half of a tag team with Doug Furnas), and the Cuban Assassin.

I went to see Enrique at the CMLL offices at Arena Mexico. They have a gym in the basement that the wrestlers use. He thought the women would be training that day, but none of them were around. I was still pretty excited, walking around the gym, taking it all in.

As I was leaving, Ricky Santana and a few of the other guys stopped by to pick up their paychecks. They asked what I was doing there and I said, "I came by to train with the women, but they're not here today, so I'm going back to the hotel."

"C'mon," Ricky said. "Get in the ring and we'll bump you around a little bit."

I was thrilled, to say the least.

It wasn't exactly a state-of-the-art training facility. The "ring" was a wrestling mat laying on the cement floor, with four wooden stakes for ring posts and garden hoses for ropes.

I got in the ring with Ricky and Kevin, and they showed me some of the most basic moves—tackles, headlock takeovers, running the ropes. We messed around for a little while and then they proceeded to take my head off with a couple of clotheslines. They didn't explain to me how to take them, but believe me, I learned to tuck my head pretty fast.

They didn't beat me up too badly—my teeth were all in my mouth, my eyes were still open—but they definitely didn't go easy on me. When it was time to call it a day, Kevin asked me if I still wanted to train with them.

It's a fine line—I had to be humble and respectful, letting them know that they had handed me my ass but that it didn't phase me. That they could beat the shit out of you, but that I appreciated it and wanted to be beat up some more. I wasn't at all freaked out by the roughness. Had I not taken judo, I might've been more shook up, but I understand that they were initiating me into the business, checking me out to see if I had what it takes.

"Absolutely," I said.

"Alright then," he said. "I've got the day off tomorrow. I'll come back here with you and we can work out some more."

Doing shows outside of Mexico City was crazy—in between the matches, all the local children would run into the ring and jump around, doing wrestling moves.

The next day Kevin and I went down there and he took me through the basic Wrestling 101 stuff. All your bumps—roll bumps, flat bumps, back bumps—plus running the ropes and flat backs. Those are one of toughest things to learn because it's mentally hard to get your head and body in sync. You have to kick your feet up and throw yourself back, while not bending your knees or trying to put your elbows down. You have to avoid landing on your neck or your ass. It's murder on your tailbone, too. Doing flat backs was really frustrating, because everything else came pretty easily to me.

I worked out with Kevin and Miguel and Ricky for a couple of days, just learning the fundamentals. After a while, we tried out a few combinations—tackle, drop down, headlock, shoot back off the ropes. It was really rough, my body bruised in places that I didn't know it could be bruised.

My trip coincided with the sixty-fifth anniversary of CMLL, so a lot of people came down for the big celebration—including a number of WWE wrestlers like Sean Morley and Savio Vega. I even got to be part of the sixty-fifth anniversary show. I came down the ramp with Los Boricuas, wearing a little *boriqua* outfit.

I also accompanied the guys on a bus trip to a show three hours outside of Mexico City. It was a lot of fun. When we got off the bus, all the town's children gathered around, surrounding all of us. They didn't know who I was—a wrestler, a wrestler's wife—but it didn't matter. They were hugging my legs, grabbing all over me.

There was also a photographer waiting for us. He took pictures of all the wrestlers, then made souvenir key chains out of them which he sold on the street. He actually made a keychain of me, which made me feel like I was really part of the show.

Doing shows outside of Mexico City was crazy—in between the matches, all the local children would run into the ring and jump around, doing wrestling moves. Then as soon as the music would start for the next match, they'd all go back to their seats. That was almost more entertaining than watching the real matches!

Back in Mexico City, I spent a lot of time hanging out at the Hotel Mont de Mar. It was like a dorm, with everyone going from room to room, kicking back with friends. Ricky Santana, Kevin Quinn, and the Cuban Assassin all shared one room, which was bigger than most of the others and had cable TV. Needless to say, that room was the main hangout for the Americans staying there.

Those guys were a wild bunch. They partied hard—definitely harder than I was accustomed to—but were all relatively respectful towards me.

In their eyes, I was nobody—they'd seen a thousand people like me, trying to break into the business. Considering what I've heard about what wrestlers do to other kids coming up in the business, they treated me great. That said, I didn't get an easy time by any stretch of the imagination. They didn't exactly treat me like their little sister.

I had never hung out with guys like them before. But my passion for wrestling made me accept my initiation with a smile. I figured, "Whatever. It's just words. They're not hurting me."

It was the same in the ring. They were rough with me, they were hard on me, but they didn't seriously hurt me. Compared to some of the stories I've heard about other wrestlers' trainings, I had it easy. It still took a very strong person to get through what I went through. Your average person wouldn't have made it.

I only trained four or five times. The rest of the time I just hung around, picking up as much information and atmosphere as possible.

My experience this time was more focused on my becoming a wrestler. Instead of having fun, experiencing Mexico, it was more about going to the building and spending time with the wrestlers, asking questions and soaking up information.

CHAPTER 18

As hard as they were, the training sessions I had with Ricky and Kevin only confirmed my desire to wrestle. In fact, it wasn't until I had that training, minimal as it was, that the idea of my being a wrestler was really cemented. Before that, it was almost like I was being cute: "Guess what, I'm going be a wrestler!" After I trained, I definitely felt like this was serious.

I was more realistic about it, though. I knew I had a long way to go before I had a fighting chance at impressing anyone enough to give me a shot.

I knew I needed to get serious. I had taken the first steps, now it was time to become truly focused on my goal. Every step that I took from that point on had to be one step closer to getting a job as a wrestler.

About two weeks after I got home, my skin started busting out in weird red spots. I went to see my doctor and he ran down the list of questions that they ask when someone comes in with chicken pox.

"Have you been around any kids recently?"

"No," I said. "None of my friends have kids. I'm never around children."

But then I thought about it a second and remembered all the kids climbing on me when I went on the bus trip in Mexico—"Actually, I did come into contact with some kids when I was in Mexico a few weeks ago."

The doctor explained that chicken pox usually takes a couple of weeks to kick in after exposure to the virus. So not only did I have chicken pox— I had Mexican chicken pox!

Chicken pox can be pretty horrible—with itching, fever, headaches— but in my case, it wasn't too bad. Of course, it wasn't too good either! There were spots everywhere, all over my body. I was pretty itchy, but I took antibiotics and that pretty much did the trick.

I was just getting over the chicken pox when Kevin Quinn called to invite me to NWA's fiftieth anniversary show in Cherry Hill, New Jersey, just outside of Philadelphia. He was going to be tag teaming with Chris Daniels in the opening match against Ace Steel and Danny Dominion. All those guys worked together in Chicago as part of the Steel Domain Training Center, which Ace and Danny co-owned.

"If you come up," Kevin said, "you'll probably meet some people that can steer you in the right direction of where to train."

Needless to say, I went to Cherry Hill. Ace and Danny had a heel manager, a little guy named Michael "The L.A. Connection" Star, so Kevin and Chris asked me to be their valet for the night.

We set up a spot where the manager would antagonize me and then I'd slap him across the face. I had no idea how to do it without really slapping him, so when the time came, I gave him the most pitiful, worthless slap ever. I didn't know that there's no way to work a slap. The only way to really make it look good is to really paintbrush him. Nevertheless, Kevin and Chris won the NWA Midwest Tag Team titles, which was definitely exciting.

There were a lot of great wrestlers at that show. There was a big Battle Royal with all the WWE developmental guys that were in training at Dory Funk Jr.'s Funking Dojo—including Kurt Angle, Test, Steve Corino, Devon "Crowbar" Storm, and Dr. Death Steve Williams. The main event was Dan "The Beast" Severn vs. William Regal. This was back in the days when Regal was in pretty bad shape from taking too many pain pills—he's

After seven days of hardcore training, my body didn't feel all that great but I did feel more prepared than I did before.

drug-free now—and he came to the ring with his boots on the wrong feet.

Kevin was right—I met a lot of people that night. Among them was a wrestler named Strawberry Fields. Her husband, Slim, had recently taken over the legendary NWA Mid-Atlantic Championship Wrestling down in Charlotte, North Carolina. Even though I only had three days of bumping school under my belt, they invited me to come down and work with them. "Oh no," I said. "I'm not ready to wrestle yet."

"That's okay," they told me. "All the girls suck. You can still wrestle for us."

I didn't care if all the girls weren't any good. I didn't want to suck! I needed to start training for real. Kevin suggested that I come out to Chicago and work with him at Steel Domain.

I flew out there in November. The Steel Domain training center was in a fairly rundown part of the city, on a street with a bunch of unoccupied storefronts. Steel Domain was pretty much the only business on the entire block. The school was small—there was a ring set up in the middle and that was basically it.

Danny Dominion and Ace Steel, the co-owners of the school, allowed me to crash on the beat-up couch they had in the training center. I was the only person there at night, and it was kind of scary. The neighborhood was pretty desolate. The only things around were a gas station and a little burrito joint. After practice ended, I would get myself a burrito, then watch wrestling tapes on the couch until I went to sleep.

Kevin would come by in the morning and we'd work out for three or four hours, just going through the basic wrestling repertoire—hip tosses, arm drags, drop kicks, sunset flips, and so forth. The regular training sessions were held in the evenings. There were maybe fifteen guys and me. It was very intensive training, but I was determined to learn as much as I possibly could in as short a period of time as possible. After seven days of hardcore training, my body didn't feel all that great but I did feel more prepared than I did before.

When I got back to Richmond, I called Strawberry and told her that I'd done some more training and would love to take her up on her offer to work some matches. I was careful to explain that I was still only a beginner—all I knew was a few basic moves and how to bump.

"That's no problem," she said. "Why don't you come down here a day or two early. We can put a match together in advance, so that you'll feel more comfortable in the ring."

I went down to North Carolina in early January. I spent a couple of days working out with Strawberry, as well as training with some of the other NWA Mid-Atlantic wrestlers. Strawberry and I got in the ring and she said, "Okay, what do you know? What do you want to do?"

"I know next to nothing," I told her. "If you show me how to do something, I'll be able to do it. But honestly, I really don't know how to work a match."

My first professional match was on January 9, 1999, at East Rutherford High School, in Western North Carolina. I worked under the name Angelica, which was the gimmick name I used when I was the valet for Kevin Quinn and Chris Daniels. Chris was known as "the Fallen Angel," so they suggested I call myself "Angelica." And it just kind of stuck.

Strawberry based our match on all the basic techniques that I was comfortable doing. We mapped it all out in advance and I had it completely memorized, from start to finish. Unfortunately, Strawberry kept forgetting everything we'd prearranged. I totally didn't know what to do. I wasn't really comfortable calling moves in the ring, and I didn't want to insult someone who had more experience than me by telling them what to do.

We managed to get through it, though, with Strawberry beating me in the end with a powerbomb.

We had a decent crowd—maybe four hundred people—because NWA ran shows at the school on a fairly regular basis. Strawberry was pretty

popular in the area—she was famous for doing tricks with her boobs. She could make them move up and down individually. That was what she'd do when she came out and got into the ring. The little boys in the crowd just ate that up.

All in all, my ring debut didn't turn out half bad. Especially considering how horrible it could've been!

Strawberry and Slim ran with a very hard-partying clique of people. They always had a wild scene going on around them. Slim owned a bunch of strip clubs throughout North Carolina, and they thought because I'd worked as a dancer that I was into the same things they were. I explained that dancing just happened to be what I did to make cash. The whole stripper lifestyle was very unappealing to me.

It was a very awkward situation to be in. I often had to be very political as far as trying to fit in, while at the same time, preserving my personal boundaries. I felt lucky to have met Strawberry and Slim—with me being so inexperienced, they were nice enough to let me work matches—yet I felt so foreign and out of place in their environment. It reached the point where I started to question my decision to become a wrestler. I definitely loved wrestling, but I began to hate being surrounded by people that I felt I had nothing in common with.

Even though I didn't click socially with Strawberry and Slim, they were extremely supportive as far as helping me to get my career started. At the same time, I knew I could only do it for so long. I knew that eventually there would come a point where our personalities really did start to clash.

CHAPTER 19

I began going down to Charlotte to get more training under my belt. There was a Mid-Atlantic wrestling school, so I'd train with the other people that were training there. Meanwhile, Strawberry and Slim kept booking me onto shows. For my second match, I worked with Leilani Kai, who was one of the most successful female wrestlers ever, a former WWE Women's World Champion.

The third show I did with Mid-Atlantic was at Union Pines High School in a little North Carolina town called Cameron. The card included a couple of local boys that had recently been signed to WWE— Matt and Jeff Hardy.

From the first time I laid eyes on them, I knew the Hardyz were something special. They'd been running their own local promotions for years, including the incredible OMEGA. I was so impressed—not only were they amazing athletes, doing all the high-flying action that later made them famous, but the fans treated them like huge superstars. They were such idols to the kids there.

The plan that night was for Strawberry and I to do the original match we'd worked out weeks ago, only this time I was going to win by reversing a powerbomb into a sunset flip. Once again, we didn't talk about our match at all. She was busy, running the show with Slim, selling her gimmicks.

Strawberry and I went out there and naturally, she didn't remember anything we'd discussed. She started calling stuff in the ring—things that I had no idea how to do.

"Punch me," she said.

"But I don't know how to work a punch!"

It went on like that, just as sloppy as could be. She knew that there was a limited amount of things I could do, but that little fact must've slipped her mind. She just kept calling moves that I was totally unprepared for.

"Fisherman's suplex!"

"What the hell? I don't know how to do a fisherman's suplex!"

The match had gone completely haywire. All of a sudden, Strawberry hit me with a powerbomb and I thought, *Okay, this is supposed to be the finish. I'm just going to stay down.*

"Kick out," she growled at me.

I kicked out as the ref counted two. We got back into it and a minute later Strawberry powerbombed me again. "Stay down," she hissed.

Okay, I thought. *Sure thing.* I was just happy to have the match over with.

I was really embarrassed about the poor quality of the match. When I was introduced to Matt, I said, "Listen, I don't want to hear it. I know how horrible it was."

But Matt was totally cool. He clearly understood that I was giving my all and that's what counted.

Meeting Matt and Jeff and the rest of the OMEGA posse really restored my faith in my decision to wrestle. We were from completely different backgrounds, but these guys were people that I could relate to.

I liked Matt right away. He told me that two OMEGA wrestlers—Shane Helms (who later became known in WWE as The Hurricane) and Jason Ahrndt (who would become the Mean Street Posse's Joey Abs) had been at my first Mid-Atlantic show. Matt had asked if anybody new was at the show. "Yeah," Jason said. "There was some new little redneck girl there."

I just thought it was hilarious. For one thing, I had never lived in anything but big cities. Those guys all lived in the middle of Nowhere, North Carolina, and *I'm* a redneck. To this day, Matt will joke about me being a little redneck girl.

I did a lot of driving in those days—a *lot* of driving. On the weekend I'd head down to Charlotte to work a Mid-Atlantic show or just do some training. Then once a week, I'd trek up to Washington, DC, to work at the Royal Palace. But because I was only working one or two shifts, I was barely making enough money to cover my gas and expenses.

One weekend, Luna Vachon came down from WWE to work a couple of shows for Mid-Atlantic. Even though I wasn't booked, I asked Strawberry if I could come down and meet her. Luna was a definite inspiration for me—she had a wild look and was a genuinely tough female wrestler.

The two of us hit it off immediately. Luna had a reputation for being kind of crazy, but I found her to be as sweet as could be. We chatted a bit and actually corresponded for a while, writing letters back and forth. She was always very encouraging, telling me to stay true to myself as far as refining my wrestling persona.

Luna worked two shows that weekend, the second of which featured the Hardy Boyz on the card. After the show, we all went to a club in Charlotte, a place called Club 2000, and from there back to Slim and Strawberry's house.

Matt and I chatted all night—we hit it off right from the start. There was an immediate physical attraction, but there was also something more than that. He was so different from most of the wrestlers that I'd met. We ended up in the hot tub together, but mostly we just talked and talked, about wrestling, about our lives. He seemed like somebody I'd definitely like to get to know.

We exchanged numbers and I called him a week or so later. I was listening to music as we talked and at one point he said, "Hey, are you listening to Hole? I love them."

I told him how punk rock and alternative music was a huge part of my life and that really knocked him out—the only person he knew who listened to alternative music of any kind was his brother! But it was nice to discover that we might have more in common than just wrestling.

Matt and I made arrangements to meet up at an upcoming Mid-Atlantic show, just outside of Greensboro. Neither of us were booked, but a couple of OMEGA guys—Jason Ahrndt and Shannon Moore—were on the card. I had a great time, hanging out with Matt and Jeff and all their friends.

Matt and I talked about how we both loved cheap little independently owned hotels, because they have more character than the generic chain places. We decided to spend the night at a place called, no joke, the End of the Road Motel. It was pretty creepy, like something out of a David Lynch movie.

The Hardyz had just started working full-time for WWE. Matt explained that the OMEGA guys would work out every Sunday at their training ring, out in the woods at their friend Tracy Caddell's house.

The next day being Sunday, we drove out to the ring. We traveled down a little two-lane road, through small towns like Seagrove, and as we got closer to Cameron, I felt this really nice, really comfortable sensation. There were farms and pine trees everywhere. I kept thinking, *This must have been a pretty cool place to grow up.*

Even though I was born and raised in the South, this was completely different from what I was used to. I spent my whole life in metropolitan— or at least suburban—areas. As we drove deeper and deeper into the backwoods of North Carolina, it really felt like I was entering into a totally alien environment. But in a good way.

There was a whole bunch of guys working out when we arrived at the ring. Jeff and Shannon I'd already met. Tracy Caddell was there, as were Johnny Yow, Rambunctious Bobby Burnett, and Little Mike Teague.

What I saw took my breath away—there was a wrestling ring *in the middle of the woods.* There were mattresses all around the ring, covered with dirt and leaves and bugs. It was wild!

All the guys were very cool to me, making me feel completely welcome right from the start. I got a kick out of how close they all were, talking about old times and busting each other's chops. They'd known each other forever, which was something that I never experienced because my family moved so many times.

We trained all day. Matt was clearly in charge, running us through endless drills. "You're going to be tired all the time if you make it to WWE," he said, "so you need to be practicing even when you're exhausted."

At one point, Shannon went up to the top turnbuckle and he did a senton bomb onto the mattresses on the ground. *Wow,* I thought. *That's a pretty cool move.*

"Okay," Matt said. "Who's next?"

"I'll do it," I said. I'd never even done a top move before, but what the hell, why not give it a try? Just as I climbed up to the top, Rambunctious Bobby Burnett came running towards me at top speed. He draped himself over the top rope and I crotched myself bad. There were no turnbuckle pads on the posts, so it really hurt. A lot!

What I saw took my breath away—there was a wrestling ring *in* the middle of the woods.

I actually got pretty angry—my first ever attempt on the top rope and this idiot crotched me! But the truth is, they called him Rambunctious Bobby Burnett for a reason. The guy is completely out of control—I don't know, maybe he needs Ritalin or something .

Of course, I couldn't let these guys see that I was pissed off or that I was in pain. The only thing to do was to get back up there and do the senton off the top to the ground. I'd never done anything like it before, but I'd watched Shannon do it, so I was able to pull it off. What a rush! I have to say, I was pretty pleased with myself.

We finally called it a day at around six-thirty—we had to watch *Sunday Night Heat* at seven. Then we went for dinner at El Chapala, a Mexican joint nearby in Southern Pines.

Matt invited me to come down and train anytime I wanted. Even if he wasn't around, there was always somebody working out there and I was welcome to join them.

Suffice to say, I was just totally blown away by all of it. There I was, in a place that was unlike any place I'd ever been, hanging out with these amazing guys—two of whom had just made it all the way to WWE. It was a revelation, especially considering how out of place I felt at Mid-Atlantic.

This was the community that I was looking for when I first got interested in wrestling. This is what I had been looking for all along.

CHAPTER 20

I started driving down to North Carolina every couple of weeks. I'd stay at Johnny Yow's trailer, which I thought was so cool. I'd never seen one before and I just thought it was so cozy. When he told me how much he'd paid for it, I could hardly believe it—what a steal!

"This is a nice trailer," I said.

But Johnny was offended—"It's a mobile home, girl."

Sorry! How was I to know?

I was only the second girl to ever work out at the ring in the woods. Lexie Fyfe, who's an indie wrestler that later became a very good friend of

Lexie Fyfe and the "Sensational" Sherry Martel with me at an indie show.

mine, came out there one time to train, but Matt nailed her with a clothesline and she chipped a tooth. She got all aggravated and never came back.

It seemed like I was on the road constantly in those days, driving from Richmond to DC for work, or to North Carolina to wrestle. One weekend Matt and Jeff invited me to join them at a show they were doing with Maryland Championship Wrestling, the promotion run by a very cool guy named Dan McDevitt, who told me I was welcome to work out at his wrestling school in Baltimore, called Bone Breakers.

I kept meeting more people and learning more about the business. I was training as much as possible, either down in North Carolina or in Baltimore. Danny also let me work MCW shows, which was where I met Joey Matthews and Christian York. They were part of the whole OMEGA posse, just great guys. They wanted to be wrestlers in the worst way. They worked their asses off! Joey and Christian were very helpful to me—they would get me onto whatever indie shows they were working.

I traveled a lot with those guys, working indie shows all over the South, including Nashville's famed Music City Wrestling. It was a ten-and-a-half hour journey for me—three and a half from Richmond to North Carolina, then another seven from North Carolina to Nashville. But Music City had a small TV show that ran on public access channels all over the country, so I felt the trip was worth it to maybe get some on-camera exposure.

These days everything is perfectly timed out in order to accommodate the various camera shots and run-ins, but Music City Wrestling was very old school—you weren't allowed to have any communication with your opponent before your match. The wrestlers would just talk things through in the ring. It was great experience for me. I learned how to get in there and think on my feet. I learned that you don't freak out if things don't necessarily go as planned in the ring, you just keep going.

I began spending a lot of time with Lexie Fyfe. Marybeth—Lexie's real name—had been in the business for a few years and had connections throughout the Southeast—places like Virginia, North Carolina, South Carolina—so we ended up traveling and working together quite a bit.

We did a show in Alabama with Sensational Sherri Martel—one of the true legends of women's professional wrestling. Sherri was a WWE Women's Champion and later became a manager, working with such greats as Shawn Michaels, Ric Flair, and Harlem Heat.

We were so excited! We wanted to get our picture taken with her, so we followed her into the locker room. She went into the bathroom and we could hear her peeing—we stood there giggling like little fans, "Sherri Martel is peeing!"

When she came out, we introduced ourselves and she was super nice. She said she would watch our match that night, so Marybeth and I pulled out all the stops to impress her. We put on a serious wrestling match—we did a lot of moves and just beat the hell out of each other. Afterwards in the locker room, our eyes were swollen, our lips were bloody, and we asked Sherri what she thought.

"Shoot," she said. "I'm glad I'm not wrestling you two. You guys kick the shit out of each other!" Looking back, I'm not really sure she meant that as a compliment!

Women like Sherri and Luna were so inspirational—they set the precedent, so the fact that they were so cool to me really made me believe that I could make it in wrestling.

I would travel all over working indie shows wherever I could. Most nights I barely made enough money to break even. At Music City, for example, the first couple of times I worked there was for a handshake. The next bump up was twenty dollars. By the time I had left there, I was up to forty, which didn't even fill the gas tank to get back home.

More often than not, I didn't get paid at all. At some point, you'd think people would say, "Screw this. I'm never going to make it to WWE." But true wrestlers have a special mindset—we're willing to put up with a lot of shit in hopes of making it.

Lexie had a few connections at ECW, so when they came down to the Carolinas for four house shows, we decided to go and see if they might let us work out in the ring before the show.

The first show was in Charlotte. We got there pretty close to showtime, so when Lexie asked if we could maybe train with some of the guys, we were told that it was too late. "But if you come back tomorrow," we were told, "we usually have a workout before the show."

The next day they were in Columbia, South Carolina, and this time, we made a point of getting there early. I introduced myself to Tommy Dreamer, who not only wrestled, but was very involved in running the show backstage.

"We heard if we came early we could work out," I told him.

"No problem," he said. "Knock yourselves out."

We went to the ring where Super Crazy and Tajiri were working out their match. I hadn't ever met Tajiri before, but he was working at CMLL when I was down in Mexico, so I went and introduced myself to him.

Tajiri and Crazy were both doing springboard moonsaults to their feet. I got in there and

"I'm glad I'm not wrestling you two. You guys kick the shit out of each other!" Looking back, I'm not really sure she meant that as a compliment!

I was actually scared out of my mind—the whole thing was out of control, from the fans to the wrestlers themselves.

started doing them too. As I was doing them, Tommy Dreamer came to the ring. "Hey, come over here," he said.

Uh-oh, I thought. *I'm in trouble.* I figured that maybe I'd been doing something I shouldn't have been doing, or I was getting in the way of the other wrestlers.

"How about you get with that other girl," Tommy said, "and put together a little five-minute match?"

Lexie and I put together a little match, which went off okay. It was nothing special. Then Tommy asked me if I wanted to get involved during that night's match between Skull Von Krush and Angel of the Baldies.

"Well, sure," I said.

I came out to the ring with Angel. We did a spot where I slapped Skull and then he hit me with a piledriver.

After the show, I was told that Paul E. Heyman—the creator and owner of ECW—wanted to talk to me. I went over to him and he very matter-of-factly told me that he wanted me to come work for him.

To be honest, I wasn't all that familiar with ECW. Mikey from Florida had sent me some videos, so I'd seen the show. Plus, I had gone up to Philadelphia with Beau and Mikey in the summer of 1998 for a fan convention at the infamous ECW Arena. I was actually scared out of my mind—the whole thing was just out of control, from the fans to the wrestlers themselves.

So when Paul E. offered me a gig, I said yes, but didn't really know what I was getting into. I just figured it would be a good opportunity to continue my education. I'd get to work on a regular basis, and get to pick up knowledge from people that had been in the business for a while and had some notoriety.

I was told that they wanted me to work a pair of shows the following Saturday and Sunday. I had a minor problem, though. I was in the middle of a storyline with Maryland Championship Wrestling and the blow-off match was scheduled for that same Saturday night. It was a mixed tag—me and Christian York vs. Joey Matthews and his manager, Platinum Nat.

I explained the situation to Tommy, "Would you mind if I fulfilled that obligation before I started working with you?"

"Of course not," Tommy said. "I completely understand. That's no problem at all."

Late Friday night, I got a phone call from Debbie at ECW. She was Paul E.'s one-woman talent relations department. She did just about everything, including booking flights for all the wrestlers.

"I've got your flight information for you," she said. "You're on the eight A.M. to Chicago out of Dulles. . . ."

"That's Sunday morning, right?"

"Oh no," she said. "*Saturday* morning. Eight hours from now."

"I'm sorry," I said, "but I can't go. I already explained that I've got to work this match in Maryland. It's been advertised and I've got to be there. Tommy Dreamer told me it wasn't going to be a problem."

"I'm not sure what to tell you," Debbie said. "You have to be there. This is your only chance."

I was totally torn. Danny McDevitt had been so good to me, giving me regular work and letting me train at Bone Breakers free of charge. I really didn't want to screw him over. Fortunately, when I told him the deal, he was totally understanding.

"I'm not mad at all," Danny said. "I'd be mad if you didn't go do the ECW show, because that's what you've been working towards."

Still, I felt really bad. I went to Chicago with my defenses already up. When I got to the building I learned that they hadn't figured out what I was going to do that night. "Just sit tight," I was told.

I hung around all day, waiting to see what the plan was. Finally the show started and I was informed that I wasn't going to be doing anything until tomorrow. I was pissed, to say the least! I had to bite my tongue to keep from freaking out—something I've never been especially good at. I tend to wear my emotions on my sleeves, on my pants, on my forehead. But I kept my anger in check.

The next night in South Bend, Indiana, I went out to the ring with Justin Credible. He had a match with Skull Von Krush and we did the same spot as the previous week—I slapped him and he gave me a piledriver.

Backstage, Paul E. told me that he'd been brainstorming a character for me. He asked me if I could ride a motorcycle.

"You're going to be this bad ass chick," he said. "You'll ride into the arena on a big motorcycle. It's going to be great!"

Bubba and me in our ECW days.

But when I got to the show the next week—we were at the ECW Arena in Philly—I was told that I'd be paired up with Danny Doring and Roadkill, the Angry Amish Warrior. I wasn't shocked, because I'd heard that things in ECW often didn't go as planned.

As it turned out, pairing me with Danny was the best thing that could've happened. He was my saving grace in ECW. He had a reputation for being an asshole—especially to girls. But for whatever reason, he was always really nice to me. He never came onto me or treated me like anything other than a friend and coworker.

The more Danny and I spent more time together, the more I came to like and respect him. His mother had recently passed away, so Danny was responsible for taking care of his younger brother and an uncle that lived with him. Even though he had the weight of the world on his shoulders, he always maintained a terrific sense of humor.

Danny, Roadkill, and I all traveled in Kill's van, which was known as the RKV—the Road Kill Van. Sometimes other wrestlers would join us, like Big Sal from the FBI, Nova, Chris Chetti, Simon Diamond and Dawn Marie, and Jazz.

One night down in Florida, we all got a little drunk and I very quietly threw up in the back of the van. I didn't tell Kill and cleaned it all up the next time we pulled over for gas. When Kill found out, he was really pissed off. I wasn't officially banished from the van, but he never forgave me. From that point on, Kill would go out of his way to be a jerk.

Danny would get very aggravated with Kill, because he disliked me so much that he was barely civil to me. "I know you don't like Amy," Danny said, "but can you at least tone it down so that we can all do business together?"

Kill always acted like I was trying to be a big star, which was totally not the case. Of course, he was totally over with the fans and all I ever did was occasionally slap someone across the face. Even if I'd wanted to, I didn't have a clue how to steal the spotlight.

I really didn't understand the politics of the business yet, but I always tried to be respectful towards everybody that worked at ECW. They busted their asses and had worked a lot longer than me. Now they were allowing me to be in their environment and I wanted to show them that I appreciated the opportunity. I was as friendly to the ring crew as I was to Tazz and the other top guys.

Which isn't to say that the top guys were always friendly to me. There was actually a small incident on my very first weekend with ECW—Bubba Ray Dudley was holding court around the ring, talking, goofing around with some of the other wrestlers. When he saw me standing there, he started in, asking me all kinds of questions. "So," he said, "you know those Hardy Boyz?"

Obviously he knew that I did, but I still answered him. "Yeah, I train with them down in North Carolina."

All of a sudden his demeanor completely changed. He went from acting all lighthearted to totally pissed off. He looked right at me, with fire in his eyes.

"You tell them that if I ever come face to face with them, I'm going to kick both their asses."

It seems that the Hardyz had done a variation of the 3D in a match that aired on WWE TV. Bubba was really hot about it, which typifies how protective the guys were of ECW.

I immediately got angry and defensive when he said that, but Bubba was one of the top guys at ECW and I was a complete and total rookie. What was I going do? Tell him he was being a dick? "You got it, Bubba," I said. "I'll pass that message along."

I called Matt as soon as I had the chance and told him what had happened. He just laughed. "They're going to kick our asses?"

Nothing ever came of it—the Dudleyz got signed to WWE not too long after that and they never said anything to Matt and Jeff.

I've always gotten along really well with D-Von. He's just a nice, sweet guy. Bubba, on the other hand, can be a little difficult. When I first got to

WWE he came over and asked, "Why did you come here? You had it made in ECW. You're never going to be anything but tits and ass here."

I pretty much responded the same way I did when he told me that he was going to kick the Hardyz' asses. "Okay, Bubba. We'll see." I mean, what are you supposed to say to something like that?

The ECW locker room wasn't exactly the most professional environment, but it served as a good introduction to the backstage politics of the wrestling business. There was always a lot of maneuvering going on, a lot of gossip and backstabbing. It often felt like there was no one in charge, so there was no one to talk to if you got into an issue. You had to fend for yourself—you could duke it out, you could shit in their bag, but in the end, it was your problem and you had to figure out the best way to deal with it.

I got along well with most of the girls there. I was always friendly with Jazz, because she's about as laid-back as they come, and it's easy to connect with people who are as low on the totem pole as you are.

Dawn Marie was nice to me from the start. I think she was given a pretty hard time by a lot of the other wrestlers when she first came in, so instead of doing the same thing to people who came in after her, she went out of her way to be sweet.

Francine—the Queen of Extreme—was one of the bigger stars in ECW and while she was always nice to me, I heard through the grapevine that she spoke negatively about me behind my back. To be fair, she had taken a lot of shit to get to where she was in the business, and if she was aggravated or bitter, I can kind of understand how that could happen. If it made her feel better to talk shit about me, I didn't care. She was always very pleasant to my face, and we never had the slightest bit of trouble working together in the short time I was there.

Ultimately, it was Danny Doring that made my six months in ECW a tolerable experience. It would have been completely different if he wasn't there. It was nice to always have one person that I knew I could be myself around.

When you're out on the road, you have to find ways to entertain yourself. You work such long hours for such little money, at the end of the day you need to blow off some steam. In ECW, we used to amuse ourselves at night by shoot wrestling on the beds in our hotel room.

There was a regular group of us—Danny, Roadkill, Chris Chetti, Nova, Big Sal, and sometimes a few others. When we were on the road, we'd often sleep four to a room—we'd pull the mattresses off the box springs so that there would be "beds" for everyone. Because we were usually in such close quarters, packed three or four to a room, shoot matches would usually break out in some form or another.

There was always a dorm room atmosphere at the hotel. You'd still be a little hyper from the show, you were in a town that you didn't know, you didn't have any money to hit the clubs or go out to eat. All you had to do is to hang around with the people that you had already been with all day long.

Like the worms back in my roadie days, the shoot fighting usually started out spontaneously. We'd be watching TV and someone would get bored during a commercial break and jump on whoever was sitting next to them. Then one of us would serve as referee, just to make sure things stayed nice and legal.

The fights usually happened on the bed, with everybody standing around like in a lumberjack match. We operated under traditional shoot fighting rules, though occasionally someone would do something illegal, like tickling their opponent. It was all in good fun.

One night we were hotel wrestling and I got into a match with Jerry Lynn. He wasn't one of the regulars, so he didn't understand that this was serious business. When we started hotel room wrestling, the shit was on! Even though it was all playful and joking around, the goal was still the same as any real shoot fight—to make your opponent tap out.

We started wrestling, and Jerry was laughing until he realized that I wasn't fooling around. He was totally taken aback. I could see the look on his face as he thought, *Oh, shit—this girl is really trying to make me tap! I actually have to get into wrestling mode!*

We tangled for a while and it kept getting more intense. Finally I got Jerry into a judo hold called a *juji gatame*—it's a straight armbar, where your hips are under their elbow. I held him like that for a little while and he couldn't stop cracking up, laughing that Minnesota laugh of his. He was shocked, I think, like, "Holy shit, this really hurts!" But there was no chance that I was letting go. The only way to stop the pain was to tap. Finally, he gave in and tapped, "Okay, okay, enough already!" Jerry thought it was funny as hell—the matches were all in good fun, but still, no one wanted to tap out to a girl.

Another time I made Chris Chetti tap out—he was just completely mortified! Chris was Tazz's little cousin and had trained with him at the House of Hardcore—also known as the Team Tazz Dojo. He had some background in amateur wrestling and judo, and was always a strong competitor in the hotel room matches. Chris made me tap a bunch of times.

Well, we were going at it and I got Chris in a judo hold that he was not going to get out of. He got so mad, screaming, "*Arrgh!* You bitch! You bitch!" as he tapped out. After I let him go, he looked at me like a guilty little kid and said, "Please don't tell Tazz."

The hotel wrestling was never alcohol-driven—we were just bored. It was cheap entertainment. We'd play around for forty-five minutes and

The hotel wrestling was never alcohol-driven—we were just bored. It was cheap entertainment.

then we'd go to sleep. "Good night. See you tomorrow at the burnt-down roller skating rink."

That was my ongoing joke—in WWE, it's easy to find the building when you drive into a city. You just look for the arena. But in ECW, we put on shows in the craziest places—conference rooms at hotels, dilapidated civic centers, banquet halls. The RKV would pull into these towns in the middle of nowhere, and I'd roll down the window and ask people, "Excuse me, do you know where the burnt-down roller skating rink is around here?"

It may sound hard to believe because so many people are such marks for ECW, but I never bought into the whole mystique behind it.

When I was first offered the job, I debated whether or not to take it. At least working on the indies, I would have had more control of my schedule. Whereas in ECW, I was at their mercy—you're either in or you're not.

No one made much money working for ECW. Most people did it for the experience and the hope that ECW would take over the world. I'd get fifty to seventy-five dollars a show, but there was no guarantee that I'd get anything. Between gas money and hotels, I was definitely paying to work there. But I didn't mind. I was doing it to continue my wrestling education.

I started my run in ECW as Angelica, but then Paul E. came up with the character of Miss Congeniality. Now, I hadn't spent much time in New York, so I hadn't been around anybody with a hardcore New York accent. When Paul E. came to me with the verbiage he wanted me to say, I could barely understand what the hell he was talking about, "You say, 'I am the Miss Congeniality of the New Millennium . . .' Okay? Ready? Go!"

I didn't know what he was saying! I didn't really understand what kind of character he wanted me to be—hell, I don't think he did either! Not only that, but I'd never done a pre-tape before. Doing vignettes was a part of the business I had never really thought about. I never really thought about the fact that I'd have to be an actress in addition to being a wrestler.

At ECW, we often filmed our vignettes—also known as "pre-tapes"—after doing a show. That meant that sometimes you had to stay until six in the morning. You'd be completely tired and then all of a sudden, Paul E. would come to you and say, "Okay, this is what you're doing. Don't hold everybody else up, it's already four A.M.!"

"Um, yeah," I said as the camera rolled. "I'm Miss Congeniality . . ."

I made my official ECW TV debut in July, at the *Heat Wave* Pay-Per-View in Dayton, Ohio. My *unofficial* debut actually happened a couple of weeks earlier—on *Raw*.

Matt told me that the Hardy Boyz were going to be winning their first-ever WWE Tag Team titles at a *Raw* taping in Fayetteville, North Carolina. Well, I wasn't about to miss that, so I drove down to the show. I was hanging around backstage when The Godfather's wife, Denise, asked me if I had any plans for the night.

"No, I'm just here to watch the show."

"Do you think you could be one of the Hos tonight? The girls that were scheduled just got here and well, let's just say they're not going to put him over."

That was her roundabout way of saying that whatever local club was in charge of that night's girls had sent over a bunch of butt-ugly strippers. Of course, there was no way I was going to say no to being on WWE TV. I had my gear in my car—a wrestler always takes their gear to a show, for just this kind of emergency.

I was excited to appear on WWE TV, but I wasn't at all nervous. I didn't have any spots, all I had to do was walk down there and clap when The Godfather got some offense. I figured that it could only be a good thing as far as my future in the business was concerned, because although I was only a Ho, at least the WWE people had met me.

It ended up being me and another girl who was there visiting friends. The Godfather's match against Gangrel was right after Matt and Jeff's, so I was standing in the gorilla position—the spot right behind the curtain where the wrestlers wait to come out—when they won the titles. I watched their victory on the monitor with the rest of the *Raw* crew, which made it all the more thrilling.

This was back in the days when *Raw* would alternate between live and taped broadcasts. The next day I called Tommy Dreamer to give him the heads up that I'd be appearing as one of The Godfather's Ho's on the following week's *Raw*.

"It might not have been the best thing for you as far as doing business in ECW," Tommy said, "but I understand that it was something you had to do."

"I did what I thought was right in the situation and I got paid out of it," I said. "If it means that I'm not welcome back at ECW, that's fine."

"Well, you'll probably catch a little flack from some of the guys, but I don't think it's going to be a problem."

I didn't care if I got some heat—WWE paid me $250 and it wasn't like ECW was footing my bills! As it turned out, no one ever commented on my Ho appearance, but the incident still reinforced the Us vs. Them cult mentality of ECW. That never made any sense to me.

Because he couldn't pay everyone, Paul E. would give these speeches to raise morale and make everybody feel as if they were part of something important. I never could swallow Paul E.'s Kool-Aid. I saw things from a more realistic perspective. I'd sit there thinking, *This is total crap. Don't lie to these guys. They have mouths to feed at home and you're telling them they're about to get paid when you know full well that they're not.*

About a month after joining ECW, an opportunity came up for me to wrestle in Peru. It was a ten-day tour for which I'd be paid $750. That was way more money than I made in ECW!

I went to Tommy Dreamer and explained that I had this amazing opportunity. If Danny was my saint as far as personal matters were concerned, business-wise, I couldn't have survived at ECW without Tommy Dreamer. I could ask him anything and he never made me feel stupid. I could go to him for anything I needed and he'd do whatever he could to help me out.

"I'm going to go," I said. "Is that cool?"

Tommy didn't exactly say no. "You can do what you want," he said, "but you've got to realize that it's probably not going look too good to the people here. You should also know that these things don't always go as planned—you might not even get paid. But if this is what you want to do, then go do it."

A number of ECW people turned their noses up at me because they felt that by leaving so soon I was being disrespectful to the company. The way I saw it was that I didn't owe them any loyalty. It's not like they were paying me a lot of money—hell, I was paying out of my own pocket to work there!

The deal was that we were going to be paid $750 and the promoters would pick up all expenses—food, lodging, the works. There were maybe twenty wrestlers going to Peru, mostly from an indie promotion called Florida Championship Wrestling. Our big attraction was a Hulk Hogan impersonator. He looked just like Hogan—if the Hulkster was half his size and twice his age! But he had the big blond mustache and mimicked all of Hogan's mannerisms to the tee.

The night we arrived in Lima, we were taken to a really nice hotel, then went out for a meal at a great restaurant. *So far, so good,* I thought.

What I didn't know at the time was that there was a feud going on in Peru between two rival wrestling promotions. The original plan was to run shows in Lima, but then our promoters decided that we would go to other cities in order to disperse the market. They booked us onto a flight to the city of Huancayo.

When we got there, it seemed like everybody in the entire city were gathered outside our hotel to get a glimpse of the American wrestlers. It was pretty cool—we were like the Beatles!

We spent two days waiting around, but finally we were told that a show was booked. Since it was so last minute, we had to do some promotion for it at a local street festival. All the wrestlers got onstage and introduced ourselves, selling the fact that we were doing a show in the area and that everybody should be sure to come down—it was going to be great!

When it came time to go back to the hotel, our car was mobbed by hundreds of people. They were banging on the windows, rocking the car to the point where I thought they were going to tip it over. The police had to come break it up. It was incredible—they acted like we were huge superstars, even though they had no idea who we were.

The show turned out to be an unmitigated disaster. It was an a huge arena, a building that was way too big for our little wrestling show. The promoters were expecting a sell-out, but there were only five hundred people there.

Instead of a wrestling ring, we had a boxing ring, which is actually not the same thing. The ropes are very different—they're not designed for what wrestlers do, so if you try to run the ropes they'll break on you. There are no turnbuckles to speak of, which makes a lot of moves impossible to do. And, worst of all, the mat is hard as hell, with no give at all.

After the show, we all went back to our hotel, where we were told that we were all kicked out. "Nobody's paid for these rooms," we were told.

We all went to one of the promoters to ask what was going on. "There's clearly some sort of mistake," he said. "But since we're leaving in the morning, how about we all try to double up into rooms?"

They ultimately paid for just one room, which was used to store all of our luggage. I slept on a lawn chair on the roof that night. *I guess Tommy Dreamer was right,* I thought. *We're getting screwed.*

The promoters had booked a massive tour bus to take us to our next show, but I guess no one had put any thought into the fact that the mountain road

I guess Tommy Dreamer was right, I thought. We're getting screwed.

we had to travel was barely big enough to handle it. The wheels of the bus literally touched the edges of the road as we drove, rocks were falling down the side as we went along. Some of the wrestlers were getting sick, looking out the window and realizing how close we were to falling off the mountain. Plus, the elevation was so high, we were all getting altitude sickness. There was actually a rest stop on the mountain where we were able to get some oxygen.

The town was like the stereotypical poor South American community—dirt roads, ramshackle houses, chickens in the street. Unsurprisingly, the hotel we were booked into was a complete dump. All the wrestlers started getting mad, saying, "To hell with this!"

I did my best to keep things calm. "Look," I said, "they've got our plane tickets, they're holding onto our passports—they're in control. Forget whether or not we're getting paid—we need to worry about getting back to the States!"

A group of us decided we'd better have a talk with the promoters. "Remember, don't piss them off," I explained. "They've got our destiny in their hands!"

The promoters were all nervous when we asked for a meeting. They were certain they were going to have a mutiny on their hands. "We're sorry that the last show didn't draw as well you'd hoped," we said, "and we're all happy to do whatever we can to try to make the next one as successful as possible."

The promoters got tears in their eyes, they were so grateful—they'd put all their money into the tour, thinking they were going to become the Vince McMahons of South America. They thought all they had to do was bring American wrestlers down there and everyone in Peru would go wild. Instead, they'd totally lost their asses.

We realized that if we were going to sell any tickets, we needed to do some last-minute promotion. The promoters got ahold of a car and we drove through the city promoting the show though megaphones—"Come see the American wrestlers!" Our little promo job seemed to be attracting attention. All of the city's children followed us around like we were the Pied Piper.

We all went for a meal before the show. It was a little outdoor café, just a cheap family place—our expenses had decreased and decreased, going from fancy restaurants in Lima to this lower-scale place. But I remember sitting there, feeling nothing but good vibes. I'd already written off the $750. There was nothing I could do, so I might as well have myself a good time. After all, when else would I ever get to Peru?

As the wrestlers ate, a little local kid walked around, asking for autographs. He had a line-ruled school notebook, filled with WCW trading cards in it. He went around, asking everybody to sign their card. All the guys thought it was hilarious. They were signing their name to pictures of WCW wrestlers. When the kid asked me, I said, "Sorry, but my picture isn't in here."

I just had to make him happy, and sign his book.

He got all upset, going through his book, crying, "No, no, I have everybody's card!"

I tried to explain that I wasn't actually on a card, but he wasn't having any of that. So I looked though the book and found the card for Fyre, from the Nitro Girls—"Oh, sorry," I said. "I must've missed it. Here you go!"

He was all smiles after that. He hung around me like a little puppy dog the rest of the time we were there.

We got to the building where the show was to be held. It was a small gymnasium, a little primitive but fine for our purposes. The show drew close to four hundred people—not bad, all things considered, but still not enough for the promoters to even come close to breaking even.

The next day, we trekked back to Lima and headed home to the good old U.S. of A. In the end, we only did a couple of shows, so I got what essentially amounted to a free ten-day vacation. There were some scary moments, but I never regretted going. I just chalked it up to another interesting life experience.

CHAPTER 21

A couple of months after I started with ECW, they struck a real TV deal with TNN and began giving out contracts. TNN wanted ECW to have a certain amount of employees under official contract just to be sure that there would be a show every week.

Paul E. offered me a deal that wasn't for very much money, but at least it was something. I was basically paying to be in ECW up until that point, and his offer would have given me enough where I'd break even, and actually make enough to pay my bills.

Around this time, my dad called to tell me that my grandma, Maga, was very ill and it didn't look like she was going to make it. Maga had always been very supportive of my wanting to become a wrestler. She always told me, "Oh, you should be a model or a movie star," but I never had any interest in those things. Being a wrestler was close enough in her eyes, so she was all for it.

I went to see her and I told her that I'd been offered this big contract and that I was going to be on TV. I made it out like I'd become a huge success. "I did it, Maga!"

She was so proud of me. "I always knew you'd make it," she said, caressing my cheek. Maga passed away not long after that, without ever seeing me on TV. That was sad—I think she would've gotten a big kick out of that.

I never did sign the ECW contract. Despite the fact that I was working regularly, I wasn't feeling especially fulfilled there. It didn't feel like I was making forward motion in my career. Everyone at ECW thought that the TNN deal was going to send them straight to the top of the business, but even if it had, I still had my sights set on WWE.

My old friend Mikey from Florida e-mailed me that Dory Funk Jr. had started running an independent training camp. Dory is a major legend in our business. He was the longest uninterrupted NWA World Heavyweight Champion ever, and with his brother Terry, one of the all-time greatest tag teams in wrestling history.

Dory's "Funking Dojo" was WWE's developmental camp for years—Matt and Jeff trained there, as well as such Superstars as Kurt Angle, Edge, Christian, and Test. But when the relationship ended, Dory and his wife, Marti, had opened their own place in Ocala, Florida, called the Funking Conservatory.

The Funking Conservatory offered a weeklong program, which included training in every possible aspect of professional wrestling. It cost $750, which included accommodations at a nearby hotel. That was a lot of money for me at the time. I was wrestling every weekend, so I really didn't have time to earn a living by dancing.

The Hardyz had told me about their experience at the Dojo and I thought it sounded like something I'd really get into. I understood that it would be extremely hard, but I also knew that it would be really effective. I decided I was going to go for it.

When I first told Tommy that I was going to attend the Funks' camp, he wasn't exactly encouraging. "Why do you want to go there when you can learn all you need to know working here?"

"I just feel it's something I've got to do," I said.

"Well Paul E.'s not going to be happy about it but I guess you've got to do what you've got to do."

My trip to the Funking Conservatory was scheduled for the morning after the first *ECW on TNN* taping at the Elks Lodge—aka the Madhouse of Extreme—in Queens, New York. After the show, we stayed late to tape vignettes. Danny and I were waiting to film our bits and it just kept getting later and later. I finally had to go to Tommy Dreamer and say, "Dude, I'm going to miss my flight if we don't do this vignette soon."

We did the pre-tape—which saw me sniffing my armpits and blaming the smell on Road Kill—and just as I was leaving, Paul E. called me aside to wish me luck at the camp. "Thanks a lot," I said and hurried out of there, just in time to get to the airport for my flight.

I liked Dory and Marti right away. Matt used to mimic Dory when we'd practice at the ring in the woods. One of the things he'd always say in his Dory voice was, "This is a good business. It's a hard business, but it's a good business." The first day I was in Ocala, Dory actually said it, and I had to keep from cracking up.

At that point, I was the only girl to come to the training camp. That week it was me and twenty guys. The mornings began with a workout, followed by some training in the ring, learning various moves and spots. Then Dory would put two wrestlers together to work a match later in the day.

We also spent a lot of time learning how to cut promos. Most young wrestlers grab the mike and act cocky—"It doesn't matter who this guy I'm fighting is. I'm going to kick his ass!" But Dory explained the basic rule about cutting a quality promo—always talk up your opponent before you trash them. It's the same thing with the actual wrestling match. You have to put your opponent over at the same time as you're putting yourself over.

Even though I'd done pre-tapes on ECW TV, I really felt as though I didn't really get the hang of doing promos until I did the camp. Playing the heel, being a little snotty bitch, came a lot easier to me than this smelly New York biker chick character that Paul E. had come up with.

The afternoon session would include more training and then your match. At the end of the day, we did what Dory called "the Dojo High Spot." Two of us would get in the ring and we'd do a series of moves—headlock takeover, drop kick, arm drag, shoot off the rope, duck, clothesline—ending in a pinfall. First, one person would give everything and the other would take it. Then the one who was giving would get out of the ring and a new person would come in and take everything from the person who took it in the first match. It would progress like that until everyone in the dojo had been in a match, taking and giving moves.

Playing the heel, being a little snotty bitch, came a lot easier to me than this smelly New York biker chick character that Paul E. had come up with.

The next morning, it'd start all over again. We'd go to the gym and then watch our matches and promos from the day before. It was a proven formula that Dory and WWE trainer Dr. Tom Prichard had come up with, and it was exciting knowing that this was the same structure that was used to teach WWE Superstars.

At the end of the week, we put on a little show so that we could experience what it was like to work in front of a crowd. It was a pretty big deal—we filmed promos, we were given entrance music, the whole nine yards.

I actually had a decent match against one of the guys. My gimmick was that I was a heel chick—I even had a heel manager, HC Loc, who went on to become ECW's "Extreme Referee." All things considered, it was a good little match. When Matt watched it, he was pretty impressed.

The show ended with a huge battle royal between all the students. In the end, it came down to me and a guy named Dave who went by the gimmick name, the Largest Man on the Planet. I thought that was a hilarious name. I mean, he was big, but he wasn't that big!

Of course, he beat me up real bad. As I lay there semiconscious, he started singing, "Good night, sweet darling, it's time to go home . . ." then picked me up for a powerbomb. But I came

With Dory Funk, Jr., just after my Dojo match.

to just in time to flip over and reverse the powerbomb into an X Factor! He went face first into the mat, then I quickly rolled him over and pinned him—one-two-three!

It was a pretty sweet way to end the week. The Largest Man on the Planet didn't mind that I was going over. We had become friends over the week, so it was fun for us to work together to close out the camp.

The Funking Conservatory was very intense, as grueling an experience as I'd ever had. By the end, my body just plain hurt. The sheer number of bumps we took was ungodly.

That said, I was really glad I'd done it. It was definitely the most progress I had experienced since my first three days training in Mexico, when I went from knowing absolutely nothing to a good understanding of the basics.

The main thing I got out of attending the Funking Conservatory was that I felt so much more comfortable in the ring. That was very important to Dory: "You have to feel like this ring is your living room."

By the end of the week, I really felt more at ease with getting in the ring and doing the moves that I'd have to do hundreds and hundreds of times if I was serious about being a working wrestler. After my last match, I told Dory that for the first time since I'd started wrestling, the ring really did feel like my living room.

No question about it—my training at the Funking Conservatory definitely took me to the next level. Quite literally, as it turned out.

At that point, I was the only girl to come to the training camp. That week it was me and twenty guys.

CHAPTER 22

Marti and Dory were as good as gold to me. He was definitely proud of how I went toe-to-toe with the guys all week long.

Marti is a real unique character and a genuinely nice person. She had a real den mother vibe about her. She was very nurturing towards the young wrestlers, always offering compliments and trying to keep their confidence up.

Marti's very into photography, and one of the staples of the Conservatory is that she always takes lots of pictures of the guys. Because I was the only girl, she especially loved photographing me. We did a few shoots while I was in Ocala. I woke up extra early, went down to the lake and

took pictures with Marti, then hurried back to the gym so I was there when Dory started work at eight.

At the end of my training, Dory told us that he would send a video of the final night's show up to the WWE office, but obviously he couldn't guarantee that anyone would look at it. As it turned out, Terry Taylor, who worked with WWE's developmental talent at the time, did indeed watch it. He asked Dory to send up videos of the other matches I'd wrestled over the course of the week.

The Funks called to tell me that WWE had shown interest in my tapes, and that I'd be smart to make a followup phone call. "Oh no," I said, "I don't want to bug anybody."

"You have to bug them," Marti told me. "Not only are they all very busy, but you've got to show them that you're a take charge person."

A few days later I called Terry Taylor. I left a message on his voicemail, "This is Amy Dumas, Miss Congeniality in ECW. The Funks told me that they'd sent somebody my tape and I just wanted to see if you had a chance to look at it." I never heard back.

In late September I went to a *SmackDown!* taping in Richmond. I was backstage, hanging out with Matt, and Terry Taylor came over to say hello. "You're Amy Dumas, right? I got your message. Yes, we saw your tapes and we really ought to talk sometime soon."

As this was going on, I realized that Bubba Dudley was standing there, watching our conversation. *Oh God,* I thought, *now Paul E. is going to know that I'm trying to get work in WWE.*

Paul E. always knew everything that was going on everywhere in the business. He had sources everywhere. There was no doubt in my mind that Bubba was going to tell him what he'd heard. I was in an awkward position—if Paul E. found out that I was talking to the talent relations people at WWE he'd be pissed, and justifiably so. I didn't want to lose my gig at ECW before I'd signed up with WWE. I had no way of knowing if WWE was even interested, so I could've ended up without any job at all.

I was so stressed, wondering what my future held. But as it worked out, I needn't have worried. Terry and I talked on the phone a few times, and even though by this time he had accepted a job with WCW, he still arranged for me to talk to Jim "J.R." Ross and Bruce Prichard—the guys in charge of WWE Talent Relations. Terry did ask if I was interested in going to WCW, but I stuck to my guns. A week later, I flew up to Titan Towers— the WWE home office in Stamford, Connecticut—for a meeting with J.R. and Bruce.

I was so nervous! I couldn't decide what to wear in order to make a good impression, so I decided to buy myself a cute little Guess? business suit. It was so not me, but I wanted to look professional.

We talked for maybe thirty minutes. They had seen my tapes as well as some of Marti Funk's photos, and they were definitely interested in signing me. The meeting was largely about them getting a sense of what I was like, a feeling for the kind of person I was. They asked me questions that they surely knew the answers to—how long I'd been in the business, who I'd worked for.

Then J.R. asked me if I'd ever worked as a dancer. I had actually talked about that with Terry Taylor in one of our phone conversations. I explained to him that it was something I'd done to earn a living over the years, but I didn't want to be pigeonholed with the stripper image.

Terry was nonchalant about it. "I totally understand," he said. "But you know, in a lot of ways, the psychology is very similar to our business. They're actually very compatible, business-wise."

Still, when J.R. asked if I'd danced, I was kind of bummed out. I really didn't want to leave them with the impression that I was just another trashy stripper. At the same time, I wasn't going to lie about it, so after a long pause, I said, "Yes I have. Is that okay? Is it a problem?"

"Oh no, not at all," J.R. said. "We were just curious, honey."

Since they didn't seem to mind that I had danced, I figured I'd also tell them something else that might affect their decision. "I'm planning to get my boobs done as soon as I leave ECW," I said.

It was something I wanted to do because of what I saw elsewhere in the business. I looked at where I wanted to be and that's the look that I saw.

When the meeting ended, Bruce and J.R. shook my hand and said that they'd like to offer me a developmental deal. It's funny—I tried to be what I thought they wanted, and in the end, they liked me because of who I really was.

Even though I wasn't contractually obligated to ECW, I explained to Bruce and J.R. that I wanted to do the right thing by Paul E.

"That's fine," J.R. said. "Time is not an issue. We're not in any rush here. You can work there for however much longer ECW needs you. If there comes a point where there's a conflict, we'll work it out."

When I told Paul E. that I was going to WWE, he wasn't remotely surprised. "I already knew that," he said.

You've got to hand it to him—the guy had spies everywhere! His phone probably rang two seconds after I'd shaken hands with J.R. and Bruce.

"Well, I just wanted you to know that I'm happy to work for however much longer that you need me to."

"There's nothing for you here," he said, trying to show me how unimportant I was. "You can leave right now if that's what you want."

I didn't quite know what to do—I wanted to get the hell out of there, but I also wanted to do what was right businesswise.

"How about we make my last appearance two weeks from now at the ECW Arena?" That made sense to me—it was a big show and it was also what you'd do at a regular job, giving two weeks notice.

Paul E. agreed and that was that. Needless to say, the next two weeks weren't exactly my most comfortable weeks at ECW. After Paul E. found out I was leaving, he had Miss Congeniality do some really gross things on camera, like biting off my own toenails with my teeth—to this day, I get loads of comments about that pre-tape, as well the time I spanked Tammy Lynn Stych with a dominatrix whip.

But by that point, I didn't care what Paul E. asked me to do—I was going to WWE!

My final ECW show saw Danny Doring and Roadkill turning on me, followed by Cyrus presenting Danny with his new girlfriend, Electra. She was super-nervous when she came out—it was her first promo and it was in front of the ECW Arena crowd. "Why have chopped liver," she said, pointing at me, "when you can have filet mignon?"

Danny thought that was hilarious. I almost lost it watching him trying to keep from laughing. Then he hit me with a DDT and took Electra out of the ring so Roadkill could splash me off the top rope. I was scared to death because I knew Kill didn't like me and I was totally at his mercy. But he was good to me. He didn't hurt me at all. As I lay there, Cyrus leaned down and whispered in my ear, "Tell Vince we said hello."

Later that night I said my goodbyes to the people at ECW. Some of the other wrestlers were very positive, wishing me luck in WWE. Others weren't so nice, saying things like, "You're not ready yet."

The saddest thing about leaving ECW was that I wouldn't be working with Danny anymore. We'd really grown to be very close friends and I was going to miss him.

More than anything else, I felt a sense of relief. I didn't know what was ahead of me, I didn't know what WWE had planned for me. My fingers were definitely crossed, but I was glad to be taking the next step forward.

CHAPTER 23

If I wasn't interested in being on TV, I probably wouldn't have gotten my boob job. I didn't have any confidence issues—I just knew where I wanted to be and I knew what everybody looked like there.

I saw who was making money. I saw what the company liked. Even though I felt that I had something completely different to offer the business, I figured I'd meet things halfway and have both.

Getting the augmentation was something that I felt would help my career. Don't kid yourself—wrestling is show business. Would I have done it

if I wasn't in wrestling? Probably not. But since I wanted to be a WWE Superstar, I thought that if I was going to do this thing, I was going to go all the way.

The first thing I did after Paul E. and I agreed on my final show was call the cosmetic surgeon to schedule my boob job. I wanted to get it done as soon as possible—I didn't know when WWE was going to want me, but I wanted to be ready when they called—so I booked my surgery for three days after my last ECW show.

I went to a plastic surgeon in Virginia Beach that a friend in Richmond recommended—let's call him "Dr. Julian." When I went for my consultation, I had to choose the size of my implants. What you do is put on different bras and try out various implants to see what feels comfortable. Obviously it's not completely accurate, because the actual implants go in under your muscles, but it gave you a sense of what it would look and feel like after the surgery.

I picked my implants and then Dr. Julian ran through all the logistics of the surgery. Finally he asked me, "Do you have any questions?"

"You've done this a few times, right?"

"I've done over four thousand augmentations," he said.

"Nope," I replied, "I don't have any questions." Really, what did I need to know? The doctor clearly had it under control.

The procedure is totally simple. I went in at one in the afternoon and was out of there four hours later.

A girlfriend of mine came down there with me, so we rented a hotel suite for the night. That way she would be able to hang out in the living room while I slept off the anesthesia. The next morning I had to stop by Dr. Julian's office for a quick check to make sure everything was okay, and then that was that. I was able to go home.

I was supposed to receive my WWE contract that day, so I was definitely excited to get home to Richmond. I was still kind of groggy from the anesthesia, and the post-surgery pain had begun to kick in. It's pretty bad—it feels like two knives have been stabbed in your chest.

As soon as I got home, I went straight upstairs to my bed. When the doorbell rang, I jumped up to answer the door. I got down maybe four stairs before my entire upper body just exploded in pain. I was basically paralyzed, it hurt so much! I started yelling to the FedEx guy, "Hold on, hold on! I'm coming!"

There was no way I wasn't going to sign that contract, no matter how much pain I was in. I managed to hobble the rest of the way down the stairs, my chest throbbing in pain. I got to the door and the FedEx guy handed me my WWE contract. So what should've been one of the most

So what should've been one of the most incredibly happy moments in my life was marred by intense physical pain.

incredibly happy moments in my life was marred by intense physical pain.

I was still pretty excited. Holding that contract in my hand made it official—I was going to be a WWE Superstar!

The pain continued for a good few days after the surgery. I actually started getting concerned, "What if I'm not going to be able to wrestle?" Fortunately, the pain went away as my body healed up and I've never looked back. My bra size is about the same now as it was before I started weight training. I think people don't quite understand that boobs are mostly fat, so they disappear if you work out in a serious way. When your body fat is low, then you don't have any boobs. Basically, I just replaced what I had in the first place.

It's always funny when I look at fitness magazines or things like *Playboy* with one of the guys. They'll see a girl that's completely skinny with big boobs and say, "Do you think those ones are real?"

I just laugh, "Hell no!"

It's physically impossible for there to be a muscular hard-bodied girl with big boobs. That's one of the things that the girls in the locker room talk about. "Boys are so dumb! They don't get it!"

Of course, most guys don't care whether boobs are real or fake!

CHAPTER 24

No one told me that I needed to be there, but I decided to go down to Greensboro, North Carolina, for the final *Raw* of 1999. I didn't want to appear pushy, but I figured, why not? As I drove down there, I realized that I wasn't going to make it there on time—wrestlers are expected to arrive at the building at one o'clock on TV days. I got worried, thinking, *Maybe I shouldn't go, because I'm not going to be showing up on time.* But then I thought, *Well, I'm not technically late, because I'm not even supposed to be there!* I kept going back and forth, back and forth, in my head and finally showed up at the arena in the late afternoon.

J.R. saw me hanging around backstage and said hello. An hour later he told me that he went ahead and put me on for the payroll and that I'd get my travel information for the following week at the next day's *SmackDown!* taping in Richmond.

To this day, I don't know what would've happened if I hadn't come down to Greensboro. Who knows where I'd be if I'd sat home thinking, *Well, they'll call me whenever they're ready for me.* But from that day on, I was officially in the loop.

The next day at *SmackDown!* I was told that the creative department were interested in pairing me with Papi Chulo, one of the few *luchadors* on the WWE roster. Of course, I knew him from my time in Mexico, back when he was known as Mr. Aguila.

They had us do a photo shoot together, just so Vince McMahon could get a sense of what we looked like together. There wasn't a lot of planning—we both just wore our own gear.

Papi and I were really excited about our new journey together, but the truth was that we weren't very high on anyone's list of priorities. Not a lot of thought went into our being teamed up. We both had red hair and tattoos—that was the entirety of the logic that went into it.

Meanwhile, things between Beau and I weren't going too well. I was on the road so much, we hardly ever saw each other. We saw each other for a few minutes when I came home, but that usually consisted of dumping my bags, grabbing fresh clothes, and heading back out again. We decided to go away for New Year's Eve 2000, so we flew to Cancun with my friend Marybeth—aka Lexie Fyfe—and her husband.

Cancun is a really fun town. The four of us got pretty drunk—it was the changing of the millennium, after all. There were people partying everywhere, in the clubs and out on the sidewalks. Marybeth and I were joking around, putting our legs in the street like we were hitchhiking. Somehow it turned into play fighting, which then turned into actual wrestling, right there on the sidewalk. We locked each other in the Figure Four and mimicked Ric Flair—"*Wooooooo!*"

People stopped to watch us wrestling. Everyone was hooting and hollering, "Yeah girl! Kick her ass!" I was really buzzed, so I told anyone that would listen that we weren't just a couple of drunk chicks, we were professionals. "Look for me on WWE when you get back home to the States," I told them.

When Ric Flair came to WWE, I actually told him this story and he said that he was extremely honored. Of course, I'm sure I wasn't the first person to get drunk and pay tribute to Ric Flair. At one point or another, every wrestling fan feels the need to go "*Wooooooo!*" at the top of their

"Yeah girl!
Kick her ass!"

lungs. It's one of those things that transcends all cheesiness.

Although our relationship wasn't that good at the time, Beau and I had a fun time together in Cancun. But once we got back to the States, I was right back out on the road with WWE. It had become clear that Papi and I were going to be a team, so I asked if we could spend some time working together at the WWE dojo up in Stamford.

The wrestlers at the very bottom of the card don't get to spend a lot of time in the ring at live shows. There's so much going on as far as putting the show together—you don't want to have two kids that aren't even on TV hogging the ring.

I thought it was important that the two of us had the opportunity to get some significant ring time together, just so that we'd be able to join together as a cohesive unit. J.R. agreed, so we went up to the dojo for a week.

We spent some time training with Dr. Tom Prichard, but for the most part, Papi and I brainstormed on our own. We wanted to have our own plans as far as moves and our overall gimmick. One thing I've learned over the years is that you've got to take the bull by the horns if you want to get anywhere in the wrestling business, or for that matter, life.

After we wrapped up at the dojo, Papi and I began working dark matches—the matches that happen before the cameras start rolling. Even though he'd been working matches as Papi Chulo—on shows like *Shotgun Saturday Night* and WWE's Spanish-language *lucha libre* show, *Los Super Astros*—it was decided that a full character overhaul was in order. He came up with the name "Fuego Dragones"—Fire Dragon. As for me, I was going to be called "Phoenix."

From the very beginning, the creative team was unsure of what kind of character I was supposed to portray. Was I Mexican? Was I American? Before we hit the ring for our first dark match, I cut a promo from the stage which I delivered half in English and half in Spanish—"*Hola,* ladies and gentleman! We are *Fuego Dragones y Phoenix!*"

Then I threw the mike down and we ran into the ring. The big finish was Papi's moonsault to the floor, followed by another one from me for good measure.

Like so much of my moveset, I learned how to do the top rope moonsault out at the ring in the woods. I'd done it a million times, but I'd never done it to someone laying in the ring. When I first started doing the moonsault with Papi, I'd freak myself out, thinking that I wasn't going to hit right. I thought my opponent had to be in exactly the right spot in order for me pull it off, but sometimes they weren't there. When that happens, you can kind of adjust yourself in the air, but it makes it much more difficult. After a while, my confidence grew and I was able to pull it off without worrying about it. On the other hand, maybe I should have—Lord knows I've misjudged my opponents on more than one occasion!

CHAPTER 25

The boys have a tradition of welcoming new-comers to the locker room with a bunch of practical jokes, known in the business as "ribs." They can often be pretty rough, but it's a time-honored way of initiating a new wrestler into the group.

Fortunately for me, the girls don't have the same tradition—which isn't to say new people are embraced with open arms. But if you don't do any-thing to piss anyone off—you don't touch anybody's stuff, you were friendly to everybody, you don't overstep your boundaries, and nobody feels like their toes were getting stepped on—then more than likely, no one is going to screw with you. You're monitored for a while, making sure you don't break any of the unwritten rules of the locker room. Finally, after a period of time, you're accepted as part of the group.

When I came to WWE, Chyna was unquestionably the women's locker room leader. Miss Kitty—the Kat, Jerry "the King" Lawler's then-wife—was Chyna's little shadow. The other girls—Jacqueline, Ivory, Terri, and Tori—were all pretty mellow.

Of all the women, I clicked best with Tori. Luna Vachon was there at the time, but we knew each other from the indies and got along real well. Possibly because of my friendship with Tori and Luna, my time under the microscope wasn't as long as it is for some people. I was at ease with them, which made the whole environment much more comfortable.

A lot of that probably had to do with my relationships with some of the boys. Obviously I was close to Matt and Jeff, and through them I had become friends with Edge and Christian. I was also friendly with Chris Jericho, because we'd bonded over our time in Mexico with CMLL.

Over in the men's locker room, Bradshaw was the leader, and I was scared to death of him! I had heard all kinds of stories, and was really worried that he was going to make my life hell. But I knew that I'd introduce myself to him on my first day there so that there would be one less excuse for him to screw with me. I took a deep breath, thinking, *Okay, just go over there right now and put your best face on.* Of course, Bradshaw was totally cool. I said, "Hello, I'm Amy," we shook hands, and that was that.

The sad truth is that women wrestlers are largely viewed as unimportant, so there's no real reason to break them in. If a girl commits an infraction that would earn one of the boys a punishment, the usual attitude is that it doesn't really matter. We're just written off.

In a way, it makes getting acclimated into the locker room a lot easier for the girls. Ultimately it's what you do and how you act that earns you the respect of others. There will be people that you form friendships with, and other people that you have a business relationship with. It's the same in any job.

One of the basic rules for a new person is that you have to introduce yourself to everyone. It's a way of showing respect to everybody that's been there before you (although, these days, with some of the new people, this seems to be a dying art). It took me a couple of weeks before I introduced myself to Triple H. He always seemed to be in the middle of something, and I didn't want to disrespect him by interrupting.

I'd see him in the hallway and I'd think, *Okay, there he is, I'm going to say hello . . . Nope, not right now. . . .*

I finally said hello to him about two weeks into my WWE career. I went

Essa & Lita.

up to him in catering—we were in Philadelphia and I went into a long monologue. "I apologize for not having said hello to you earlier," I said, "but you always looked so busy. Anyway, my name is Amy and I just wanted to introduce myself to you. . . ."

Triple H just smiled, letting me know that it was no big deal. In fact, he didn't seem to care one way or the other. We chatted for a few minutes and he was totally friendly.

Triple H was personally involved with Chyna in those days. Joanie—Chyna's real name—was also a fairly intimidating presence. She didn't give me a hard time, but she didn't speak to me for a good while. It felt like she was intentionally not looking at me. She would have her head down and I'd say, "Hey Joanie, how are you doing today?" She'd glance at me, give me a nod, but that was about it.

A lot of people would be bothered by that kind of behavior, but I didn't care. She had taken a lot of shit to get to where she was in the business, so if she wanted to behave in that way, it was no big deal to me.

Even though Matt and I were hanging out a lot outside of work, in the beginning I tried not to spend too much time backstage with the Hardyz. I didn't want to make them feel like they had were responsible for me, and I didn't want anyone thinking I was riding on their coattails.

Mostly I hung out with the dark match clique—Essa Rios, Steve Bradley, Tom Howard. I usually rode from show to show with Tori or with Jason Ahrndt (aka Joey Abs) and the Mean Street Posse. Jason and Matt had had a personal falling out by this point and were no longer best friends. But the Mean Street Posse—Jason, Rodney, and Pete Gas—were really nice to me. They had gotten a hard time when they first started, so they made a point of making other people feel welcome.

Papi and I spent a few weeks working dark match after dark match. Papi's *lucha* style didn't really fit into the WWE format, especially seeing how the Light Heavyweight division was essentially in limbo.

The WWE Light Heavyweight Championship has pretty much the same history as the Women's title—nobody cares about it, so it comes and goes. When Papi and I first started, the Light Heavyweight belt was held by Gillberg—literally.

For those of you who don't remember him, Gillberg was an indie worker named Duane Gill who was brought into WWE in 1998 to goof on WCW's big superstar, Goldberg. It was a great gimmick—Gillberg was a scrawny little bald guy, probably one hundred pounds lighter than Goldberg. His entrance was hilarious, with a couple of guys holding sparklers instead of Goldberg's big fireworks display.

Eventually the joke got old, and Gillberg left WWE, taking the Light

Heavyweight title with him. He continued to work at independent shows around the country, acting like he was a big-time WWE Superstar. In February, creative brought Gillberg down to the *Raw* tapings in Austin, Texas, to drop the belt and put the Light Heavyweight Championship back in the mix.

The plan was for Gillberg to come out on *Heat,* claiming that he was the greatest WWE champion in history because he'd held onto the Light Heavyweight belt for such a long time. Then Christian would come out and beat him for the title.

Unfortunately, Christian was involved in an angle with Edge. Just before showtime, creative decided that that storyline took precedence over the Light Heavyweight title, so writer Brian Gewirtz came to us and said, "We're going to start you guys tonight."

My initial reaction was "Really?" I was surprised that Papi and I would've even crossed anyone's mind.

It was pretty last minute, maybe three hours before the show started. Even though Papi and I had been working dark matches for a few weeks, we hadn't coordinated our outfits in any way. But I wanted to make sure we looked good for our big *Heat* debut. Papi had been wearing red tights, so I went to the seamstress and asked her if she could do something with this red cat suit that I had. She cut it into a little top and pants instead of one solid thing. Even though our outfits didn't exactly match, at least we looked like a cohesive unit.

In this business, you have to take the initiative. Chris Jericho has a saying which I completely agree with—"It's easier to ask for forgiveness than to ask for permission." Every time a new girl comes in, they'll say, "No one told me what to wear. No one told me what to do."

"They're not going to," I tell them, and they invariably look at me like I'm a huge bitch. But the fact is, once you've made it to WWE, you should be able to show some initiative. Wear what you want to wear. We work for a wrestling company, not a fashion company. Figure it out on your own.

You have a choice. You can either take the ball and say, "Cool. I can do whatever I want," or you can doubt yourself and say, "Oh well, they didn't tell me who to be or what to do." Not having the courage to be creative and tweak or invent the way you want to project yourself has been the downfall of many people in the business. It's sink or swim.

The fact that we were a last minute addition to the show was a good thing in my eyes. I've always worked well under pressure. I do my best work when I don't put a lot of planning into it. My whole life has been like that—I get an idea and then run with it.

So when we got the word at four-thirty, I thought, *Alright, let's get ready to go out there.* I got my outfit made, Papi and I brainstormed a little bit, and before I knew it, we hit the ring. A lot of people would've buckled under that kind of pressure. Whereas that's when I start to thrive.

It was a great way to debut. Papi and I stood in gorilla as Gillberg hit the ring and issued his challenge. "Tonight I'm putting out an open challenge to any Light Heavyweight in that locker room that thinks he could beat me," he bellowed. " 'Cause there ain't one."

We didn't know what our entrance was going to be, if Howard Finkel was going to announce us or if there was going to be any music. Bruce Prichard said, "Go!" and we went running down the ramp to some generic entrance music.

The match was quick as could be. Papi gave Gillberg the tilt-a-whirl head scissors and then hit him with the moonsault—one-two-three! Then I hopped up on the top and gave Gillberg a moonsault of my own. Papi grabbed the belt and we headed out of there. As we walked up the ramp, I looked at the camera and celebrated. "Yes!"

When we got to the back, Shane McMahon came over to us and said, "Great job. Don't ever look at the camera again."

I didn't know that I wasn't supposed to do that. It was another example of something that no one tells you, you're just supposed to know.

"Okay," I said. "Thanks."

There was one other issue—we didn't have names yet. Papi had been Papi Chulo for some time, but they wanted this new character to be a fresh start. No one really liked the names we'd been using, Fuego Dragones and Phoenix, but they also hadn't come up with anything better. The attitude was, let's send them out there and we'll figure it out later. When we went out, we were told that *Heat* announcers Michael Cole and Kevin Kelly would say "Who are these challengers? We don't even know who these people are!" On the following week's show, we'd get a proper introduction.

But as things tend to happen in WWE, plans were changed and our names were written into the commentary that they did in postproduction. As we hit the ring, they introduced Papi as "Essa Rios," followed by a little discussion about me.

"Who's that lady at ringside?" asked Kevin Kelly.

"She's known as Lita," answered Michael Cole.

"I'm in love with Lita!"

Of course, no one bothered to tell me—I found out I was Lita by watching *Sunday Night Heat.* I had seen a reference to "Essa Rios and Lita" on the Internet, but I just assumed that whoever was writing the *Heat* spoilers made the names up. When I heard Michael Cole call me "Lita," I thought,

I guess the Internet was right. Then I thought, *Ick. I don't like it.* Everything was going so great except for that rotten name.

I didn't know where the name Lita came from until very recently. I was in the Stamford studio, chitchatting with Adam Penucci, the producer who puts together all of our amazing video packages. He's just incredibly talented. We were talking and Adam said, "Did you know that I named you?"

"Nope," I said. "I never knew that."

It turns out that Kevin Dunn—our executive producer—sent out an e-mail to everyone in WWE, asking if anyone had any suggestions as far as names for these two new wrestlers that were making their debut on *Heat.* Adam offered the name "Lita," which he thought was a kind of Spanish twist on "Lolita."

While I didn't like it at first, I've gotten used to it and it doesn't bother me one way or the other. To me, I'm still Amy. It took about a month before I began responding to Lita. I heard it and I'd have to take a second to remember, "Oh, right. They're talking to me."

CHAPTER 26

I was on cloud nine after Essa Rios and Lita made their triumphant debut, but was brought back down to earth as soon as I returned to Richmond.

Something was wrong with Cody—it started out as a bad limp, so Beau assumed he'd twisted his leg in some way. But it quickly got worse, to the point that he could barely turn his head without yelping in pain. Within twenty-four hours, Cody couldn't even walk.

I immediately made an appointment with a specialist. The doctor injected Cody with a dye to see if there was something wrong with his spine. He discovered that the disc between his third and forth vertebrae was slightly bulging.

"But that shouldn't be causing him this much pain," the doctor said. "He should be able to walk. We can do surgery to remove the bad disk and fuse his vertebrae together, but I'll be honest—there's only a fifty-fifty chance of it helping."

I was so worried. I didn't know what to do. I thought about it a while and decided to go ahead with the operation. I wanted to be sure that I did everything I could for Cody.

After the surgery it seemed like nothing much changed at all. Cody was paralyzed. The doctor said that, because of the initial trauma of the swelling and then the surgery, it might take a few days to see any results.

A week passed, but nothing changed. Cody's vital signs were completely fine, but he couldn't move at all. It was awful—his eyes were so sad, it seemed like he'd lost all of his thirst for life.

I knew that I had to consider putting him to sleep. I decided to bring him home from the hospital, so that I could spoil him for a couple of hours before I did what I had to do. My local vet agreed to come to my house and euthanize him there.

When I called the specialist to tell him my plan, he was very understanding. "You're not making the wrong choice," he said, "but just so you know, Cody's attempted to move for the first time since he's been here. He didn't get very far—he didn't even get himself up off the floor—but he tried."

Well, if that was the case, then I clearly had to wait a little longer before doing anything rash. I went and visited him in the hospital every day. We tried to help him walk by lifting him up with slings under his chest and his legs. At first it didn't seem to be doing him much good, but little by little, he started to get better. After about two months of physical therapy with the slings, Cody was able to walk on his own. He was tentative at first, and he couldn't go for very long because his muscles had atrophied, but eventually he was as good as new.

Obviously, the whole experience was devastating for me. I was finally succeeding as a wrestler and then this horrible thing happened to Cody. It was just heartbreaking, but it really put things into perspective for me. As important as wrestling is to me, there's always more to life than show business.

Something a friend said at that time has really stuck with me: "When two spirits are so strong," she explained, "one often steps aside in honor of the other." Basically she was saying that, given the timing of all that was going on, it was like Cody was trying to bow out gracefully. I was going to be super busy and he was going to pass on so that I could begin this new chapter of my life. It was true—I had barely seen him with all the traveling I'd been doing. But I didn't want him to go! From that moment on, I made sure that Cody became a top priority.

The whole drama with Cody also enabled me to look at another part of my life and made it easier to do something that should've been done a long time ago. When Cody was in the hospital, I'd go and visit him twice a day every day that I wasn't on the road with WWE. But when I was gone, Beau—who Cody and I had lived with for a long time—never even bothered to go see how he was doing. That hurt me so much. It also made me angry—Beau knew how close I was to Cody and by not helping me take care of him, it felt like he didn't care a damn about me. It was the final straw. Our relationship had been growing apart for a while, and Beau and I finally split up for good.

Breaking up with Beau was something that needed to be done. We'd completely drifted apart. We were only still together because it was safe and comfortable. I justified it by getting upset that Beau wasn't there for Cody when he needed him, but the truth was that the relationship had been over for a long while, and it was time that I acknowledged that fact and moved on with my life.

My relationship with Beau didn't end on the best possible note. Looking back, I should've ended it long before. Beau was rightfully suspicious of Matt from the beginning, and once I decided to hook up with Matt, my heart just wasn't in the relationship anymore. I don't think it was very cool of me to have lied to Beau, but that's just something I had to learn on my journey.

On the other hand, I think every action in life has a reaction—immediately after we split up, Beau met the girl that he has since married. So in a way, what happened between us turned out for the best. We're both in very happy relationships. Things just have a way of working out.

As important as wrestling is to me, there's always more to life than show business.

CHAPTER 27

In a way, Essa Rios and Lita were a mistake. We weren't meant to get over. But for some reason, the audience attached to us very quickly.

The WWE crowds were very hot back then. The energy you'd feel in those arenas was unbelievable. There was something about our chemistry together that made them cheer from the second we debuted. You couldn't really put a finger on what it was, but the crowd was into it right away. That's not something that happens all the time.

Essa is a very natural performer—he just goes with the flow and doesn't think too much about

what he's going to do. I think the crowd sensed that we weren't contrived, that we weren't going out there trying to make a big impression. We were just doing what we do.

From the overall vibe to the flashy *lucha*-style high spots, Essa and Lita were very different from what was going on at the time. Wrestling often repeats the same characters over and over again, but you couldn't exactly compare us to anyone else. It was a breath of fresh air, and the crowd tends to respond to something new and unique.

We were told to have a kind of Frick and Frack relationship, with me mimicking Essa's moves, but other than that we were pretty much on our own. Since we were left to our own devices, Essa and I just tried to come up with the most exciting spots. The week after we debuted on *Heat,* we were in San Jose for our first *Raw* appearance. It was Essa against Crash Holly for the Light Heavyweight Title.

I'd never seen a hurricanrana done off the apron, so we incorporated it into the match—Crash ducked outside to the floor, so I nailed him with a hurricanrana and tossed him back in. Then Essa hit him with a suplex and a moonsault for the one-two-three. It was innovative and exciting, and the crowd responded. From there on in, the hurricanrana off the apron became one of my signature spots.

I didn't put a whole lot of thought into who Lita was. Lita is similar to a lot of WWE characters in that she's basically a more extroverted, flamboyant version of myself. The lights and the music and the people everywhere just kind of brought her out of me.

Don't get me wrong—I'm always watching old wrestling tapes or flipping through magazines or watching music videos, and any number of those elements enter into my character. But I don't consciously imitate the things that I see—I just kind of absorb everything and let Lita happen naturally.

Keeping Lita spontaneous and honest is very important to me. Sometimes I'll watch a tape of myself and I'll do something awkward or ridiculous, but it doesn't bother me. Those moments are worth it for me to have a natural flow to my general aura. I just do what I do, and if occasionally I get caught looking stupid, I'd rather have that happen than be constantly worried about what I look like or what I'm doing out there. I think that if you worry too much, then things begin to look controlled and contrived all the way through.

Even though we were getting great reactions from the live crowd, Essa and I mostly appeared on *Heat* and *Jakked,* working with people like Taka Michinoku and Sho Funaki, Scotty 2 Hotty, and Bob Holly.

I could never quite tell what was going on in Essa's head. He was totally nice, but I had no clue how he felt about me, if I aggravated him, or if he hated being paired with me. We looked out for each other, but I honestly never knew if he liked me.

It wasn't until my video—*Lita: It Just Feels Right*—was released that I finally discovered how Essa Rios felt about me. The things he said were incredibly sweet and generous. The first time I saw it, I was completely moved. It made me feel so good.

A couple of weeks after Essa won the Light Heavyweight Title, we were at the Georgia Dome in Atlanta for *Raw.* We were scheduled to take on Joey Abs and the Mean Street Posse in the eighth segment of *Raw,* but right at showtime, they moved us to *Jakked.*

I always refer to the time after the doors open, but before the shows starts, as "the calm before the storm." I usually use that time to clear my head, put on my makeup, and mentally prepare to do my thing. Sometimes I just spend the hour listening to music through my headphones while thinking about what I'm doing that night. I like to get any unrelated distractions out of my head so that when it's Go Time, well, I'm ready to go!

Believe me, every wrestler has had The Nightmare—your music starts playing and you realize your boots aren't laced, you're as far away from gorilla as you can possibly be, and Vince is screaming at the top of his lungs, "Where the hell is Lita? You know what, I don't care . . . *she's fired!*" Then you wake up in a cold sweat to find out you have another hour before your alarm clock goes off—you didn't miss your match and you still have a job.

We looked out for each other, but I honestly never knew if he liked me.

That night was as close as I've ever come to living the nightmare. Since the eighth segment of *Raw* takes place at roughly ten-thirty and *Jakked* starts at around eight, all of a sudden I had two-and-a-half hours less time to get ready than I'd anticipated. People were literally knocking on the locker room door, yelling at me to get my ass to gorilla. As a result, I ended up going to the ring completely frazzled.

The plan was for Essa to go over Jason—I had to moonsault him, then Essa and I would both dive outside onto Pete Gas and Rodney with crossbodies off the top. The Posse were cool about it, but I was having personal issues about having to job Jason out like that. He was one of the people that really helped me get to WWE and now I had to punk him out.

When I was working out at the ring in the woods, Jason would spot me on everything I did because he was the biggest guy there. Jeff and Shannon Moore were more inspirational, because we all shared a similar style. I'd watch them do moves and say, "Ooh, I want to do that!" But I attribute a lot of my confidence to Jason because he was so huge and I knew he was never going to let anything bad happen to me. I always felt safe, so it was easy to say, "Okay, I'm just going to do this move," whatever it was. I knew Jason was always going to be there.

In the match, Essa did his moonsault and then I did mine. As I hit Jason, my knee went right into his ribs. "Oh God," I said, "I'm sorry!"

"Get up," Jason said. "Go! Go!" He knew I had to go dive onto the Posse.

When we got back to gorilla, I just started crying. I was so upset that I'd kneed Jason, even though he barely felt it. WWE road agent—and former Freebird—Michael Hayes saw me standing there bawling. "What the hell is wrong with you?"

"It's just that Jason helped me so much," I sobbed, "and I didn't want to do that to him."

Michael turned to Matt, who was also standing there. "What's wrong with her? She's doing that girly shit."

Then he looked at me and said, "Listen, you're here in WWE. You're getting a push. There's nothing to be upset about. Get over it. Now."

I realized Michael was right. I had no reason to be upset. Sometimes in our business you have to job out your friends. It's just the way it is.

A few weeks later, we were in Trenton for *SmackDown!* Essa was booked for a title match against Jeff Hardy—my first-ever match against one of the Hardyz. Of course, Matt accompanied Jeff to the ring. It was a great feeling, being out there with the three people I felt most comfortable with.

That match saw the beginnings of a rift between Essa and me—we were starting to miscommunicate. The ref warned me not to get involved, but I hit Jeff with a moonsault anyway, causing Essa to get disqualified.

It was especially fun working with Jeff, because I was comfortable exchanging ideas and interacting with him. With everybody else that Essa and I had faced, it was often awkward asking them if they were cool with me doing a moonsault or a hurricanrana on them. The idea of a girl doing something physical to a guy other than a nut shot was a new concept. With the exception of Chyna, most girl-on-guy physicality was of the traditional damsel-in-distress-trying-to-escape variety. It was still very rare for females to do offensive moves to guys. Fortunately, most everyone was okay with it.

There's no way I'll ever be able to thank all those guys enough for what they did for me. What they allowed me to do was definitely the thing that catapulted me to the next level. The thing that made Lita such a popular character was the way I interacted with the guys. In a lot of ways, it changed the face of the business.

Amy's Girl's Club: Makeup & Hair—What Works For Me

Cheap Must-Haves
- *Wet 'N' Wild #666 lip liner*
- *Cover Girl Perfect Blend black eyeliner pencil*
- *Maybeline Great Lash mascara*

Expensive—but worth it!
- *MAC powder pigments*
- *MAC Studiofix powder*

Tips and Techniques
- *I like to multi-use products, like using my blush on cheeks, as well as an eye highlighter.*
- *I have tried a million different hairdyes—every drugstore brand and*

most salon brands. As far as drugstore stuff, I like Feria, as well as Rouge Romantics. My favorite salon hair dye is definitely Goldwell Elumen. All red dyes fade, but Elumen kicks ass!

- *A red color-enhancing shampoo used once or twice a week will be your best friend as far as keeping your color looking fresh.*

- *False eyelashes give me an instant headache—they're way too heavy for me, but really do add drama. Instead, I recommend cutting the eyelash and putting falsies on the outer corner of your natural lash-line.*

- *To really open up your eyes, try a light shimmery powder in the inside corners.*

- *I rarely wear lipstick. Mostly I stick to liner and gloss. But for adding longevity and fullness to your lipstick, try this: line your entire lip and fill in, leaving the center bare or lighter, depending on how dark a color you choose. Then highlight the center of your bottom lip with a gloss.*

- *Don't ruin your skin with the real sun—try a bronzer with a light shimmer.*

- *Do not fear sunless tanner. They've come a long way since they first came out. I'll use just about any brand, but I especially like Origins Faux Glow for the face.*

- *When applying foundation, powder, or tanner, do not stop at the jaw line. Always extend the product down your neck and onto your chest so you aren't two-toned.*

- *When traveling and removing makeup, I love premoistened towel-ettes. They are convenient, and take off makeup without being too rough on the skin.*

- *I switch up facial cleansing and moisturizing products, but love the Aveda All-Sensitive line, Kiehl's Cucumber Toner, and Creme de la Mer moisturizing creme.*

- *I often switch up the perfume I wear, but some of my favorites include BCBG Nature, Happy by Clinique, Demeter Tomato, and Demeter Grass.*

- *Most importantly, always feel free to experiment! Be creative!*

CHAPTER 28

After I broke up with Beau, there was very little reason for me to stay in Richmond. I considered moving back to Atlanta and staying with my mom for a while. My only necessities at the time were a twenty-four-hour gym and a convenient airport.

In April, just as I was debating where to move, Jason Ahrndt was sent off to WWE's developmental territory in Memphis. He asked me if I'd like to move into his condo in Sanford, North Carolina — about fifteen miles north of Cameron. Matt and I had been growing closer and closer, plus I'd made a lot of good friends in the area, so I decided to take him up on his offer.

Matt & Jeff.

I did worry that moving to North Carolina could prove to be a potentially awkward situation. I really didn't want to overstep the boundaries Matt and I had created for ourselves. I didn't want him to feel like he was responsible for me.

But Matt was cool with it. Like everything else in our relationship, it was just part of a natural progression. Up to that point, things between us were very loose and casual, more like friends than anything romantic. But once I got down there, we settled into a really nice groove. Not too long after I moved, Matt and I were officially a couple.

The process of getting there was slower than any couple I have ever known. The evolution of our relationship was completely natural. Sure, we hooked up when we first met, but we were friends first and foremost. It was a slow, easy progression from there to becoming officially committed. Looking back, I wouldn't want it any other way.

I don't want to jinx anything, but our relationship is just so relaxed and steady. I see people that seem so sickeningly in love that it's gross, and yet a year later they're in the middle of a paternity battle. I feel as though Matt and I have those same over-the-top feelings, but we just express them in a more realistic way. Instead of everything being so dramatic, our relationship is very realistic.

Which isn't to say that we aren't passionate—far from it! Things between us are never even the least bit boring. I just think people often mistake drama and craziness for excitement and passion. It doesn't have to be like that. At least that's how it is with us.

Matt's only long-term relationship before me was with wrestling. That was the only thing he was ever truly committed to. As a result, he's not exactly a candlelit dinner kind of guy. It's not a bad thing, but sometimes I wish he was a just a little more romantic. I'm not a mushy person, not by a long shot. On the scale of mushy girls, I'm definitely on the lower end. But at the same time, I'm not devoid of all mushiness.

As our time together has gone by, Matt has definitely evolved. It's going to take a while longer, but he's getting there. I remember talking to a friend about Valentine's Day and she asked, "What do you think Matt is going to get you?"

"Nothing," I said. "But it's okay—I enjoy giving him gifts."

"That's not right," she said, but I figure if him not knowing what to do on Valentine's Day is the biggest problem we have, then I've got it pretty damn good. I'm certainly not the type of girl to try and train him or turn him into something he's not. "I don't mean to pick on you," I told him, "but even one flower or a card would be nice. I know it's kind of cheesy, I know that you love me, but it would mean a lot to me."

Slowly but surely, he's beginning to understand. He's come a long way since our first Christmas together, when I got a clothes hamper, a filing cabinet, and a lamp.

The thing is, Matt is a very practical guy. For Matt, those gifts meant as much as a framed

The fans might envision us in some charter jet but, the truth is, we're usually in a rented Taurus, driving to a cheap motel in the middle of nowhere.

picture of Cody, a beautiful bouquet of flowers, and a framed picture of the two of us. He genuinely stressed out about what to get me. "I was trying to think of what you needed," he said.

"If I need something I'll go get it for myself," I explained to him. "A Christmas gift is an occasion to show how you feel."

I always get a little carried away with Christmas gifts. I gave him a stocking one year and he was so excited. "I never had a stocking," Matt said. "That's so sweet."

Matt's childhood was so different from mine. He grew up in an all-male household. Mr. Hardy did a great job raising his sons, but he's not the kind of guy to bake Christmas cookies.

Matt has definitely begun to show signs of a romantic side—he got me a very pretty bracelet for my birthday last year and it made me so happy. I was so proud to show it off—I showed it to Debra and she was so sweet. "You see, honey," she said. "We've started to convert him."

The truth is, the more time goes by, the stronger the bond between Matt and I becomes. We just keep getting better and better.

Anyway, after I moved to North Carolina, it seemed silly not to ride with Matt and Jeff. It just was the most comfortable situation for me— they were my best friends there.

Traveling with those guys was very similar to my experience on the road with Fifteen. We did it in a rental car instead of a beat-up van, but otherwise, we always traveled pretty bare-bones. The fans might envision us in some charter jet but, the truth is, we're usually in a rented Taurus, driving to a cheap motel in the middle of nowhere.

It's funny, because WWE has always used the three of us to represent the rock 'n' roll element of the business, and when we'd run into people at truckstops or restaurants that didn't watch wrestling, they would always ask, "Hey, are you guys in a band?"

We could never resist screwing with them. We'd claim to be one of those faceless alternative one-hit wonders, where people knew the song but didn't have a clue what the band looked like. "Maybe you've heard of us," we'd say. "We're Eve 6."

The more we traveled together, the more Matt, Jeff, and I grew comfortable with each other. From noon, when we had to be at the building, to midnight, when the show ended, our time was community time with everybody in WWE. Otherwise, the rest was ours, it was personal time. It's one of the unique things that I really love about being a wrestler. Most people wouldn't see six-hour drives as being a perk of the job but to me, it's something really special that you just don't get on any other job.

As with many of my best experiences, traveling with Matt and Jeff was like being part of a little secret world that nobody knew about. By and large, the three of us were a closed community. Occasionally we'd go for a meal after a show with Edge, Christian, Jericho, or The Hurricane, but then we'd be on our own again. Our personalities fit to where the three of us would accommodate our travel to fit our individual needs. Any other personalities added into the mix could potentially complicate the scenario. The last thing you want to do on your off time is walk on eggshells around people that you're not one hundred percent comfortable with.

In our business, the off time is crucial. Things get so intense, you need time to decompress. You don't want to worry about saying something in front of someone who might take it out of context.

We had our roles and responsibilities within our group—Matt was the leader, and I was the copilot. I'd be in charge of looking at the map and changing the CDs while Matt drove. Jeff was responsible for having the booking sheets on him so that we'd know where we were going. He was also very good at packing the truck—he has excellent puzzle skills! All in all, it was an ideal arrangement.

Matt and Jeff are the classic brother combination. On the road, Matt was always the older authority figure and Jeff was the detached childlike youngster. "Okay," Matt would say, "where do you guys want to eat?"

Jeff would sit in the back, not saying anything, so Matt and I would pick a restaurant. Then when we pulled into the parking lot, Jeff would just sit there.

"Jeff, are you coming in?"

"In a little while."

Most of the time, he wouldn't even come into the restaurant, he'd just sit in the car.

We always tried to figure things out as a group. If Jeff had said, "I really don't feel like stopping tonight. Let's just get fast food," that would've been factored in as an option. But since he chose not to offer his input, Matt and I had to make decisions for the three of us, and that always made Jeff feel like he had no say in what we did.

There were times where Matt would get so aggravated with Jeff, either from his lack of input or from his inability to ever be on time. Jeff would get in the car a half-hour later than he was supposed to, which made Matt snap at him, "Come on! Quit being so irresponsible!"

A minute or two later, Matt's calm, logical side would take back over and he'd try to reason with Jeff. "Dude, if you're going to be late, could you please call us? That way I could've used the time to fill the car up with gas instead of just sitting here."

Jeff would just sigh, "Yes, Matt."

We would play stupid games in the car and have really long talks about our views on life and all kinds of different stuff.

I would try to cut their confrontations off at the pass, like a mom trying to keep peace among the family. Matt was the strict dad and Jeff was well, *Jeff.*

More often than not, though, the three of us got along great. We would play stupid games in the car and have really long talks about our views on life and all kinds of different stuff. They were the most comfortable conversations I've ever had, because I knew I wasn't going to be judged on what I said. The opposite was true, as well—my opinion of Matt or Jeff wouldn't change based on anything that came out of their mouth.

One of our games was "What If?" We'd make up weird scenarios and then try to figure out what life would be like if . . .

For example, one of us would ask, "What if you didn't have a mouth and had to talk with your eyes?"

Then we'd start pondering that crazy concept—How could your eyes talk? Would they make a sound? Would it be a clicking, like Morse code? And how would you eat?

It all sounds completely nuts, but it was a way of passing time in the car. We had hours to kill, so we could just say a bunch of silly nonsense that we couldn't say with any other people in the car. It was a profoundly comfortable environment. The three of us were as relaxed as we could possibly be, which was often quite a relief after spending the entire day and night backstage. It was nice just to be able to kick off my shoes, put my feet up on the dashboard, and relax.

If you look at the fundamental character qualities of Matt and the fundamental character qualities of Jeff, I'm right in the middle. Matt is logical and levelheaded and totally in control of his emotions. Jeff, of course is the exact opposite, a free spirit to the Nth degree.

I love Jeff so much, he really is like a brother to me. Until I met Matt and Jeff, I was always the youngest person in my group of friends. I was always the baby—I hung out with older people, I dated older guys.

When I first met Jeff, he was twenty-one years old, but he struck me as much younger. As I got to know him, I realized that we were very in tune with each other. Matt was more like a teacher, someone that I was eager to impress. But Jeff was totally sweet and totally mellow. He didn't show signs of stress. Plus he always does his own thing, which is very much how I've tried to live my life.

From the first day I trained at the ring in the woods, Jeff was a huge inspiration to me. He encouraged me to not be afraid to try new moves. I don't get scared easily, but I was in a foreign environment. I wasn't invited to the ring in the woods as a friend—I was there as a fellow wrestler. This was very much their turf, and I was very worried about playing by their rules.

It wasn't anything he said. Jeff didn't go out of his way to be motivational. He was just naturally supportive. We were talking about standing frankensteiners onto someone's shoulders. I didn't think that I could jump up that far. "It seems so high."

"No, man," Jeff said. "I think you could do it."

"Can I try it on you?"

"Sure, I don't care."

I jumped up so high that my pubic bone hit him in the face and busted his lip.

"See," he said. "It was easy."

"God, Jeff. I busted your face! I'm so sorry!"

"Oh, whatever. It's no problem."

He was just so nonchalant. Some people might have told me, "Be careful, because you could try to jump up and land on your head." But every time I asked Jeff, "Do you think I could do this?" his answer was always the same—"I don't see why you couldn't."

I've always loved Jeff's innocence, his way of not worrying at all about what other people think. He's completely unconcerned with looking cool. He's not worried about looking stupid. He's wonderfully uninhibited and totally at home in his own skin. He is who he is and he doesn't give a rat's ass what anybody thinks. I've always been comfortable with myself, but Jeff is the real deal. When I'm around him, I feel even more carefree and creative than I usually do.

Jeff was an alternative kid as far as Cameron, North Carolina, went, but I've always been curious about what he would've been like if he'd grown up in a big city. Because Jeff never had an opportunity to meet people that were in tune with alternative culture, he had to make his own. He never got to meet punk rockers and artists and all-around weirdoes. He's entirely self-made, which makes him cooler than cool in my book.

Everybody knows that Jeff is really into playing music, but just as high on his list of interests is digging. Whenever fans come up to me, in restaurants or in Wal-Mart, they always ask about the other members of Team Extreme. They'll ask, "Where's Jeff?" I always have the same response, "Digging holes and filling them back up."

The people look at me like I'm the crazy one, but that's the God's honest truth. There's nothing Jeff likes to do more than moving dirt around and building life-sized anthills and things like that. There's no rhyme or reason to it, either. He'll be sitting in his trailer and all of a sudden say, "Man, it'd be cool if there were a bunch of hills out front and a bunch of tunnels in back." Then he gets up, walks out the front door, and starts making hills and tunnels.

I remember when Matt first told me that Jeff bought a Bobcat. Now, Jeff is a big animal lover, he has all kinds of pets, including a boxer, a prairie dog and a South American raccoon, but a bobcat seemed pretty excessive.

"He did?" I asked. "How much was it?"

"They're twenty thousand," Matt said, "but I think Jeff got a good deal on it."

"Wow," I replied. "Where is he going to keep it?"

"Probably just over at his house."

"What about when he goes out of town?"

"My dad likes it, so he'll probably keep an eye on it."

"Does he have to keep it locked up?"

"No, he'll just probably keep it out back in the shed."

"But won't it run away?"

"What?"

"The bobcat, won't it run away?"

Matt looked at me like I was nuts. "A Bobcat is a *tractor,* not an animal!"

Honest to God, I thought he meant that Jeff was getting a real wild bobcat. In the world of Jeff, it would've made perfect sense. It wouldn't surprise me in the least if he said, "I'm getting a cougar to keep out in back."

As much as I love Jeff, in a business capacity he can be very aggravating. It's been pretty well documented, but Jeff is habitually late. I'm not talking about ten minutes late or a half-hour late. It can be anywhere from six hours to an entire day late.

When Team Extreme were traveling together, Matt and I would be in charge of getting Jeff from place to place. Before we went to bed, we would call Jeff in his hotel room and say, "We're going to meet in the lobby at seven A.M."

"Okay. No problem."

We'd call him at six-thirty—"Are you awake?"

"Okay. I'm up."

Then we'd call again at six-forty-five, just to be sure—"Are you about ready?"

"Okay, I'm getting my stuff together."

We'd call at six-fifty-five to tell him we were going downstairs, but this time he doesn't pick up the phone. Then we'd call his cell phone, but still no answer.

We'd call again and again, until he finally picked up. "We're in the car waiting for you."

"Okay. I'll be right down."

By that time, it was already seven-thirty, and Jeff would come down, put his bags in the trunk, and climb into the backseat just like it was seven-oh-one. He never said, "I'm sorry but I overslept," or "Thanks for waiting." Nothing.

Jeff can be incredibly irresponsible, but I guess that's just the negative side to his being a free spirit. We will always have a bond, but in the past year or so Jeff has become very distant. He tends to isolate himself, so we don't hang out as much as we used to. In fact, it doesn't seem like Jeff hangs out with much of anyone these days.

My Top Ten Favorite Restaurants

1. *Chevy's*
2. *Yamato's in Sanford*
3. *Outback*
4. *Quizno's*
5. *Cracker Barrel*
6. *Waffle House*
7. *Tripps*
8. *Jamba Juice*
9. *Taco Bell*
10. *Tortillas in Atlanta—R.I.P.*

CHAPTER 29

We were doing *Raw* "in the shadow of New York City"—also known as the Meadowlands in New Jersey—when Essa and I were informed that he'd be dropping the Light Heavyweight title that night in a match against Dean Malenko. The agent for the match wanted a spot where I'd do something off the top turnbuckle onto Dean's Radicalz pal, Eddie Guerrero, on the outside.

"Maybe you do a crossbody off the top and have Eddie catch you," he said.

It was one of those occasions where I wonder if the person coming up with these spots watches too many cartoons! Eddie and I stood there looking at each other, thinking, *Not in a million years. It's just not going to happen.*

There was no way in hell Eddie could've caught me off the top. Granted, he's pretty thick, but he's just not that big. When you come off the top, you come down with a lot of force. Brock Lesnar is probably the only person that could catch me like that.

"What about off the apron?" I suggested. "That's a little more realistic."

"No, that's not all that impressive because it's not as high."

"Okay, how about I come off the top and Eddie catches me in the ring?"

"No, we need it to happen on the outside."

Finally Eddie and decided that I would go to hit him with a hurrican-rana, except he'd catch me and reverse it into a powerbomb.

We went to try it and instead of powerbombing me like he would anyone else, he put me down gently, like he was placing a newborn baby in a carriage.

"That going to look like shit," I said.

"I don't want to really powerbomb you," Eddie said "It'll hurt."

"You don't have to drill me. How about you change the direction as soon as I straddle your shoulders and just drop me?"

"Okay, no problem."

"Do you want to try it in the ring," I said, "because that way it'll be safe."

We got into the ring, I came off the top turnbuckle, Eddie caught me and drilled me WHAM! right into the mat.

I don't think he meant to hurt me—I've seen Eddie do a million power-bombs and he does them like that every single time. He knocked ninety percent of the wind out of me, but I got up and managed to sputter, "That was fine. It didn't hurt at all."

"Are you sure?"

"Totally. Should we do it again?"

"Okay."

We did it again and the same thing happened—Eddie totally knocked the wind out of me. All I could think was, *Boy, if it was this bad in the ring, it's going to hurt like hell when he powerbombs me onto the floor!*

That night as I came off the turnbuckle, I knew it was going to be bad. After Eddie caught me and slammed me onto the floor, I felt like my shoulder was on fire, though I didn't think I'd done any real damage. As I laid there, I remember thinking, *I'm glad that's the last thing I have to do tonight, because I don't know if I can get up.*

Essa didn't see what had happened because he was tied up in the ring, losing the Light Heavyweight title to Malenko. When he came out to help me up, he lifted me by my injured arm. God, it hurt, but I just pulled it away and held my shoulder in as close as I could.

When we got back to gorilla, everybody said, "Wow, that was a hell of a bump. Are you okay?"

"Yep. Sure. No problem. I'm great."

I went back to the locker room and it took me forever and a day to change my clothes. I walked back out and was hanging around, watching the monitor. People kept asking me, "Are you sure you're okay?"

I continued to play it cool. "Oh yeah, I'm fine."

Meanwhile, my shoulder was tightening up and it was getting harder and harder to move my arm. When the show was over and it was time to leave, I went over and asked Tori if she'd mind giving me a hand with my bags.

"We've got to get a trainer in here to check you out," she said. "You can't just leave like that."

It was suggested that I might want to see François, a shiatsu masseur that worked for WWE at the time. Half the locker room swore by him, but the other half would hold a crucifix in front of them and run the other way if he came near them. It was a fifty-fifty split—he could either make you feel better or make it so you couldn't move at all.

I went to see François the next day at *SmackDown!* "It's out, baby," he said, putting his hands on my shoulder. Everyone was "baby" to François— it must be a French thing. He popped my scapula back in, and right away, I felt better. The WWE trainer had made me an X-ray appointment for later that day, but after François did his thing, I decided to blow it off. "It's fine now," I told Bob Clarke, who works at WWE's Talent Relations department. "I can move again."

Bob pulled me aside. "Don't ever go to François before you've been seen by a doctor," he said. "What if you had broken something? Who knows what could've happened?"

"Okay," I said, and went to my X-ray after all. Everything looked fine and that was that. My shoulder ached for a good ten days or so, but the pain was nothing compared to how much it hurt that first night.

Even though my shoulder was still bothering me, I worked Jacqueline— who was the WWE Women's Champion at the time—at the Saturday and Sunday house shows. It probably wasn't the best thing to do to heal my shoulder, but I was still new, so I worried about saying no to anything I was offered. Plus, the house show money was great!

On Tuesday, we were in Milwaukee for the *SmackDown!* tapings. The agent came to me and said that since Jacqueline and I had been having good matches at the house shows over the weekend, they wanted to see how it played on TV.

Even though it was going to my first official singles match, I was actually unhappy about it. I liked being with Essa and I was hesitant to do anything that might take away from that.

I didn't care that Jacqueline was going to go over—I actually like her a lot. She's a very straightforward person, she doesn't bullshit you. I had heard of her reputation for working stiff—not pulling her moves—but it didn't bother me. I had always trained with guys, so I wasn't worried about getting beaten up. I knew I'd be able to hold my own.

It just felt kind of pointless. In every show there are a few segments that need to be filled at the last minute. That match was definitely filler, what they call a "collapsable segment." If the show is heavy and any of the other matches have gone long, then you don't work. If the show is light, your five-minute segment might have to stretch to eight minutes. It's TV—you just never know.

My match with Jacqueline was one of those things that happens all the time in WWE—you're thrown into a match for no particular reason. They could've made it a lot more interesting with just a couple of little tweaks, but I wasn't in any position to complain.

A week or two later Essa and I were told that we would be working an angle with Eddie Guerrero and Chyna, with Essa challenging Eddie for the WWE European Championship. That was cool—the European title was the next step up from Light Heavyweight on the WWE ladder.

But when I first heard about the plan, I thought for sure that Chyna was going to squash it. I later found out it was her idea—Joanie was smart, and liked the idea of having another strong woman to work with. I was actually the first woman to ever do an offensive move on Chyna. We had a TV match leading up to the *Backlash* Pay-Per-View and I did a cross-body off the top to the floor on her.

Eddie's clean and healthy now, but at that time he was having troubles with drug addiction. Unfortunately, there were moments during our angle together that he was pretty out of it. The day of *Backlash,* we were talking over that night's match with our agent, Michael Hayes, and Eddie was basically unconscious. The four were sitting there in catering—Eddie was passed out and Essa barely spoke English—but Michael just went on talking about the match as if nothing was wrong. Chyna and I kept exchanging looks, like, "Is this really happening?" It was a very weird scene.

Unsurprisingly, the match wasn't a five-star classic. Stuff was screwed

I wore big, clunky heels and had to stuff my bra with Styrofoam just to be silly. There was plenty of room, of course—Chyna's dress was way to big for me!

up right and left. Before we went out for the match, there was a huge sign in gorilla that said DON'T TOUCH THE SPANISH ANNOUNCE TABLE—Triple H and Shane McMahon were going to get Rock Bottomed through it later on in the show.

There was a spot in our match where I was supposed to climb to the top, then Chyna would throw me off and I'd gut myself on the guardrail. But when the time came for her to give me the big shove, Eddie and Essa's positioning caused us to be in a different corner than we'd originally planned and I fell right towards the Spanish announce table.

As I fell, all I could think was, *I'm going to ruin the main event!* I didn't know how fragile the table was, but I wasn't going to be the one to break it. When I landed, I barely touched the table—it didn't break, thank God, but my bump looked like shit.

I was bummed about that—at that point in my career, I wasn't working many matches other than what I did on the outside. When I was actually physically involved in the match, I was determined to always take the best bump possible for the other person. After all, so many people had done the same for me.

I also wanted to make sure that Chyna was cool with everything I did—that I didn't do anything that made her look stupid, and that I was there right when she needed me to be somewhere. I wanted her to want to keep working with me.

Ending up by the Spanish announce table, the one side we weren't supposed be on, was potentially a situation where a lot of people would get pissed off. But Chyna was cool—she just laughed about it. I thought, *Whew! I'm not in trouble with her!*

At the end of the match—Eddie beat Essa with the Gory Special—I stripped off Chyna's prom dress, which was hilarious. The next night we were in Baltimore for *Raw,* and I came down to the ring wearing the dress and mimicking Chyna. I wore big, clunky heels and had to stuff my bra

with Styrofoam just to be silly. There was plenty of room, of course—
Chyna's dress was way to big for me!

Needless to say, Eddie and Chyna came out and beat us up. In the end,
Chyna ripped the dress off me, leaving me standing there all embarrassed
in my bra and panties.

That was really fun for me, because I hadn't gotten many opportunities
to do things that were comical or over the top. I still haven't—I mostly just
do my thing.

**In mid-May, I heard Vince was planning on breaking up Essa and
me. I felt so bad, because I knew they weren't going to do anything
with Essa. He had helped me so much.**

Our breakup started at *Raw* in Indianapolis. Essa was tag teaming with
The Godfather against Perry Saturn and Malenko. Before the match, I
caught him hanging out in the locker room with The Godfather and his
Hos. Instead of acting all jealous, I said, "It's all cool." But then, at the end
of the match, when Essa went to the top for his moonsault, I knocked him
off and Saturn hit him with a brainbuster for the one-two-three.

The next night on *SmackDown!* was my last-ever match alongside Essa.
Of course it was against Matt Hardy. Midway through the match, the two
of them were going at it on the outside. Matt went to hit Essa with a right,
but my soon-to-be-ex-partner pulled me in front of him as a shield so that
Matt ended up nailing me in the face. At the end, Essa got distracted after
accidentally bumping me off the apron and Matt landed the Twist of Fate
for the win.

Essa got all angry, blaming me for the loss. He tossed me into the ring
and hit me with a powerbomb—my pants actually came down a little and
you could see my ass crack—and a moonsault. Then the Hardyz came
running back in, took Essa out, and carried me up the ramp.

When we got to the back, Michael Hayes was pissed off that Matt had punched me. "You're not supposed to hit a girl," he yelled. "Now we're not going to be able to show the match on TV!"

The rules about violence against women don't make a lot of sense. If Essa had shoved me into Matt it would've been okay, but because Matt actually took a swing and punched me in the face, it was a total no-no. If Matt had hit me and then came over to see if I was alright, that also would've been acceptable, because it would've been clear that it was inadvertent.

In the end, though, it seemed that Michael Hayes had overreacted. The match aired on *SmackDown!* without a single cut.

The plan from that point was to team me up with the Hardyz. Creative said that they kept seeing me hanging around with Matt and Jeff, and it simply looked like we belonged together. The idea was that I wasn't going to play the traditional female role of valet. I was going to be the best friend, the Hardy Girl.

Of course, no one knew exactly when it was going to happen, and in WWE, you can never be sure of anything until the second you walk out from behind the curtain. I spent the next couple of weeks hoping that nothing was going to change and it was still going to happen.

The setup on TV was to show me backstage watching every Hardy Boyz match on a monitor, cheering them on. And since I wasn't with Essa anymore, I began getting used more in the Women's Division. We did *SmackDown!* in Buffalo and the show featured a Women's Battle Royal for a number one contender shot against the then-champion, Stephanie McMahon-Helmsley. It was all the girls—me, Kat, Terri, Ivory, and Jacqueline, with Tori as the special guest referee.

The match ended with me hitting Ivory with a snap suplex and the moonsault for the win and the title shot. I called out Stephanie, but Tori clobbered me. Then Steph ran out and pinned me to retain her championship. It was your classic McMahon-Helmsley Era screwjob.

That match is most significant for being the debut of one of my trademarks. I had gone shopping with a few friends in Atlanta a few weeks earlier, and that night, I was showing off my purchases to Edge. I put on this outfit—it was actually what I wore in my very first promo pics, a tin-foil red top and red rocker pants with big bell bottoms. I came out and asked Edge what he thought.

"Well, not like this," I said, realizing that my black thong was showing out of my pants.

"I don't know," Edge said. "I think it looks pretty cool like that."

"You think?"

"Oh yeah. I really think you've got something there."

I thought about it and decided that it would be a great way to change up my look after I split up with Essa. After the Battle Royal, I was in the back, chatting with Jerry "the King" Lawler.

"That was a really good match tonight," he said, "but did you know your underwear was sticking out of your pants the whole time?"

"Oh my God," I said. "It was? I'll make sure I do something about that, That's pretty embarrassing."

I thought certainly he was kidding—obviously I knew that thong was showing. It wasn't just like it was a tiny bit sticking out where maybe I didn't notice. The King walked away like he thought he was doing me a big favor. It turned out I was doing *him* a favor—my thong supplied him with an endless amount of material.

Since then, the thong thing has become part of my overall image. As you'd imagine, I have hundreds and hundreds of different thongs, though I probably have ten or twenty favorites that I wore on a regular basis. To me there's nothing especially sexy about it—it's just a fashion accessory, a way to add some color to whatever else I'm wearing that day.

The next Monday we did *Raw* in St. Louis. Linda McMahon came out and made one of her occasional housecleaning appearances and declared that Stephanie had to face me in a real title match.

It was a short little fight, largely because Steph wasn't yet ready to wrestle a full match. She got bumped off the apron, and when referee Teddy Long went to check on her, Kurt Angle ran out and hit me with the Olympic Slam. Stephanie got back into the ring and pinned me.

Even though I didn't win, getting a title shot was definitely a big deal—at least it was a much bigger deal than the first time I went for it against Jacqueline. That was in the days where the Women's Championship was in this Jacqueline vs. Ivory limbo, where the two of them battled for it, back and forth, over and over again. It had really lost all meaning.

But during the McMahon-Helmsley Era, Stephanie stole the title from Jacqueline and the Women's Championship began to build up some value again. It was so aggravating—Steph would walk around with the belt on her shoulder, acting so proud, even though she didn't do anything to actually win it.

It made people crazy! People would come up to me on the street and say, "I want you to kick Stephanie's ass so bad!"

The McMahon-Helmsley faction was so hated at that point. To be part of the top storyline on the show—even in a minor role—was pretty exciting. It was a definite sign that I was moving up from the bottom of the card.

My Fave Clothing Brands

- *Bug Girl*
- *Kik Wear*
- *ILLIG*
- *Serious*
- *Trip*
- *Thrift store clothes and a pair of scissors!*

My Fave Clothing Stores

- *Trash & Vaudeville (New York City)*
- *Commander Salamander (Washington, DC)*
- *Junkman's Daughter (Atlanta)*
- *Red Balls (Melrose, CA)*
- *Serious (Melrose, CA)*
- *SOHO (Mexico)*

My Fave Shopping Areas

- *Little Five Points (Atlanta)*
- *Montrose (Houston)*
- *South Street (Philadelphia)*
- *St. Mark's Place (New York City)*
- *Sunset Boulevard and Melrose Avenue (Los Angeles)*
- *Haight-Ashbury (San Francisco)*

CHAPTER 30

I had only been a WWE Superstar for a few months, but I was already getting an incredible reaction from the crowd. That kind of thing doesn't happen to every new wrestler.

I knew things were going well for me when I began seeing signs about myself out in the crowd. There were nights when it seemed like every single person in this arena had a Lita sign. I would take my time going down the ramp so that I could read as many of them as possible. There are always lots of puns on my name, like "Follow the Lita." One sign that sticks out as an all-time classic read "I Want Lita in a Pita," with a picture

of my face on top of a falafel. Matt and I still laugh about that one! I'm amazed sometimes—the amount of creativity the fans put into making their signs blows my mind. It shows just how devoted they are.

In a way, I didn't really get to enjoy my early success, because I worried that any sign of my getting off on it might be perceived as being too big for my britches. I was the first woman to get a big reaction from the fans since Sable had left the company, and unfortunately, the manner in which she parted ways with WWE led to my behavior being put under a microscope. The office was very sensitive about any girl starting to think that she was bigger than the company. I was actually called aside by management a few times to check that I was still humble, that I hadn't gotten a big head. They wanted to nip things in the bud or cut things off at the pass—before there was even a bud to nip or a pass to cut.

As a result, I was careful never to appear to be gloating or acting cocky about my popularity. Anytime someone put me over, I totally played it off like it was no big deal. "Oh, they just like my outfits."

It's funny, because later on, I became somewhat overexposed and people started trash-talking me, saying "Lita's not all that. All she can do is two moves!"

That made me want to turn around and brag right in their faces. "Hey, I changed the face of women's wrestling! What did you do?"

It was great that I was able to open their minds and show them that there were other kinds of women out there.

Things were moving so fast, it was hard to even digest what was happening. I felt really lucky and I was having a great time. That's really all that mattered to me and I just went with it.

There was a realism to my character that people responded to. Women like Sable, or on the other side of the spectrum, Chyna, were such cartoon characters. But Lita was somebody that they could actually relate to as a real person.

Fans tell me that they think of Lita as a big sister or one of their best friends. There's a real personal connection that they feel. I'm sure some of my fans are also, say, Madonna fans, but they probably don't feel as close to Madonna. They love her albums and they love seeing her on MTV, but they don't feel like Madonna is a real person that they could talk to and hang out with. With me, they know that I'm really just like them. I'm just Amy.

It was so thrilling for me to talk to female fans who would tell me that I was the reason they watched wrestling. For the most part, the women who watched—or the girlfriends of the guys who watched—liked some of the male wrestlers because they were cute, but always hated all the girls. But when I came along, female viewers had someone they could connect to, just like I responded to Rey Mysterio. That always meant the most to me—not guys telling me that they thought I was hot, but girls that were into what I was doing.

In terms of the guys, I was a very different sex symbol than what they were used to. I loved the fact that the same guys that were drooling over Sable were now into me. Talk about night and day! With the exception of Chyna, the only sex symbols in wrestling had been these blonde Barbie doll types, which I most definitely was not. It was great that I was able to open their minds and show them that there were other kinds of women out there.

All of a sudden, I started getting a huge amount of fan mail. When it first started showing up, I was really blown away, and as I got more and more popular, the fan mail just rolled in by the bagful. It's a very moving experience, seeing all those letters and postcards and pictures and gifts, realizing that so many people were moved by my character.

They were coming from people aged eight to eighty, male and female. What was interesting to me was that, because I don't talk much, people were responding to something physical, to my overall vibe. It was as if they felt what I felt coming down the ramp, like they were getting into my head and feeling all of my excitement.

A lot of the mail I receive tells me how people have been inspired by me. There's no single thing that moves them—it's mostly just a feeling that they pick up from me. Girls always tell me how watching me has encouraged them to follow their dream—whether it's to become a wrestler or an actress or a doctor.

I think it's really cool to be a source of inspiration for other people, especially when those people are able to apply it to their own lives. There are maybe fifty different wrestlers in WWE, but millions of TV viewers. Obviously they can't all become wrestlers, no matter how motivated they are. So it's important that I can encourage others to succeed in their own lives, their own worlds. Life is hard work, and if identifying with Lita's passion makes things easier or lights a fire under peoples' asses, then I'm all for it!

My fans don't just send letters—they've also given me many wonderful gifts. I've gotten hundreds of drawings of me, some of which are incredibly intricate, which tell me that they spent an awful lot of time thinking of me. It's so cool to have people that you don't know drawing you. It's fascinating to see all the different interpretations of who I am and who the fans think I am.

The gifts I've received from fans range from things people have made, like paintings, to diamond earrings. I've gotten ungodly amounts of stuffed animals! People also send me a lot of videotapes, usually of themselves wrestling. One person sent me a tape of old 7 Seconds live footage—that was awesome!

Even Cody gets a crazy amount of gifts—collars and bones and toys, all kinds of fun doggie stuff!

I try to write back to as many people as possible, but I just don't have enough time. I hope the fans understand that it's impossible for me to write back to all of them. I don't have an official fan club set up; I don't have a staff to help me answer my mail. My P.O. box is just me.

When I injured my neck, I received an unbelievable amount of get well cards. There were literally tons! One guy sent me a card every week after I got hurt, just wishing me well. He said he's going to do it until I come back.

That's powerful stuff. It shows me how dedicated my fans are, especially considering how fast-paced our business is. The second you're off TV, most people forget about you. Whether it's wrestling or children starving on the streets, the American mentality is out of sight, out of mind. So the fact that, after I stopped wrestling, the fan mail kept coming and people were still standing in long lines to meet me at appearances really says a lot about how much they must care about me.

CHAPTER 31

I was in the locker room before a show when Tori—not Torrie Wilson, but Tori of D-Generation X fame—came to me and said, "All the Divas have to go to New York for a photo shoot."

I didn't know what she was talking about. "Who the hell are the Divas?"

"We are," Tori said. "All the girls, we're WWE Divas."

I thought that sounded so gross. It made us sound like we were like the Nitro Girls, nothing more than cheesecake. I saw myself as one of the guys—we all have the same schedule, we work for the same company. Why are they wrestlers and we're Divas?

I have a huge sweet tooth—in fact, I probably have more than one sweet tooth.

To me, it takes away the individuality of the girls by lumping us all into one group. Everybody is their own character, but by making us all Divas, then the more people are going to look for similarities. Since the idea of Divas first started, I think the girls have gotten less unique. Granted, there are a lot more of us now, so there are less roads you can go down to keep us all separate. But the more the girls are grouped together, the more they bite off of each other's image.

It was a strange concept to me and to this day, I try to use the word "Diva" as little as possible. It's such a girly, superficial term. It puts you on a pedestal, which I don't like at all.

Obviously if I'm going to go and get my boobs done, I understand women's role in the business. Regardless of how different my character is, there's still a sexual element involved. Men come to the show, they drink beer, of course they want to see girls in not a lot of clothes.

I didn't become a wrestler so that I could model tiny little outfits, but at the same time, I understand that it's part of my job. When the time came for us to do the Divas in New York photo spread, I opted not to express my distaste for the whole affair.

The shoot was a very weird experience. There I was, in the middle of freaking Times Square, wearing practically nothing, with all these fans standing around hooting and hollering. At first I tried to play it cool, chatting with the fans. But as the day went on, I began feeling awkward and uncomfortable. I had to act like there was nothing wrong. I don't mind posing in a studio environment, but it really sucked doing it out in the street with an audience watching. It wasn't a great day for me. It was something that I hope I never have to go through again.

That was the first-ever Divas shoot. It was a strange dichotomy for me—at the same time as I was pioneering what a woman could do in the wrestling ring, I was also being used for cheesecake.

By the way, I *hate* cheesecake! I have a huge sweet tooth—in fact, I probably have more than one sweet tooth. I'd eat nothing but steamed

I always tell the photographer to just shoot away—no countdowns or warnings. I don't care if my hair is in my face or anything like that.

chicken and veggies all day long if I knew that at two A.M. I could sit in my hotel room and eat chocolate cake or peanut butter cookies. *Mmmmm!* I think those things just taste better at night, though maybe they just taste better when you shouldn't be eating them. But no matter how much I love sweets, I really do hate cheesecake.

Anyway, each Diva's layout is different. In November 2000, we went to Hedonism in Jamaica—that was my first bikini shoot and there's not much you can do to study up on how to do it. Again, it took me a little while to warm up, to get used to being in front of people with not a lot of clothes on.

What I like about the Diva shoots are that we're given some choice of what we wear so you get a sense of each girl and their different personalities. All the girls have their own style and you can see it in the pictures. For example, Trish Stratus' shots are very carefully posed— her arms and legs are always perfectly pointed, her muscles perfectly flexed. Whereas my pictures come across spontaneous and natural, the same as I am out in the ring. I always tell the photographer to just shoot away—no countdowns or warnings. I don't care if my hair is in

Noelle Carr does everything she can to get the perfect photo.

my face or anything like that. I try to look like a real person who just happens to be having her picture taken in a glamorous location.

An extraordinary amount of work goes into the Diva spreads. There are photographers and makeup artists and assistants, all there on the beach with you. It's not just you and a guy with a camera. It's a huge project.

Noelle Carr is WWE's Managing Editor of Photography, and the Diva shoot is very much her baby. She puts so much effort into getting it all together. Noelle gets the various resorts—like Hedonism in Jamaica—to sponsor us; she arranges for all these different clothes manufacturers to give us suits; she coordinates the makeup artists, the camera crews, everything.

Noelle's so cool. She's got a lot of spunk. I always want to do the best work that I can for her because I know how much she's put into it.

WWE tries to make the Divas' layouts look like a big old slumber party, with all us girls frolicking in the sun and surf, but the reality is complete-ly different. There's usually a planned activity of some kind that the TV crew films in order to further enhance the slumber party vibe, things like swimming with dolphins or doing a trapeze act or shooting up cans in the desert. It looks like a lot of fun but we have to rush over to the dolphins in between shoots, spend just enough time for the crew to get the footage, then it's back to work.

In truth, the girls have hardly any interaction—we're too busy working! We wake up at four-thirty in the morning to get ready, then shoot the whole day until the sun goes down. Then we rinse the sand out of our clothes, get some dinner, and go to sleep early so we can wake right back up and do it again.

I always enjoy seeing the finished product, because you can see all the hard work and energy that went into it. The pictures always turn out great. It's become our *Sports Illustrated* swimsuit issue, yet we have a totally different flavor.

When the first Divas magazine came out, I was surprised to see myself on the cover. I've got to admit, I wasn't expecting it. It's cool to see yourself in pictures that are completely different from who you are normally. I just look at the Diva shoots as stuff for my scrapbook.

The worst part of the Diva shoots is that they always make for a rough week—house shows on the weekend, then two nights of TV, then straight down to the island for three days of shooting, then back to the States for *Survivor Series* and two more nights of TV. By the time I finally get home, I'm completely ragged out.

The perception is, "Hey, you went down to the islands, it must have been a vacation," but the truth is, being a Diva is hard work. It's almost ridiculous to call three days on the beach hard work, but it really is!

My Favorite Junk Food

- *German Chocolate cake—and just about any cake besides ones with fruit or cheese*
- *Crème brûlée—even better with berries!*
- *Breyer's Mint Chocolate Chip ice cream*
- *Little Debbies—especially Nutty Bars, Swiss Cake Rolls, and Star Crunch*
- *Peanut butter cookies—or just about any other cookies*
- *Anything with marshmallow*
- *Boston Market corn bread*
- *TCBY White Chocolate Mousse yogurt*

CHAPTER 32

After a few weeks of teasing my involvement with the Hardy Boyz, the time finally came for me to become part of their team. Matt and Jeff were going to have a match with T&A—Test and Albert—and then they were going to lose due to interference from T&A's bitch manager, Trish Stratus. When T&A put the boots to the Hardyz after the bell, I would run in and take out Trish to make the save.

We got stuck in St. Louis the night before the match—there was a big snowstorm and our flight to Chicago was cancelled. There were a few

options, like getting on the standby list for the next flight, or flying to Milwaukee and then driving to Chicago. We decided to just drive the whole way.

We weren't too worried about when we would get there because we knew that the whole show was going to be a little late due to the problems at the airport. It wasn't a bad drive, maybe five hours, and we finally arrived at the building just after the doors opened at five-thirty.

When we got there, Michael Hayes—our agent for the match—told me that they wanted me to do something to Trish. Since things were running late, there wasn't time for us to practice doing a moonsault on her, so Michael suggested, "How about a leg drop?"

I'd never done a leg drop before, but I'd seen Matt do it a thousand times. As usual, I thought, *Why not? I can do that.*

The Hardyz and T&A had the match, I did my run in and as I stood on the second rope to drop the leg on Trish, I realized, "I don't know how to do this."

Of course it was too late to turn back, so even though I didn't know what was going to happen, I knew that I'd better do something. I jumped off and WHAM! landed my ass right onto Trish's face.

Oh shit! Trish was still very green at that time and Michael Hayes was always saying that I had to be careful not to hurt her. Fortunately, my ass hitting her in the face didn't do any damage—I didn't break her nose or even bruise her up. It could've been a lot worse. Trish was totally cool

Fortunately for me, that was one of the rare nights where I got to whip Trish. The second I hit her with it, I knew it was cutting her up.

about it—she understood that she was the new girl and that she had a bunch of dings and knocks coming to her.

For all intents and purposes, that night was the beginning of Team Extreme. Our official debut as a threesome was in Memphis against T&A and Trish at the next *SmackDown!* That match was actually pretty historic—the first-ever mixed six-person tag match.

It was an okay TV match—I hit the moonsault on Trish, but the ref was distracted by the four guys brawling on the outside. Then Albert got me with the Baldo Bomb and pulled Trish on top of me for the pinfall.

The feud between Team Extreme and T&A and Trish was a lot of fun. The crowds were so into it—they really wanted to see me and Trish get at each other—and that made us all give it our best. We all wanted to continue to evoke that response from the crowd.

What also helped to make it play so well was that the drama was kept high, but the wrestling was relatively simple. Both Trish and I were new. We were both very limited in what we could do, so our spots were carefully choreographed. We weren't out there putting together twenty-minute matches. We were able to work off of our emotions and the energy from the crowd and it played out great.

There's no reason to stretch people beyond what they can do. That's become one of the problems with women's wrestling in today's WWE. To me, there's no need to have Torrie Wilson and Dawn Marie out there in bikinis exchanging hammerlocks and headlock takeovers. It just looks like amateur hour. Going out there in bikinis and trying to act like serious wrestlers is ridiculous. The crowd doesn't buy that shit. They know it's horrible. Well, at least *I* know it's horrible.

The Team Extreme vs. T&A and Trish feud went on for weeks. One unforgettable moment was on *Raw* in Albany, when the Hardyz were having a match against the Dudley Boyz and Trish threw me off a ladder through a table.

We had brainstormed all day about how to do it. Everybody kept making suggestions that were just not plausible, like Trish powerbombing me off the ladder. "That's not going to happen," I said.

Finally Matt came up with the perfect plan. T&A did a run in and took out both the Hardyz and the Dudleyz, resulting in the match being declared a no contest. Then Albert set up the ladder while Test laid me out on a table. Trish climbed up top and was ready to frogsplash me, but I got off the table and climbed up after her. We exchanged blows on top of the ladder, I tried to superplex her, and she ended up shoving me off so I went backwards through the table.

It was pretty scary, because I couldn't see where I was going. All I could do was hold my breath and cross my fingers. There wasn't a lot of precision in how I landed—my butt hit the mat and my head and upper back went through the table.

It was a huge adrenaline rush, but I think it's important for people to understand that no matter how you slice it, going through a table hurts. A lot! It takes a lot out of you, like getting into a minor car crash.

People always assume that things are gimmicked so that the wrestlers won't get hurt, but that's definitely not the case. For example, one of the staples of my feud with Trish was her taking a strap to me. Let me tell you, that's no picnic. Getting whacked with a belt repeatedly hurts like nobody's business.

There was one night where we didn't have our usual leather strap, so Tom Prichard gave us the belt off of his pants. It was brand new and really stiff. Fortunately for me, that was one of the rare nights where I got to whip Trish. The second I hit her with it, I knew it was cutting her up. I could see this look in her eyes, like, "You are freaking killing me with that belt."

It was rough—I had to whip her all the way from the ring, up the ramp to the back. I probably had to hit Trish with that belt twenty-five times.

When we got to the back, I just looked at her and shrugged my shoulders, "Sorry about that."

At the *Fully Loaded* Pay-Per-View in Dallas, Team Extreme and T&A and Trish had the first-ever Six-Person Intergender Tag match. The difference between a mixed person tag match and an intergender tag match is that in an intergender match, the men and the women are allowed to go at it.

It was a really hot match. The crowd was with us all the way through. I had a lot to do that night. I tagged in and hit a tornado DDT on Test, followed by a crossbody off the top onto Albert—if you watch the tape back, you can see me patting Baldo on the leg, thanking him for catching me and taking the move from me!

Then I went back up and got a near fall on Test with a hurricanrana. After he kicked out, he powerbombed me and let Trish tag in. She got on top of me for the pin, but I got a shoulder up and we went at it for a few. Finally, I hit her with a superplex, then went up top for the moonsault—one-two-three!

The *Fully Loaded* match was also memorable because Team Extreme debuted one of our coolest moves that night, the triple suplex. After we hit it, Matt and Jeff did one of their signature spots—they'd do a double team move, then get all fired up and tear their shirts off. Well, this time, I watched them do it, got all fired up myself, and ripped my top off. The crowd went crazy! It was a classic Team Extreme moment.

Matt always likes to claim—and I'll go along with it—that Lita and the Hardyz were the true innovators of intergender wrestling. There was some male vs. female stuff before us, but nothing with the excitement and energy of the things we did.

It was a huge adrenaline rush, but I think it's important for people to understand that no matter how you slice it, going through a table hurts.

CHAPTER 33

The feud between Trish and myself had gotten so popular that creative began trying to figure out ways to mix us into the other big storylines. There was a great *SmackDown!* match in San Antonio where I teamed up with Chris Jericho against Trish and Chris Benoit.

I was pretty psyched to work with Jericho. We first met before I came to work for WWE. I was hanging out backstage at a house show and we had a brief conversation about my time in Mexico City. He had also worked for CMLL so we had a number of mutual acquaintances. We just had an

Chris Benoit respected my skills.

instant bond—we have similar senses of humor and were compatible as friends right from the start.

For me, the highlight of that match was giving the hurricanrana to Chris Benoit. He wasn't known for having much female offensive interaction in his matches, so I felt very honored for him to agree to work with me.

On the next *Raw*—in Atlanta—I teamed with The Rock against Trish and Triple H. At the end of the match, The Rock gave Trish a spinebuster and then pointed to me and the turnbuckle—"Now you go up there and do your thing"

The problem was, Trish was laying a good distance away from the corner that he pointed to. Of course, there was no way to say, "Um, Rocky, she's actually a little closer to that other corner. Can you move her in?" so I got up on top, trying to look confident. *I might be apologizing for this in a couple seconds,* I thought, *but there's not much I can do about it now.*

I pushed off and hit the moonsault over more than half the ring to land on Trish for the pinfall. Somebody must've been looking out for me that night—or looking out for Trish.

That match was pretty exciting—I'd only been in WWE a few months but I had already gotten a chance to work with the main event players. It's always a thrill to work with the top guys, especially in a high profile match. The stakes are raised so that I have to give my best and then some.

My goal when I work with guys like Triple H or The Rock is simple—I don't want them having to work extra hard to baby the girl. When Triple H has to clothesline me, I'm already feeding for it before he has to tell me to get ready. I want him to have one thought when he gets to the back, *Working with Lita sure was easy.*

I got to work with Triple H again the next night at *SmackDown!* in Birmingham, Alabama. There was a six-person no-DQ tag match—I teamed with the Dudley Boyz against Triple H, Stephanie, and Kurt Angle. I blasted Triple H with a flipper and the crowd went nuts. That was a total rush!

At the end, Triple H gave me a Pedigree, then dropped Steph on top of me for the pin. I really love taking the guys' finishers. I've taken most of the big ones—the Pedigree, the Walls of Jericho, the Gore from Rhyno. My favorite finisher is the Stone Cold Stunner, because you get to bounce around after Stone Cold hits you with it. You have to be careful to time it right. Fortunately, I've done a good job when called upon to take a main eventer's finish.

The important thing about that tag match was that it kicked off my run towards the WWE Women's Championship. Stephanie had held the belt hostage for one hundred and forty-seven days, which really put the spark back into the title chase.

Steph was definitely intrigued by the idea of being a wrestler, even though I don't think her dad really wanted her to do it. She really wanted to prove to herself, her dad, and the fans that she could carry her own in the ring. She had always done a good job when she got involved in other people's matches, but it's a lot different when you're out there in the ring on your own.

As we built towards our title match, Steph started training in Stamford with Dr. Tom. I went up there a couple of times so that she could master some of the spots that were going to be in our big match, like the tilt-a-whirl.

Vince came by one evening and Steph was all excited to tell him what she'd done that day. "Do you want to know what we worked on today, Dad?"

"Nope," he said. "I don't want to know."

Vince wasn't being mean—he just wasn't thrilled about the idea of his little girl going out there and wrestling. He was definitely concerned about her getting hurt.

We finally had our match on August 21, in Lafayette, Louisiana. It was a very big deal—the only time two women have been involved in the main event on *Raw*. I was super-nervous before the match. I came down to the ring first, followed by Triple H, Kurt, and Stephanie. Triple H came at me and got in my face to intimidate me. It looked like he was saying something like, "You're going down, you little bitch!" But in reality, what he said was, "Just breathe and relax."

It took everything I had not to smile. I had to stay in character, acting like I was frightened, but inside I was thinking, *That's so sweet.*

Steph handled herself pretty well, considering that this was her first real wrestling match. Early on, I gave her the tilt-a-whirl, just like we'd

Luckily, she wasn't knocked out—she was more startled than anything else. I've been there.

practiced, but she didn't quite take it right and landed on her head. I was very concerned when I saw her laying there afterwards.

Luckily, she wasn't knocked out—she was more startled than anything else. I've been there. You're thrown off your game for a second. You think, *Oh my God, I'm hurt! Wait a second— am I hurt?* But because things are moving so fast, you just decide to worry about it later. Steph was tough—she kicked out and we kept going.

Having Triple H and Angle at ringside didn't make it easy for me—at one point, I got Stephanie with a snap suplex, then went up top for the moonsault, but Kurt pushed me off. The Hardyz came running down about halfway through the match, just to even up the odds.

The Rock—who was the Special Guest Referee—got involved in the finish, hitting Steph with a Spinebuster. Again, he signaled for me to get up top for the moonsault. Unlike the previous time, when he did that in the tag match with Trish, Stephanie was at a very reachable distance and I landed a perfect moonsault—one-two-three! I was the new WWE Women's Champion!

Before the match, Matt and Jeff were told to get

me out of the ring as quickly as possible so that Triple H and Kurt weren't stuck with their thumbs up their asses while we celebrated. So as soon as the bell rang, they grabbed me and we ran up the ramp. As soon as we got to the stage, the Hardyz put me on their shoulders and basked in the crowd's applause.

When we got back to gorilla, Vince was furious! He wanted a shot of Rocky raising my hand in victory, but because Matt and Jeff were concerned about hurrying me out of there, they never got the shot.

But that couldn't take away my excitement at winning the title. It was built up so perfectly. It was especially satisfying because it signaled that the Women's Division was being taken somewhat seriously.

I ended up holding onto the Women's Championship for close to three months—a perfectly respectable run. That was the only time in my WWE career that I've held the title. The perception in the back is that I'm already over with the fans, so I don't need it. They can use the title to elevate other people.

CHAPTER 34

As much as it was fun for me to team with people like The Rock and Chris Jericho, it always made me a little sad. To me, Team Extreme was a threesome—Matt and Jeff and Lita.

Lita had become a hugely marketable character, but in a lot of ways, it had very little to do with what went on in the ring. When I'd get interviewed I'd try to redirect the focus to the Hardyz—"They do all the work," I'd say. "I just do one move. Really, I'm not that great, but Matt and Jeff are!"

"Oh my God! Lita just hit the ladder!"

Of course, Matt and Jeff were totally cool. They never acted resentful of my success. I'm sure it would've been very different if the same scenario happened and I was part of a team where I wasn't such close friends with the other guys.

SummerSlam 2000 was held in Raleigh and it was a very big deal for Matt and Jeff. Not only was it basically their hometown, but they had been told that they'd win the WWE Tag Team Championships. Unfortunately, it didn't work out like that, but that couldn't take away from the fact that the highlight of the night was one of the greatest matches in WWE history—TLC: table, ladder, chair.

My first involvement came about halfway through the match. Everybody was down except for Edge and Christian. They started heading up the ladder towards the straps, so I ran in and pushed them over. Then when Matt took that unbelievable backwards bump through a two-table stack, I came back out to see if he was okay. When I bent over to check on him, Edge speared me onto the floor. My head hit the ladder that was laying there and just about knocked me silly. As I lay there, I could hear people reacting—"Oh my God! Lita just hit the ladder!"

I also remember thinking that the impact of my head hitting the ladder made a very cool sound. It hurt, of course, but I knew it couldn't be too bad if I was able to recognize the fact that it sounded good.

Fortunately, I didn't hit one of the sharp corners, so I didn't get cut—it was just a goose egg. That was good, because the doctor that was working backstage was famous for stitching people up with no anesthesia. I didn't want any part of that!

I think TLC was one of the all-time classic matches in the entire history of professional wrestling. In the end, what people remember is not who pulled the belts down, but that the seven people involved busted

I consider myself
as tight with Edge and Christian as I
am with any of the boys.

their asses to create something truly special.

As a member of Team Extreme, I've probably worked with Edge and Christian and the Dudley Boyz more than anybody else in WWE. I consider myself as tight with Edge and Christian as I am with any of the boys. Apart from the North Carolina contingent—Matt, Jeff, Shannon Moore, and The Hurricane—I'd say my closest friends in the business are Edge, Christian, and Jericho.

Those guys are just so easy to get along with. We all share common interests. More importantly, I feel like we're all on the same page as far as how we view the world and the wrestling business.

As for the Dudleyz, I get along with them much better now than when I first met them in ECW. D-Von has always been nice; he's just a naturally friendly guy. Bubba and I have actually found a comfort zone—he's the kind of person that likes to screw with people, but if they don't kick and scream and tell everybody that he's giving them problems, then they end up on his okay list.

The *SummerSlam* match was the first time I was officially integrated into the TLC Boys Club. I might've played a minimal role, but I'm still the only girl that's ever been part of a TLC match. That's quite an honor—any one of the guys could've said, "We don't want the girl involved" and the girl wouldn't have been involved.

Not only did the guys let me get involved in the match, they let me sit there while they were putting it together. Even though I only had one

Christian.

or two spots, they allowed me to listen in as they mapped out the entire match.

Being able to sit in as the boys put their matches together has meant a lot to me. I learned so much that way—about putting together a good match, about psychology, everything about the business from top to bottom. I could never thank the guys enough for that. It showed that they understand that I'm actually interested in wrestling.

Some girls would rather be told when to get up on the apron, when they need to take their bump, and then go and get their hair done. Their attitude towards the rest of the match is, "If I'm not involved in that other stuff, then I don't need to know about it."

The Hardy Boyz finally won their second WWE Tag Team Championships in a Steel Cage match against Edge and Christian at the next Pay-Per-View, *Unforgiven*. The creative team's attitude was that the Hardyz were so over with the fans that they didn't need the titles, but Matt and Jeff really wanted the titles.

It was a brutal and bloody match, as Cage matches often are. My involvement was giving Christian the hurricanrana off an eight-foot ladder. That move was, without a doubt, the most frightening thing I've ever done.

The afternoon of the show, Michael Hayes insisted that I demonstrate the move before the Pay-Per-View went live. I tried to get out of it, operating under the theory that if I hurt myself, I'd rather have it happen in front of twenty thousand screaming fans than in an empty arena.

"Sorry," Michael said, "but I need to see it done before I approve it to be in the match."

I really wanted to be part of the match, so I agreed to give it a try. God, it was so scary. As I was doing it, I couldn't feel where my body was in the air. Usually I have a pretty good sense of where I am when I do the hurricanrana, but coming off the ladder totally altered my perspective. It was impossible to get any real momentum, because the ladder could've fallen over at any time if I didn't distribute my weight correctly. Plus, I was worried that I might hit the ground in some haphazard fashion, or that if my aim was just the slightest bit off, I would drive my head right into the ladder.

When I landed, I had no idea if I had pulled it off. I stood there, trying to catch my breath, thinking, *What did that look like?*

"It was great," Michael Hayes said. An hour later, Shane McMahon decided that he wanted to see me do it. "Fine," I said. "I'll do it again."

Christian and I went up the ladder and it wasn't any less scary the second time. I still couldn't feel where I was, I couldn't tell how far my head was from the ladder.

When the time came to do the hurricanrana during the match, I was very apprehensive. Even though I'd managed to pull it off twice that afternoon, I was still scared.

It ended up going perfectly. The 'rana off the ladder was an awesome spot that I'm very proud of. Being involved in a TLC or a Cage match is always somewhat bittersweet for me—the boys get twenty minutes of amazing action and I get one cool fifteen-second high spot. While I'm unbelievably honored to be a part of them, I would love to team with Matt for a whole Ladder match or a whole Cage match. I really feel like I can do it and I hope that someday I get that chance.

Matt and I have had a number of discussions about one day working together as the first real intergender tag team. We've talked about doing it as a heel couple, like Bonnie and Clyde or Mickey and Mallory from *Natural Born Killers.*

The idea is so intriguing to me. The male/female tag team has never been done before. No question, I'd have to really step up. To be in a serious in-ring partnership with Matt, I'd have to be at the very top of my game in order to make it work. He's a total perfectionist, especially when it comes to wrestling. He takes it very seriously and even though we're a couple, he never bullshits me or coddles me in any way. When Matt tells me my work was good, I know it was damn good.

God, it was so scary. As I was doing it, I couldn't feel where my body was in the air.

CHAPTER 35

The hardcore feud between Jacqueline and myself was a very underrated piece of business. Ivory and Tori had had the very first women's hardcore fight, but what Jacqueline and I did out there took it to the next level.

It kicked off with a pre-taped segment on *Raw* in Washington, DC, where we beat the living hell out of each other backstage. It was an unbelievably violent fight, especially for two women. At one point, Jacqueline threw me into a chain link fence and I went down. She was supposed to climb up onto an eighteen-wheeler, then splash me from off the top of the truck. So I stayed down, still

selling as I waited for her to climb up there. All of a sudden, she kicked me hard, right in the side of my head—POW! Not only was it a stiff kick, I had no idea that it was coming. I just felt this blinding smash to my temple and actually blacked out for a couple of seconds.

When I came to, Jacqueline was on the hood of the truck, so I climbed up there and we exchanged blows until I shoved her off onto the floor. I tried a moonsault off the hood, but Jacqueline managed to roll out of the way, grab a fire extinguisher and blast me in the face as I came down onto a big pile of cable. Believe me, even though I had something to break my fall, doing a moonsault off an eighteen-wheeler while being blinded with a fire extinguisher is very scary.

There I was, crawling around, covered in fire extinguisher chemicals. I couldn't see or breathe—it was in my eyes, in my throat. You'd think that was enough, but no, Jacqueline had to keep going. She took a garbage can lid and pretty much beat my brains out. She must've hit me ten times! It was just brutal.

The following week I was able to get revenge in a legitimate hardcore rules match on *Raw*. It wasn't easy, though—Jacqueline didn't fool around in there. She smashed me with the handle end of a hair dryer, which gave a big goose egg. I also took a DDT onto a baking sheet and the edge caught me above my eyes, leaving a nasty bruise, like a line right across my forehead.

The performance aspect of wrestling works two ways. Sometimes you exaggerate how much something hurts, then other times you play it down...

Eventually, I pulled out a ladder and we fought up there for a bit. Then Jacqueline went to give me a crossbody off the top, but missed because I blinded her with the fire extinguisher. That was funny—she was walking around the ring, taking wild swings at the air.

After that, I was supposed to hit her with a stop sign, but I couldn't find it, so I just grabbed whatever was closest to me—in this case, the baking sheet—and whacked her with that for the three count.

I'm not a huge fan of working hardcore. The fans are so desensitized at this point, they don't react to garbage matches nearly as much as they do to my moonsault or hurricanrana, and those things don't leave me with eggs all over my head.

The worst part is that people don't seem to understand how much of what we do can hurt. You get hit in the face with a hair dryer, then feed up into a frying pan. Believe me, it's no walk in the park!

The performance aspect of wrestling works two ways. Sometimes you exaggerate how much something hurts, then other times you play it down—if Jacqueline hit me in the head with a trash can lid in real life, I wouldn't have gotten up and gone after her. I'd have laid there on the ground, going, "Oh my God, I can't see straight!"

On the other side of the coin is the bra and

panties match—those, of course, were Trish's specialty at that time. The two of us got into one after I was teamed with the Acolytes for a match against T&A and Trish at *No Mercy.*

But before the match even began, T&A attacked Bradshaw and Faarooq in the back. I watched it go down on the TitanTron, and as I ran up the ramp to help them, Trish and T&A hijacked me and kicked my ass.

The next night on *Raw,* I went to Commissioner Mick Foley and demanded a match with Trish. "How about a bra and panties match?" she said.

"I don't care if it's a bra and panties match," I replied, "I don't care if it's in a mud pit. I just want to beat your ass."

I liked how they set it up—it wasn't inconsistent with my character. My only concern when creative told me I was going to be beating Trish in a bra and panties match was to find a bra that I wasn't going to fall out of.

I've been pretty fortunate in that respect—I've only popped out of my top one time. The girls usually tape ourselves into our bras with double-sided tape. It's actually wig tape for men who wear toupees, and as you'd expect, taking it off is pretty unpleasant. On the night I popped out, I had been told that I wasn't going to be doing much on the show, so I decided not to tape in. It was no big deal—I heard several guys in the front row go, "Oh man, we just saw Lita's boob!" and pulled my top back up. I just considered myself lucky that the camera didn't catch it!

CHAPTER 36

When J.R. put his *Can You Take the Heat?* cookbook together, J.R. asked all of the wrestlers to submit recipes. Unsurprisingly, half of the boys proposed recipes for things like protein shakes, egg white omelets, and plain boiled chicken with steamed broccoli. He ended up having to incorporate a bunch of recipes that had very little to do with the Superstars who allegedly made them all the time—not that I doubt that Kane loves to bake his Red Velvet Cake!

I was still working with Essa Rios at the time, so I submitted a recipe for a Mexican-influenced ceviche, which was definitely a favorite food of mine—I probably ate it three times a week back when I was in Mexico. When the cookbook was released, it also featured a recipe for "Lita's Spicy Black Beans with Onions and Bacon." I'd never even seen that recipe until I opened up the book!

After *Can You Take the Heat?* was released, five WWE Superstars were invited to go on *Live with Regis* to prepare dishes from the book. It was Stone Cold Steve Austin, Kurt Angle, Triple H, Chyna, and myself—which was pretty good company to be included with.

I had never really thought much about doing that sort of celebrity appearance—I was so into being a wrestler. I didn't decide to become a wrestler because I wanted to be famous. To me, what was appealing was that wrestlers get to travel, they get to be physical, they get to wear cool outfits. I never thought, *I want to be a wrestler so that I can become a big TV star.* The idea that people would recognize me or that I'd get free dinner when I went to Cracker Barrel never even occurred to me. I certainly never saw myself appearing on morning talk shows!

When I got to the *Live with Regis* studio, the producers had pre-prepared the bean dip. I guess they felt that the ceviche was too complicated. There wasn't much point in arguing. It was easier to just go along with what they wanted. So the first time I ever made my "Lita's Spicy Black Beans with Onions and Bacon" was on live TV!

The producers also suggested I do one of my wrestling moves with Regis, but I didn't want to do that. Not only was it a lame talk show cliché, I was worried that it would take up my whole segment. The appearance would end up being about Regis' shtick and not about me.

"The moves I do are really complex," I hedged. "I doubt there's anything we could do that Regis would be comfortable with."

I got lucky—the producer agreed with me, so we ended up doing a bit where Regis asked me to show him the moves I was famous for.

"I usually jump off of the top rope and do something called a moonsault," I said. "Maybe I can get up here on this cook-top counter and show you . . ."

"No, no, we don't have to do that," Regis said. It was funny, and definitely a little more unorthodox than the usual host-in-a-headlock bit.

When I went back to the green room after my appearance, I met Regis' other guest for that morning, Melissa Joan Hart. I remembered her on *Clarissa Explains It All*, so I decided to introduce myself.

"Just wanted to say hello," I said, offering my hand. "I'm Amy, how's it going?"

"Oh," she said, barely looking up. "Hello."

She didn't even shake my hand. It was clear that she was totally impressed with herself. Her "Hello" was more like, "Okay, now you can tell all your friends that you met me."

Of course, I couldn't care less. I was only being friendly. All I could think was, "Hey, if you want to play 'Who's A Bigger Celebrity?' how about we go out on the street and see who gets recognized more...."

It was an interesting period for me. Chyna had been the female face of WWE for a while, but things were changing and I found that more and more attention was being focused on me. It was around this time that I was contacted by the Braverman-Bloom Company, which is an agency that works with some of the wrestlers. They told me that a lot of people were expressing interest in doing business with me, from high-profile entertainment projects to sponsorship deals outside of WWE.

I basically just listened to what they had to say—I certainly wasn't about to make any deals that might upset the balance of my relationship with WWE. One thing I knew for certain was that I didn't want there to be any backstage whispering about my conversation with Braverman-Bloom, so I pulled Vince McMahon aside at *Raw* in Albany to tell him what had gone down.

Vince said that he was definitely aware that there was a lot of buzz going on about me. In fact, he'd recently been getting a lot of calls from *Playboy*. It seems they were interested in shooting me. Very interested.

"I just want you to know that it's entirely your decision," Vince said.

"Thanks for telling me," I replied, "but my initial reaction is that I don't think it's for me."

I also felt that by appearing in *Playboy* I'd be thrown into a category with all the other girls that had posed for them.

It wasn't because I have any issues about being nude—I felt that doing it might alienate some of my fans. One thing I've always been proud of is that my fans relate to me as a real person, and appearing in *Playboy* might hurt that connection.

I also felt that by appearing in *Playboy* I'd be thrown into a category with all the other girls that had posed for them. I didn't want to give up my individuality in that way. Plus, it had already been done by Sable and Chyna. I would have loved to have done something as big and controversial as Chyna's appearance, but on a completely different plane.

Vince meant what he said—there was never any pressure for me to do it. That was the last I ever heard about posing for *Playboy*. Looking back, it's impossible to know if I was right or wrong not to do it, but I've never regretted my decision.

Lita's Mexican-Style Ceviche

1 ½ pounds fresh scallops, cut into bite-size pieces

¾ cup freshly squeezed lime juice (from 5 to 6 limes)

1 cup chopped red onion

3 medium fresh tomatoes, peeled and cut into wedges

½ teaspoon coarse sea salt

Pinch of oregano

3 tablespoons olive oil

⅓ cup chopped cilantro

4 leaves iceberg lettuce

1 avocado, peeled, pitted, and sliced into wedges

Place the scallops into a wide, shallow, glass casserole, and pour the lime juice evenly over them. Cover and place in the refrigerator for 2 hours, stirring occasionally. Add the rest of the ingredients, except the lettuce and avocado, and marinate for another hour, stirring occasionally. Line 4 chilled wineglasses with the lettuce leaves, then top with the ceviche. Garnish with avocado wedges. Or serve on tortillas or with crackers.

Makes 4 servings.

These Are a Few of My Favorite Foods

- *Steamed tofu*
- *Black beans*
- *Guacamole*
- *Steamed dumplings*
- *Steamed spinach*
- *BBQ—sweet and smokey, not the vinegary Carolina style*
- *Artichokes*
- *Broccoli*
- *Tomatoes*
- *Onions*
- *Garlic*
- *Sushi*
- *Fajitas—no green peppers!*
- *Vinaigrette dressing*
- *Peanut sauce*
- *Cottage cheese w/ pineapples*
- *California-style burritos*
- *Miso soup*
- *Yellowish-green bananas*
- *Ceviche—of course!*

CHAPTER 37

On Halloween 2000, I arrived at the building in Rochester, New York, for *SmackDown!* and was told that I'd be dropping the Women's Championship that night in a Four Corners match with Trish, Jacqueline, and Ivory. There was no warning—not that I needed a warning—just a simple, "Okay, this is what we're doing tonight...."

The decision was made in order to give Ivory's new character some steam. She had just joined Right to Censor—the heel faction that parodied WWE's arch-enemy, the Parents Television Council.

Ivory was so excited to finally have something to do. She was technically a heel before joining RTC, but the only character direction she was ever given was, "Be a bitch."

She didn't know why she was a bitch—why she was mad? Why she didn't like any of the other girls? All she was told was, "Be a bitch." So when she became part of RTC she finally had a why for her actions, which is all she needed.

We ended up feuding through the next few weeks, leading up to a Title match at *Survivor Series*. That month was just crazy busy—the *Divas in Hedonism* photo shoot was during the week leading up the Pay-Per-View, so we flew down to Jamaica, spent three days taking pictures, then flew straight back to Tampa for *Survivor Series*. It was just exhausting!

When it came to putting our match together, Ivory and I had very different opinions about how we wanted it to go. "Let's do a lot of wrestling," she said. "Let's show everybody that girls can really wrestle."

"Let's not," I said. The truth is, as good as both Ivory and I are, we're not even close to the guys. For whatever reason, two girls working a real wrestling match just doesn't have the same intensity.

Ivory had been running her RTC gimmick for a few weeks, but was still working through some wardrobe changes. That night she was wearing a long skirt with granny boots, regular street boots with little wooden stacked heels.

Early in the match, I gave her an ensiguiri kick and as she bumped, her heel connected with the corner of my left eye and busted me open. I knew it was cut the second it happened. *Damn,* I thought, then gathered myself together, *Okay. I'm busted open. It's no big deal. Keep going with the match.*

I had no problem continuing the match, though I could feel the blood pouring down my face. I was kind of worried that Vince was going to be angry with me—a woman shouldn't be cut open like I was and then keep doing cool high-flying spots. On the other hand, the ref wasn't being told to stop me, so I kept on doing my thing.

If nothing else, I knew that all that blood definitely looked cool as hell. Since I was going to lose the match, at least I'd look good going down. The only thing that bummed me out was that I was wearing a black mesh shirt. All I could think was, *This is the worst shirt ever for seeing blood!*

My getting cut changed the whole tone of the match. Instead of talking about how Ivory was kicking my ass, J.R. and the King made a very big deal about how tough I was. J.R. totally put over the fact that, even though I had blood pouring from my eye, I "never gave up."

When I got to the back, Stephanie was right there, waiting for me in gorilla. "Are you okay?" she asked.

Early in the match, I gave her an ensiguiri kick and as she bumped, her heel connected with the corner of my left eye and busted me open.

"Yeah," I said, "I'm fine."

"Great, great. Can we get a camera crew over here?"

"Listen, Steph. I want to call my mom and tell her I'm okay."

"No problem," she said. "We'll just put the camera on you when you call."

I was kind of aggravated about that—they couldn't allow me five minutes to check in with my mom to tell her that I wasn't too badly hurt. The attitude was, "We're doing a TV show here. We've got to turn this into a TV moment."

In retrospect, I'm glad they taped it. It was a very cool segment that felt very genuine, probably because it actually was real. You could actually hear my mom on the other end of my cell phone.

After we called it a wrap, I went to get stitched up. Miss Kitty, who wasn't exactly one of my close friends, was in the locker room and volunteered to come hold my hand when I went to see the doctor.

"That's really not necessary," I said, but Kitty wouldn't take no for an answer. "Fine, come with me."

Dr. Bob, who's one of the doctors WWE uses backstage, told me I had to get four stitches. He's a good guy. He was acting as if his own daughter had gotten busted open. He took his time, making the most careful stitches possible. I could tell that he was actively trying not to hurt me. He didn't pull the stitches very tight, which actually caused it to scar a little bit more than it would have if he'd made them super-tight.

Kitty screamed like a maniac every time Dr. Bob poked the needle through my eye. "Oh my God, I can't believe it! Your skin is stretching so far before they push it through! I can't believe you're just laying there like that!"

Just go away, I thought, as Dr. Bob put another stitch in. I had my eyes closed and when I looked up, I could tell Dr. Bob was all nervous, trying not to hurt me any more than he had to. I thought that was so cute. "You're doing a great job," I said. "It hardly hurts at all."

"Thanks," he said. "I really appreciate that."

It was like our roles had flipped—I was laying there, getting this big cut on my eye stitched, but I was trying to calm the doctor down!

I was feeling pretty burnt out around that point. Wrestling is an unusual business—there's no breaks, no vacations. With very few exceptions—like Christmas—we work fifty-two weeks a year. When people ask me, "Are you ever going to get a vacation?" I always say, "I sure hope not, because the only time you get a vacation in this business is when you're injured."

You have no choice but to go into auto-pilot. You can't give yourself a chance to breathe or even the option to slow down. There's no time to think about how harsh you are being to your body. I'm not even including the

bumps you take in the ring—I'm talking about the schedule and the overall lifestyle of travel and work followed by more travel and more work.

But when you become a wrestler, you have to go into it understanding that you have a limited amount of time in your career, so you can't afford to slow down. Between the house shows and the TV tapings and the photo shoots and personal appearances and autograph sessions, it simply never lets up. At best, you get two days at home each week, and those are catch-up days. You wash your clothes, you pay your bills, and you pack your bags to go do it all again.

It wasn't until after I injured my neck that I was able to really appreciate just how hard the life is. The first time I went to TV with Matt after my surgery, I was completely exhausted. It's such a long day, flying in the morning, driving straight to the building then working from noon to midnight. Even though I was just hanging around with nothing to do, by the end of the day I was completely wiped out. "I don't know how you guys do it," I kept saying, even though I knew exactly how they do it.

CHAPTER 38

Team Extreme's feud with Dean Malenko and the Radicalz went on for months, but it started off as a total fluke. We were in Ames, Iowa, for *Raw*— the Hardy Boyz and Chris Jericho were scheduled to take on Dean, Chris Benoit, and Perry Saturn in a match that night, so we shot a pre-tape to give it a little meaning.

We were standing outside of the locker room. Malenko came over to me and said that he'd noticed the way I'd been looking at him. "I know you better than you know yourself," he said.

"Are you right- or left-handed," I asked, "because you look like you need some entertainment. You ought to go home and entertain himself."

Just as I turned away and headed into the locker room, Benoit, Saturn, and Eddie Guerrero came out, slamming the door into my head.

"Maybe we should help her up," Malenko said.

"Just leave her," said Benoit.

When Matt and Jeff came out of the locker room and saw what had happened, the two teams exchanged words and the Radicalz ended up beating the Hardyz down.

The pre-tape was good. The creative team liked the on-camera chemistry between Dean and myself. They thought there were lots of possibilities in continuing the angle.

Working with the Radicalz was very different from what Team Extreme was used to. When we worked with people like Edge and Christian, we were all good friends and that made it easy to exchange ideas on how to make things as interesting and exciting as possible. We definitely got along with the Radicalz, but they were all business every step of the way.

Dean Malenko is a very funny guy. He loves to joke around in the back. That being said, when it's time to talk about work, he talks about work. I prefer that—I need to focus when I'm discussing business. I can't be thinking of one liners to zing back to Dean as he tells knock-knock jokes. Not that I don't appreciate his knock-knock jokes.

He was always very encouraging in terms of my wrestling. If there's one thing about Dean that stands out, it's that he's always serious about wrestling.

Working with a female to the extent that we did was completely different from anything that Dean had ever done before. Nevertheless, he was actually very giving. He went out of his way to highlight me without burying himself. He put a lot of thought into what we were doing, to make everything we did look as good as it could be.

We had a match the next night on *SmackDown!*—Team Extreme vs. Malenko, Saturn, and Guerrero. The finish had Matt and Jeff brawling on the outside with Eddie and Perry. I landed a moonsault on Dean, but Terri—Perry's "girlfriend" at the time—distracted the ref long enough for Eddie to frogsplash me and pull Dean over me for the pinfall.

Dean brought me flowers on *Raw* the following Monday. He apologized for what happened on *SmackDown!* then asked me out on a date.

"Can I think about it?"

"Of course."

"Okay, I've thought about it," I said and slapped him right across his face.

He caught my hurricanrana, reversed it into a powerbomb, then he slapped on his submission hold, the Texas Cloverleaf.

But Dean was persistent—he offered me a shot at his Light Heavyweight title, with the stipulation that if he won, I had to go out on "an evening (I'd) never forget."

Those pre-tapes were exciting for me—it was one of the first times that I was actually the focus of the segments, as opposed to just standing there with Matt and Jeff saying, "Let's go get 'em!" It was a great opportunity to develop my character, which was a lot of fun.

Dean and I ended up having a good little TV match. I got some decent offense on him, but in the end, he beat my ass. He caught my hurricanrana, reversed it into a powerbomb, then he slapped on his submission hold, the Texas Cloverleaf. I had no choice—I had to tap out.

As a result, the next night on *SmackDown!* I had to go out on a date that I'd never forget. Dean walked into the Hardy Boyz' locker room dressed in a tux, carrying a dozen roses. "Don't wait up," he said.

We were in New York City that night, so our date started out in the back of a taxi. Then we went to a restaurant called Nick & Stef's, which is a very nice steakhouse that's attached to Madison Square Garden.

"It hurts me to look at you," Dean said as we sat at the dinner table.

"It hurts me to look at you," I replied.

"Your eyes are like two rising stars," he said.

"How would you know? You've been staring at my chest all night."

In the next segment, I was at the table with a big plateful of steak—along with lobster, shrimp cocktail, salad, the works.

"When I said order anything on the menu," Dean said, "I didn't mean *everything*. But I'm glad you have a good appetite—you'll need the energy for later."

Dean kept the lines coming as I ate, telling me that he was everything I could possibly want in a man. Finally I told him that he was right. "I want you," I said. "I want you now."

"Check please!"

From there, we went to this shitty hotel that was within walking distance from the Garden. It didn't look too bad from the lobby, but it was a real dive, one of those by-the-hour joints. The rooms were terrible—tacky décor and paper-thin walls.

The segment started with me coming out of the bathroom in a robe, which I opened to reveal a sexy bra and panties. Dean was laying on the bed and his jaw just dropped. "I just have one question for you," I said. "How does your wife feel about you being a sneaky two-timing bastard?"

Dean told me not to worry about that, then turned out the lights so that the room was pitch dark.

"I like the lights on," I said.

"Okay," he said, and turned them back on to find the Hardyz standing there. Matt hit him over the head with a champagne bottle, then Jeff threw the bed over on him. It was hilarious!

"I promised you a night you'd never forget," I laughed, and we left.

Shooting the vignettes was a big ordeal, but I knew as we did them that we were doing something memorable. It was great to do something that was completely different from the usual backstage pre-tapes. Plus, it was going to add a lot of dimension to the story.

The following week in Birmingham, Alabama, was the *Armageddon* Pay-Per-View—Team Extreme opened the show in an Intergender Elimination Match against Dean, Perry, and Terri. The match ended with everyone eliminated except me and Dean. Near the end, he superplexed me off the top and as I hit the mat, I felt a sharp pain shoot down into my legs.

My back was hurting the next day at *Raw,* but all I had to do in our match against the Radicalz that night was get blasted off the apron by Malenko, so I decided to ride it out. *I just need some rest,* I thought. *If I make it through tonight and tomorrow, I'll get a few days off and it'll be fine.*

But when Dean pulled me off the apron in our match, it felt like knives were stabbing into my back and down into my legs. For one scary moment, I actually couldn't feel my legs.

Now I was worried, but still didn't want to let anyone know that I might be injured. The next night at *SmackDown!* I was booked into a match against Ivory, which ended up being just rotten. Not because of my back—it was just one of those nights. The plan was that Ivory would surprise me with a roll-up for the three count, then I'd pop up, shocked that she beat me, as she scurried up the ramp. But after she pinned me, I honestly couldn't get up. I just laid there in pain. I finally had to do the classic Tommy Dreamer sell and use the ropes to pick myself up off the mat. When I got to the back, Michael Hayes told me how horrible the match was. "It wasn't a good night for Lita," he said.

"No shit, Michael," I said. "Thanks a lot."

Back in the locker room, I put ice on my lower back. It was very, very tender. It was hard to even walk around. All I could think about was going home and going to bed.

I was so happy when I finally got home the next day. It was only for one night, because I had to go do a couple of media appearances before that weekend's house shows, but at least I would get to sleep in my own bed!

But then Bob Clarke, the Talent Relations liaison who schedules doctor's appointments, called—"Your flight's not leaving until four," he said, "so I scheduled a seven A.M. bone scan for you in Raleigh so we can see what's going on with your back."

I'd really been looking forward to sleeping late before I had to go to the airport. "I'm sorry, Bob," I said, "but I just can't make that appointment. I really need to sleep."

"It's already scheduled," he said. "Seven A.M. is the only time they can do it and they're doing you a favor by squeezing you in.

"Well, I'm not going!" I was being a total brat. My schedule for the next week was absolutely hellish—I'd have to go from my media appearance to house shows to two days of TV. Then from there I had to go to California, where the Hardyz and I were scheduled to shoot our Chef Boyardee commercial, followed by more TV. It was never going to end and I was not happy!

"Look, Amy, you can go because I'm telling you to go, or I can have J.R. call you and have him tell you to go. Either way, you're going to get your back checked out."

"Fine," I said, "I'll go!" Then I lost it and just started bawling like a little girl. It was a combination of things, from the back pain to just being burnt out after working nonstop for a year. I was so looking forward to sleeping in—that was going to be the highlight of my week!

After I got off with Bob, I immediately called Matt.

"I don't know if I can do this," I sobbed. "There's no end in sight and as thankful as I am for everything, I'm only one person."

Matt was great—instead of downplaying my problem and trying to come up with a way to fix things, he simply offered sympathy and a shoulder to cry on.

The bone scan showed two cracked pars in my back. Since I was scheduled to host *Raw* from the *World* in New York the following Monday, Bob Clarke made me an appointment to have an MRI done on my back. As I sat in the waiting room, my cell phone rang. It was someone from WWE, asking me for my bra and underwear sizes.

"Why do you need to know?" I asked.

"I don't really know. I guess they've got you doing something in your bra and panties tonight at the World."

"Well, I don't know how comfortable I am with this. I'd better talk to someone in creative."

I had the MRI done—it turned out that in addition to the two cracked pars, I also had three bulging and herniated discs in my back. It was just one of those things that happens to wrestlers. It flares up occasionally and then goes away again.

That pissed me right off—I felt that parading around in bra and panties was completely contradictory to the Lita character.

From there I went directly to the *World,* where I was informed that I'd be giving Dean Malenko a very special Christmas lingerie show. That pissed me right off—I felt that parading around in bra and panties was completely contradictory to the Lita character.

"You're doing it because you know Dean is watching," I was told. "You're teasing him."

"I don't know that I would really want to be teasing him," I said. "He's beaten me up a lot lately."

"Well, we got such positive response to the hotel room segment where you were in your underwear. It was really great to see Lita's feminine side."

I was steaming at this point. "Look, I'm very happy about the positive feedback, but my being in bra and panties doesn't make any sense in this scenario."

"We're just doing what we're told."

"I don't care. I need to speak to someone in creative before I do anything."

I called one of the boys—they were in Greenville, South Carolina—and said, "Find me a writer now!" Even though it wasn't his segment, Michael Hayes got on the phone with me. He didn't know what was going on, but he sat there and listened to me bitch.

"I understand what you're saying," he said, "but I don't think there's anything we can do about this right now. Just go ahead and do it and we'll worry about it later."

So I did it. I stood there in red, white, and green bra and panties on the stage at the *World*—I was completely uncomfortable. I felt very cheap and totally embarrassed. The *World* was a very intimate environment. Usually when talent went there, we'd warm up the crowd, interact with them a bit, then do the little fifteen-second live segment. This time, I had to go out onto the stage three times—though it seemed more like fifty! I felt that the crowd could sense just how uncomfortable I was, and were almost reluctant to cheer and catcall me. It was like they knew Lita wasn't the type of girl to respond to that kind of reaction.

The worst part of it was that it made no sense whatsoever. Why would I pose in my lingerie if I was scared of him? Why would I be teasing him if I wasn't interested in his advances? Wouldn't I just stay away from him? Why am I going to act like I'm seducing him and then slap him at the end of the pre-tape?

The next morning I flew down to Charlotte for *SmackDown!* When I got to the building, Vince and Stephanie pulled me aside to tell me how great they thought the segment was. I guess they'd heard rumblings that I was unhappy, so they decided to make me feel better.

"I thought it was phenomenal how you were a little shy in the beginning," Stephanie said.

"I was freaking embarrassed," I explained. "It just didn't make sense to me."

"Well, it came across great," she said. "We're really really happy with it."

From that point on, the storyline began to develop serious inconsistencies, which was aggravating as hell. Things changed from one day to the next. My theory is that if a storyline is hard for me to follow, how can I expect the audience to understand what's going on? If I've got twenty questions, then the audience is going to have fifty. It was very frustrating, but at the same time, the storyline had people talking, so I didn't want to ruffle any feathers.

The day before the Hardyz and I flew out to Los Angeles to shoot our Chef Boyardee commercial at Big Bear Mountain, Bruce Prichard came to us and said, "Since you're going to be out west, you'd be doing us a big favor if you'd appear at a Ultimate Pro Wrestling show."

Obviously we couldn't say no. We flew all night, grabbed a couple of hours sleep in an airport hotel, and were driven out to the UPW show in Santa Ana where Team Extreme faced a UPW tag team called the Ballard Brothers and my old friend Lexie Fyfe.

Seeing Marybeth was the only good thing about doing the show. She's a real friend, which isn't something to take for granted in the wrestling business. She didn't turn on me when I got a job in WWE, and she's never shown the slightest bit of resentment.

Indie shows tend to drag on forever, so we didn't leave there until after midnight. From there we took a limo to Big Bear for the commercial shoot. We got to our hotel at around four A.M., slept for a few hours and woke back up for an eight A.M. pickup to take us to the set.

God, we were all just beat! Plus, my back was still killing me. But once we got out there and got going, it turned out to be a very unique experience. The air was crisp, the sun was shining, and I was able to forget about how tired I was.

When the shoot ended twelve hours later, we got back in the limo, went to the airport, and took the red eye back east to Chattanooga, Tennessee, to tape the Christmas episode of *Raw*. No joke—when we got to the building, it felt like we hadn't had a night's sleep since we'd seen everybody last. It was a long, long week.

That night the Hardyz took on Malenko and Benoit. After the match, Dean puts Matt in the Texas Cloverleaf. I tried to help, but Benoit grabbed me and locked on the Crippler Crossface. The paramedics came out, setting up an injury angle for me so that I could take it easy on

Because I rarely get to spend a week doing anything other than work, I've found the best thing to do during my vacation time is just stay home.

my back for a week or two. The next night we did *SmackDown!* in Nashville—Matt and Chris had a great match together—and then it was finally Christmas break. A whole week off!

Unfortunately, I didn't go home and sleep for three days. My mom actually came to Nashville and then we drove back to her house in Atlanta for the holidays. It was nice—I love spending time with her—but it wasn't the break that I needed. Granted, I wasn't working but I also wasn't at home, in full vegetable mode.

Since then, I've made my mom come to visit me for Christmas. Because I rarely get to spend a week doing anything other than work, I've found the best thing to do during my vacation time is just stay home.

That was the end of my first year in WWE—it's amazing, looking back and seeing how much I did in such a short period of time. It's hard to digest the magnitude of what's happening to you because you're so busy all the time. There's no time to stop and think about how it felt, to soak it all in, and examine your life. You're too busy just staying alive. In hindsight, I wouldn't have had it any other way!

CHAPTER 39

The first *Raw* of 2001 was in San Jose, California—it was Chris Jericho and the Hardyz vs. the Radicalz. After Chris got the pinfall on Benoit, I attacked Dean, who then grabbed a concessionaire's tray and covered me with hot dogs and mustard—it was horrible!

When we first booked the segment, the plan was for Dean to grab a tray from a nachos vendor and cover me with cheese. Somewhere along the way, that changed to hot dogs and mustard. I had no issue with getting covered in food—my problem was that I hate mustard. I mean, I really hate it. Just the smell of it is enough to make me gag.

It was all over me, too. There was disgusting yellow mustard everywhere, dripping down my arm—it was so revolting! I wore a pink net shirt and the mustard actually turned it orange! God, it was gross.

I went back to the locker room to clean up and as I showered, Malenko snuck in to spy on me. "Get out of here," I said as Matt and Jeff came in to see what was going on. They pretty much beat him senseless—Jeff held Dean's leg while Matt whacked it with a chair, setting up an injury angle so he could go and get his knee scoped.

We actually shot the shower scene twenty minutes before *Raw* went live. Then I quickly dried my hair and put on my makeup so I'd be ready in time for the show.

They told me that they were going to show me from the waist up, but when they played the shower segment, you could totally see my ass. I was wearing a thong, and looking back, that was my big mistake—I should've worn surf shorts or something to ensure that they couldn't show my butt. Still, I felt as though I'd been taken advantage of. Another thing to chalk up to "shit happens."

Malenko returned a few weeks later—*Raw* was at the Meadowlands and Team Extreme had a match against Benoit, Perry, and Terri. I was glad that we followed through with the storyline when Dean came back. Too many angles just get forgotten when someone needs a few weeks off because of an injury. In our case, we not only picked up where we'd left off, we carried all the way through to a logical ending.

We did *SmackDown!* at Nassau Coliseum. It was Matt vs. Perry Saturn. I was on the apron, and at the finish, Matt accidentally pushed Perry into me, sending me into Dean's arms. He planted a big kiss on me, full on the mouth, but I paintbrushed him and grabbed the mike.

"This has got to stop," I said. "I've got to admit I've pulled some cheap pranks on you, but it's a little hard to resist because you're such a sucker. They say what a woman wants most from a man is a ring. Well, I want you in the ring next Monday night on *Raw.*"

That was the first time I ever cut a promo in front of a live crowd. I was pretty nervous beforehand. I was concentrating so hard on what I was supposed to say. When Dean kissed me, I just stood there staring at him. Perry was laying there on the floor and he started buzzing me, "Slap him. Slap him."

Oh my God, I thought, *he's right,* and slapped the taste out of Dean's mouth. *Whack!*

I really hated the promo—Stephanie had hired a couple of women writers to work with the girls and that's what they came up with. They were gone shortly thereafter, of course. All I really cared about was that the Dean and Lita feud was finally—finally!—coming to an end.

The plan from day one had been to build to a blow-off match between me and Dean, with Dean putting me over. So much had gone on since then, so many twists and turns that I didn't always agree with, so all I cared about was putting an end to the storyline. At that point, I was just glad that no one came to me and said, "Okay, you and Dean are going to go to Vegas and elope. . . ."

Our big blow-off match was on *Raw* in St. Louis. I didn't have very much offense—I actually beat Dean's ass much more over the course of our feud—but it resolved the storyline once and for all.

In the end, Dean went to slam me to the mat, but as he swung me around, my foot connected with the ref's head, knocking him unconscious. He hit me with a vertical suplex, and as I lay there, he went outside for a chair. Right then, Matt came running in through the crowd, nailed Dean with a chair shot of his own, then slid out of the ring just as the ref came to. I crawled on top of Dean for the pin—one-two-three!

Dean was totally cool about putting me over. Of course, it wasn't exactly a competitive match—he mostly just beat me up until Matt got him with the chair shot. I think he also knew that most people would forget about the match results—they'd only remember what happened next.

Matt and I stood there in the middle of the ring, celebrating my victory, when all of a sudden, he kissed me. The crowd popped big—I was totally psyched, thinking, *If they thought that was great, they're going to love what happens next!*

I just stood there in shock at what he'd just done. Matt got all embarrassed and started up the ramp. I ran after him, grabbed his shoulder, spun him around, took a thoughtful pause and kissed him back—a huge, long lip lock. Sure enough, the crowd just went insane. The cheering was just ridiculously loud. I felt so great about that. *Cool,* I thought. *We got 'em.*

We got back to gorilla and everybody was all smiley, congratulating us on a job well done. Watching the show back, Jerry "the King" Lawler was in rare form on commentary, "She's eating him up, J.R.! She's swallowing him whole!"

Some people had been worried that it wouldn't work, but The Kiss, as it's come to be known, was one of those rare occasions where it all came together perfectly—the storyline, our timing, the camera shot, everything. It's one of my proudest WWE moments.

The Kiss was the next logical step in the evolution of Team Extreme. Matt and I were both a little hesitant about making our personal lives public, but after we were told how it was going to develop, we were totally into the idea. It wasn't just a little pre-tape where we kissed and that was

that—it was a well thought out scenario that would definitely get the fans talking.

The Kiss got such great audience feedback that the following week they wanted us to do it again. That's classic WWE—if something works, then do it again and again and again until no one gives a damn anymore.

Team Extreme were in a meaningless little match against the Hollys. We were told to jump around celebrating our win, then make out like Matt had been on a trip and I hadn't seen him in a month.

"Why would we do that?" we asked. "It's not like it was a high drama match."

"Well, the crowd loved it last time," we were told.

"Okay," I said, "but it's going to get old quick."

I was worried that we'd burn out the relationship gimmick without ever really developing it. If we kept up that pace, we'd end up as heels—Matt and Lita, the annoying couple that's always making out for no reason. It would have been no time at all until we started getting booed out of the buildings for kissing and slobbering all over each other after every match.

Matt and I had so many ideas for things we could do as a couple. We suggested things like getting filmed in the shower together—we thought it could've been sexy as hell. Obviously I wouldn't suggest things like that if I was paired with someone who wasn't my real boyfriend. But since Matt and I really are together, why not take advantage of that fact?

It's sad—creative spends so much time trying to force unique TV moments to happen, and yet they always blew off our ideas. We really could've done some great things if we were given the opportunity.

Top Ten Foods I Really Really Hate

1. **Mustard**
2. **Pickles**
3. **Mayonnaise**
4. **Green peppers**
5. **Watercress**
6. **Carrots**
7. **Cucumbers**
8. **Sour cream**
9. **Sausage**
10. **Brown bananas**

CHAPTER 40

Things in WWE began to change in the weeks leading up to *WrestleMania X-Seven*. We arrived at *Raw* in Washington, DC, and who do we see hanging around backstage but my old boss, Paul E. Heyman. ECW had finally gone under and Vince had brought Paul E. in to replace Jerry "the King" Lawler—who had quit the week before over a dispute involving his soon-to-be-ex-wife, Miss Kitty.

I'd heard rumors that Paul E. was coming. I had no idea what was going to happen, but I had a feeling it might get interesting.

That episode of *Raw* saw us teasing some kind of discontent between Team Extreme. I was on my way out to the ring to take on Ivory and RTC, but first I stopped by the locker room to wish Matt and Jeff luck in their title match against the Dudley Boyz.

"Where are you going?" Matt asked.

"My match is next," I said.

"Well, we're not going to let you go out there by yourself," Matt said. "C'mon, Jeff."

"What about our conversation?" Jeff said.

"This is more important," Matt replied. "We'll talk about it later."

My match saw the tension between the Hardyz growing—I did a crossbody onto Ivory on the outside. RTC—Val Venis and Steven Richards—started beating on me, but the Hardyz came down the ramp to make the save. Jeff went to run the rail, but instead of hitting Val, he accidentally clotheslined me.

That was the only time I took one of Jeff's big moves. Running the rail is one of his signature spots, but I've seen a lot of guys get out of the way when he does it to them—I was going to make sure I was right there.

Matt got all pissed off at Jeff for nailing me, which was supposed to create some tension between them for their match later on in the show. It didn't amount to much, though—they won the WWE Tag Team Championships for the fourth time that night.

A couple of weeks later, we were in Cleveland for *Raw* and Vince called everybody into a meeting. He informed us that he had just bought WCW. "Nobody else was going to buy it," he explained, "and I really feel that it's important to maintain some competition in our business. Now obviously, their product has suffered a lot recently, so we're going to work to bring the WCW brand up to our level of quality."

The plan was to keep WWE and WCW as two completely separate entities. "We're going to bring the WCW brand level up," Vince said, "without bringing the WWE brand down."

In addition, Vince explained that it would provide all kinds of opportunities for us, "When your career has taken all the paths it can on one show," he said, "you can go to the other brand and have a whole new start."

Well, it seemed like a good idea at the time! Vince has a real way of rallying the troops. We walked out of the meeting, thinking, *Maybe this is going to work out alright.*

At the ten o'clock hour, Vince made his big on-air speech about buying WCW, with a split-screen linking us to the last-ever *Nitro* in Panama City, Florida.

Team Extreme were then given the plum position of following one of the most historic moments in wrestling history. We were joined by Chris Benoit for a match against Team ECK—Edge, Christian, and Kurt Angle. It was essentially a teaser for *WrestleMania X-Seven* the next week, where the Hardy Boyz were facing Edge and Christian and the Dudley Boyz in TLC II.

Edge and Christian's good friend Rhyno ran in at the end of the match and gored the hell out of Matt. I climbed into the ring to see if he was okay, and Rhyno gored me as well.

I was really looking forward to *WrestleMania* that year. *WrestleMania* is different from every other Pay-Per-View. It's the biggest production of the year, it's where the major angles end and new ones begin. The heat's definitely up at *WrestleMania*—even in a limited role like I had, everybody tries to give it everything they've got.

WrestleMania X-Seven was a very big deal for me. I had attended *XVI* with Essa Rios, appearing at the fan *Axxess* convention, but we weren't part of the show. This time I was going to be taking part in one of the night's most eagerly awaited matches—TLC II.

I only had a small role on the show as part of the TLC II match between the Hardyz, the Dudleyz, and Edge and Christian, but I was featured in the promotional poster alongside Stone Cold, 'Taker, and The Rock. I was pretty excited when I saw it for the first time—I thought, *Check me out, I'm on the poster with the big guys!*

The Pay-Per-View was at the Houston Astrodome, and a couple of days before the show we held a pep rally at Fort Hood, Texas—the largest military base in the world. I went down there with Undertaker, Bradshaw, Trish, and Jacqueline. Because a lot of the military people couldn't take off to go to *WrestleMania,* we brought a small piece of *WrestleMania* to them. It was our way of showing WWE's support of the military, a fun way to say thank you for how hard everybody there works and for what they give up to defend our country.

The night before the show, we all met up to discuss the match. I was totally blown away by the massive size of the Astrodome—it's just unbelievably impressive. I stood there, soaking it all in, imagining what it was going to be like the next day when it was filled with seventy thousand screaming fans.

In the first TLC, I did the only run-in. This time, all three teams had an equalizer—Edge and Christian had Rhyno, Bubba and D-Von had Spike Dudley. Before the match there was some debate over the order of the run-ins—some people wanted Rhyno to come out last because he was going to do the most damage, but Matt argued that my coming out last

would provoke the biggest reaction. I didn't get involved in the discussions. I just sat there. "Tell me when you want me to come out," I said, "and what you want me to do, and that's what I'll do."

It was decided that I'd be the third and final run-in. Matt was absolutely right—when I came down to the ring, I got one of the biggest pops of the night, which was very exciting.

Because of the size of the stadium, the *WrestleMania* ramp was super long. I didn't want to leave anyone hanging, so when the time came for me to hit the ring, I had to haul ass all the way. Edge was on the ladder, going for the belts, so I quickly slid into the ring and pulled him down. Watching the show later, J.R.'s commentary was inadvertently hilarious, "There's Lita, jerking Edge off the ladder."

Rhyno caught me right as I jerked Edge off. He was about to gorilla press me, but Spike came up behind him and hit him with a nut shot. I gave Rhyno a hurricanrana then grabbed a chair and smashed it over Spike's head.

I gave that chair shot everything I had. As a rule, girls give crappy-looking chair shots and I was determined to make mine count. I whacked Spike good—you could see the shape of his head in the way the chair was bent. I was really happy with the shot, but at the same time, I felt kind of bad. *Poor Spike,* I thought, *I wouldn't want a chair bent over* my *head!*

After the chair shot, I was on fire! I tore off my hot pink top and turned around to find the Dudleyz, who got me with a 3D. That was it—I was done. No one gets up from the 3D. Just ask Bubba.

I was very pleased with my first *WrestleMania.* TLC II was a stone-cold classic match, and I'm proud to have played a small part in it. Some people consider *X-Seven* to be the best *WrestleMania* of all time. It's definitely my favorite.

CHAPTER 41

After living in Joey Abs' condo for about a year, I began to want a bigger space. Not just for me, but for Cody. I wanted him to be comfortable in his surroundings. After all, he was home a lot more than I was.

I was starting to make decent money, so I was able to get out of debt and put a down payment on a small house in Sanford. It was a really nice place—the best thing about it was that there was a good-sized backyard for Cody.

Since I was gone so much, I had a few people that would keep an eye on Cody. One of them was my friend Renee, who I'd met right when I first moved down to Sanford. She was the checkout girl at the local Food Lion supermarket. I was buying groceries and she seemed nice, so I asked her for some directions—I needed to change my driver's license and wanted to know where to find the local Department of Motor Vehicles.

It turned out that Renee and I had a couple of mutual acquaintances. We became friendly and she started watching Cody on a regular basis.

Renee was still living at home with her folks, so we decided that she would have her own room in my new house. That way she could stay there and take care of Cody when I was out on the road.

I was so busy during those days that I barely had any time to buy furniture for the house. All I had when I first moved in was my bed, a tanning bed, a TV, and a Stairmaster. My mom got me a dinette set so that I didn't have to eat on the floor or on my bed, but that was it. It was maybe eight months before I found time to buy a couch. The sad part is that it didn't bother me at all. I was gone so much I hardly noticed it.

Buying the house was just the best feeling. For the first time, I could plan my life for more than a few months into the future. I never planned ahead before—I just let stuff happen. It was nice to know that no matter what happened, I had a safe comfortable place to live.

It was also cool to have a place to accumulate stuff. I'd never cared about material things, I'm the complete opposite of a pack rat. But over the years I'd begun thinking, *Damn, I wish I had saved that,* so it was nice to have the space to begin gathering up all my WWE memorabilia—my posters and action figures, my photo scrapbooks, and so forth.

I really love my house. I'm sure there's a lot of people that will be reading this that think, *Oh, Lita's a big TV star, she must live in a mansion.* That is the farthest thing from the truth. It's just a nice modest house, exactly the right size for my needs.

I could've bought a much more extravagant house, but I didn't see any reason to go overboard. I'm a very conservative spender, and the fact of the matter is that at about fifteen hundred square feet, this house is still ten times bigger than anywhere I've ever lived on my own.

All I really cared about was having a calm, cozy place where I could come home to relax. It's got everything I need—a backyard for Cody, a spare room for Renee, and a washer/dryer. Honestly, it couldn't be more perfect.

CHAPTER 42

If the weeks before *WrestleMania* were strange, the time that followed was positively weird—all the WCW people were coming in, The Rock left to make *The Scorpion King,* and Stone Cold Steve Austin turned heel.

People were just refusing to boo Stone Cold. It was totally his decision to turn, but the fans weren't buying it. To them, Stone Cold was the cool guy that flips his boss off. They weren't interested in hating him.

Creative decided that they needed to get some heat on Stone Cold, so they had him beat up Michael Cole and J.R. It didn't matter—he still was getting the loudest pop of the night.

Which is where I came in.

The logic was that beating up a defenseless girl—a girl that the fans love—would evoke the heel heat that they wanted. "I'll do whatever I've got to do," Steve said when they told him they wanted him to beat my ass. "I'm not afraid to go there."

I felt the same way. I was honored just to be involved in the segment. Team Extreme got booked into the *Raw* main event against Stone Cold, Triple H, and Stephanie McMahon-Helmsley. At the end of the match, Matt and Jeff were brawling on the outside with Stone Cold and Triple H. I pulled Stephanie into the ring, gave her a Twist of Fate, went up top for a moonsault—one-two-three!

I was standing triumphantly over Steph when Triple H came running back in and whacked me from behind. He gave me the Pedigree, but then Matt came in and tackled him into the corner. As all that was going on, Stone Cold grabbed a steel chair—he hit Jeff over the head, then took Matt down with a shot to the back. He kept beating on Matt, sticking him with the edge of the chair. When he paused to soak in the crowd's boos, I crawled on top of Matt to protect him.

I looked up at Stone Cold, "Please don't do this." He was a heel, but he would never hit a girl. Right?

Wrong. Stone Cold went totally psycho and proceeded to lay a particularly nasty beating on me. He hit me with all his usual gusto, on my back and my stomach, my elbows and my knees.

After a couple of minutes, Triple H grabbed me by the hair, dragged me around the ring—"The Caveman Spot," we called it—then held me up while Stone Cold gave me the Stunner. While I was psyched to take a Stone Cold Stunner, I was bummed that I couldn't bounce after he hit me because I was supposed to be unconscious.

Raw went off the air with Stone Cold drinking his beer as he stepped all over the lifeless Team Extreme. The show ended but the crowd continued to go nuts, chucking all kinds of trash at Stone Cold. I was pretty nervous laying there. I didn't want any of it winging me in the head

As I lay there, I was happy to realize that the plan had worked—the fans were pissed off at Stone Cold. The wrestling audience is so smart, and if you can make them do what you want them to do—whether it's cheer or boo—then you've done your job. That night, Team Extreme did their job. They took a shot using us in a main-event capacity and we totally held up our end of the deal. We got the exact response we were all hoping for.

When we got to the back, there were congratulations all around. Vince came up to us and told us what a good job we'd done. Both Triple H and

Stone Cold were really appreciative. "Thanks a lot," Stone Cold said to me. "You sure are a tough girl, because I wasn't holding back at all."

The office was clearly happy with the way the angle turned out, because the next day in Philadelphia, Jeff won the Intercontinental Championship from Triple H. I wasn't physically involved in that match, because I was supposed to be badly injured from the beating I took on *Raw*.

Of course, I was still at the show. That afternoon, I ran the stairs in the empty arena while Jeff and Triple H were in the ring discussing their match. That's one of my favorite things to do in the hours before showtime—I run up and down the stairs in the stands. It's a great way to work out when there's no time to go to the gym. You never know when you'll be needed, and that way I'm right there if someone needs me.

I was pretty excited for Jeff—any time a member of Team Extreme did well, it looked great for the rest of us. I watched the match from gorilla so I could be there to congratulate him when he got to the back afterwards.

The next day we had to go from Philadelphia to film our visits to the *Tough Enough* training facility in Stamford. As a token of how well we'd done on *Raw* and *SmackDown!* Matt, Jeff and I were invited to travel via Air McMahon—Vince's private jet.

That plane is something else—it's like a limousine with wings. It's small, there's only room for twelve passengers. There are two benches where you slide this way and that on takeoff and landing. You definitely feel special and important when you're flying in it.

The whole McMahon family flew with us and there was just a really warm, friendly vibe. We all hugged when we got off the plane. It was nice—it felt like we were really appreciated for the work we'd done.

I have a good relationship with all the McMahons. We're not pals—it's all business—but it's cordial and professional. It has to be very straightforward, especially with Vince, because his time is so limited. So if you've got something to say, you've got to say it. There's no time for beating around the bush. I've always felt pretty comfortable about going to him with any comments, questions, or concerns. I feel sorry for anyone that doesn't, because that's the only way to get the ultimate straight answer.

We didn't spend too much time at Trax—the *Tough Enough* training facility—because Matt and Jeff had to go down to Florida for house shows. But we were definitely glad to do it, just to get a glimpse into what the whole *Tough Enough* thing was all about. There was a negative buzz going on among the WWE wrestlers about the show—some kids win a contest and they're going to be in our locker room?

I had always been extremely humble about how quickly I made it to

WWE. Granted, I busted my ass to get there, but it was only a year after my very first professional match. Most of the boys had worked on the indie circuit for ages before they'd even gotten a hint of recognition—they had years of experience behind them when they finally got to WWE.

There's a long tradition of paying dues in this business and a lot of the boys felt that the idea of a TV contest to get a WWE contract was just plain wrong. It was a carefully controlled environment, where their training was less about what they learned in the ring than it was about how it played for TV. Plus, they lived in a mansion and got to go on a vacation—a far cry from sleeping in their cars and making eight-hour drives just to get ten minutes of ring experience.

As a reality show, it was all well and good—*Tough Enough* was fine as far as character development was concerned. But overall, it made a mockery out of what everyone in the locker room had to go through in order to make it to the top of the business.

CHAPTER 43

Chyna and I had become good friends over the months since I first came to WWE. I had a lot of respect for her. She'd truly broken a lot of ground for women in the wrestling business, she had a strong work ethic, and above all, Joanie had a very goofy sense of humor, which was right up my alley.

I think she had similar feelings about me. She could tell that I really cared about wrestling, and that I was willing to work as hard as any of the boys in order to put on a good match. That mutual respect eventually grew beyond wrestling, where we could talk about makeup and fashion and boyfriends.

Joanie was going through some hard times—both political and personal—that were really affecting her life in WWE. It was pretty clear to everybody that her days at the company were numbered.

"We're at a dead end for you creatively," Vince told her. "You've been the Intercontinental Champion, but to be honest, you're never going to be the World Champion. What we want is to expand you into the Women's Division."

She threw out all kinds of ideas for things she could do, but there was no getting out of it—creative wanted her in the Women's Division and that's where she was going to go. She was not happy about it, to say the least.

Chyna squashed Ivory at *WrestleMania X-Seven* to win the Women's Title, and then proceeded to plow though the entire Women's Division. Eventually, it came down to me. Other than Chyna, I was the only woman in WWE that had had regular in-ring interaction with guys.

Going into the *Judgment Day* Pay-Per-View, I had a bad feeling that all the stress that was going on in Chyna's life was going to affect our match. It was a potentially volatile situation. Everybody tiptoed around her backstage—she was moody as hell and no one wanted to be the one to piss her off.

I was miserable—initially I felt that a feud with Chyna would be a big step up for me. She'd worked hard to establish her "Ninth Wonder of the World" persona, and to make people rethink women's roles in wrestling. I thought that any heat that I could get off of her would show that I was the future of women in wrestling. But now I was stuck in this awkward position of having to work with someone that no one wanted anything to do with.

The day of the Pay-Per-View was just awful. No one even wanted to make eye contact with her. And since I was working with her, the people that were usually friendly towards me were avoiding me. It was terrible. I kept thinking, *Can someone help me out here? This is supposed to be the next step in my career!*

Wrong.

Since Chyna and I were both babyfaces, I watched a lot of old tapes of classic double babyface matches to find spots that we could use in our match. But Chyna didn't want to give up too much offense, so as a result, we had a very average match. Even though I was the only female to ever have a competitive match with her, I wish we could've torn the house down. Unfortunately, we didn't.

The only thing that helped matters was that J.R. and Paul. E. sold the hell out of me on commentary. "No woman has ever taken the fight to Chyna like Lita did tonight," Heyman said.

That whole period was a very frustrating time for me. I feel as though WWE missed out on a golden opportunity by not passing the torch and putting the title on me. I know the connection I have with the people will be there whether I hold the belt or not, but considering the circumstances, I feel it would've been the right business decision for all involved.

I had been told that there were all kinds of plans for me, but somehow they just fizzled out. When Chyna's contract wasn't picked up, the Women's Championship seemed to disappear with her into oblivion. Worse was the fact that Chyna had squashed the whole Women's Division to get to me, which didn't leave a lot of credibilty to those of us who were left.

Joanie and I stayed friends for a while after she left WWE. We would chat on the phone, but I began getting uncomfortable with the fact that all she wanted to talk about was how great she was doing. I felt like she was only talking to me so that I could report back to the locker room, "Hey everybody, Chyna is doing great!"

It was an awkward situation—it wasn't my responsibilty to be Joanie's political connection to the locker room. I'm not saying she had to tell me all her personal business, but I had enough to worry about on my own.

I'll always have a lot of good feelings and real respect for Chyna—she accomplished some amazing things in this business—but the last thing I needed at that stage of my life was a superficial friendship.

With Chyna gone, there was no clear women's locker room leader. Ivory tried to call a meeting of all the girls, but I thought that was just silly—there didn't need to be any reestablishment of some kind of hierarchy. I felt that we should just all do our own thing. If two people had a problem, they could deal with it amongst themselves. Then the WCW Invasion happened, and overnight, everything in WWE changed—from the way the show was booked to the dynamic of the locker room.

When Torrie Wilson and Stacy Keibler first showed up, I basically ignored them. I was still under the impression that WCW was going to be a separate entity and that the mixing of WCW people into our roster was only a temporary thing. As far as I was concerned, the Blondes, as we called them, were just visiting.

The Blondes had zero wrestling experience, but WWE had hopes of turning these girls into wrestlers. There were two schools of thought on how to get Torrie and Stacy into shape. Some of the agents totally coddled them—they'd work out in the ring and everybody would say, "That was so good!" like they were babies learning how to walk.

**I had been told
that there were
all kinds of plans for me,
but somehow they
just fizzled out.**

I was of a different mind altogether. How were
they going to learn anything like that? The more
they were told that their horrible work was okay,
the less likely they were to improve. "Good?" I'd
say. "That was bullshit!"

The Blondes needed to be trained in the
basics—bumping, selling, and feeding. I spent
some time working with them in hopes of one
day being able to have a decent match. I wasn't
comfortable with the idea of sacrificing my
credibility by going toe to toe with them in the
ring—at least not right off the bat, and especially
not on live TV.

Trish and I teamed up against the Blondes in

the first ever bra-and-panties tag team match at the *Invasion* Pay-Per-View. My thought was to keep it simple—stomps in the corners, some choking, some kicking, and that's it.

That's exactly how we booked the *Invasion* match—nice and simple. Most of the spots revolved around taking off our clothes. Initially it was a little more complex, but before the PPV started, I talked with Torrie and Stacy.

"Are you sure you're comfortable with what we're doing out there?" I asked.

The two of them looked at me like deer in the headlights. They were clearly terrified.

"Okay," I said, "here's what we're going to do . . ."

Basically, I reworked some of the spots, taking out anything that had a high probability of getting messed up and replacing them with simple slaps and chokes and kicks.

"Oh my God," Stacy said. "Thank you! I love that so much better."

As it turned out, the match went quite well. I made a point of being connected to them so I could talk them through the match and make sure we were all on the same page.

Trish and I did the bulk of the wrestling work in order to keep the crowd hot—we even hit a Poetry in Motion on Torrie. At the end, I did a moonsault on Stacy, then pulled her pants off for the win.

After the match, Trish and I walked backwards up the ramp, pointing

I pulled her to me like we were having a celebratory hug, but in reality, we were both freaking out that she was this close to getting seriously hurt.

and laughing at Torrie and Stacy—"Ha ha! You're in your bra and panties!"

The *Invasion* stage design was very different from the usual setup. There were two separate entrances opening onto half-circles—the WCW people came out of one side and we came out the other. Both half-circles melted into one ramp in the middle, and behind them there were these big empty pits. It looked kind of like a big crazy Y.

When we got to the top of the stage, Trish came inches away from stepping backwards into one of the pits—she had one foot completely off the stage and was just about to fall in when I saw her and grabbed her hand. I pulled her to me like we were having a celebratory hug, but in reality, we were both freaking out that she was this close to getting seriously hurt.

"Oh my God," Trish said as we hugged, "I almost fell in there!"

"Oh my God," I said holding her close, "I know!"

We got back to gorilla and everybody was congratulating us for having a good match, but we were both past it. "Did you see that? Trish almost fell!"

The match was the farthest thing from our minds—we were just happy that Trish didn't get killed!

The week after the *Invasion* Pay-Per-View, Matt and I took on Torrie and our pal The Hurricane on *Raw*. I made a point of getting together with Torrie to work out a couple of very simple spots, one of which was giving Matt a nut shot as he hooked Hurricane for the Twist of Fate. Then Hurricane was going to roll Matt up into a small package for the three count.

The whole finish depended on Torrie doing her part and then getting out of the way. Unfortunately, when the time came, she hesitated as Matt waited for her to hit him. She finally gave him the low blow, but then just stood there petrified. "Go!" I yelled at her, "Go!" She ran off, but it made the finish look completely awful.

When we got to the back, Matt and I were both furious. Matt's so passionate about wrestling and can't stand to be made to look bad when he's out there giving it his all. Torrie apologized, but I think she was surprised at just how angry we were. My guess is that if she missed a spot in WCW, the attitude from the guys was, "No problem, babe," followed by a smack on the ass.

But that's not how we do things in WWE. This is not the minor leagues. We're professionals here. Whatever else you do, you don't screw up a finish.

The next weekend WWE was in Las Vegas for a house show. After the show, a bunch of people went out to Studio 54 at the MGM Grand Hotel—it was me and Matt, Tommy Dreamer, Chris Jericho, Sean O'Haire, Torrie and Stacy, and a bunch of the other guys.

I wasn't really in the mood to go out. I just wasn't feeling the party vibe—yet. I decided to jump-start the evening by knocking back two quick shots of tequila. I wanted to get a quick buzz going, because otherwise I was going to be a real stick in the mud.

We were all hanging out in the VIP section—Tom Jones was also there, though he wasn't partying with us. It wasn't long before people started recognizing us and buying rounds of drinks. Suffice to say, we all got pretty loaded. Torrie was giggling and having a great time, and I found myself still aggravated that the new girl had messed up the finish on Monday night. I decided to go remind her about it.

I went over to her and started in on her. As I was talking, I saw Stacy and Matt out of the corner of my eye. She was dancing fairly close to him, talking in his ear—the music was so loud, you had to yell to make your-self heard.

"Anyway," I said to Torrie, "you really can't screw up again . . . hold on a sec, okay?"

I reached over and smacked Stacy in the back of the head with all of my strength. She's so skinny—she went right down! She looked up from the floor—like, "What the hell just happened?"—and saw me standing over her.

"Ha ha," I smiled. "Just kidding."

I turned back to Torrie without skipping a beat. "The guys give us a great opportunity every time they allow us to get in the ring with them," I continued, "and you really ought to be grateful . . ."

The Blondes looked at me like I was crazy. They both started laughing nervously. Stacy was definitely frightened, but she also got the "Keep away from Matt" message—loud and clear.

The look on Matt's face was priceless—he just shrugged his shoulders, like, "Hey, I had nothing to do with it!"

Since then I've grown to really like Stacy—she's really bubbly and a genuinely sweet person. She's not the kind of person I usually get along with. You really have no choice but to embrace her for who she is. Otherwise you'd have to kick her ass for being so aggravatingly nice!

Torrie is a little more reserved, but we get along just fine. Things were a little rocky in the beginning of our relationship, like a feeling out process, but now there's no heat at all between the two of us.

Both of the Blondes have grown quite a bit since coming to WWE. They really didn't have much of a choice.

CHAPTER 44

One of the biggest honors of my career was being featured in *Rolling Stone*. If I could've picked any magazine to be in, that was definitely the one. I actually became pretty friendly with the journalist, Harry Thomas. It was just a short piece, but I felt Harry did a great job. The editor of *Rolling Stone*—who was not a wrestling fan—agreed, and assigned Harry to do another more detailed story about me

Harry came out on the road with Team Extreme in September, driving with us from *Raw* in San Antonio to *SmackDown!* in Houston. Unfortunately, the article never ran—when Harry finally submitted it, the world was a very different place.

We had driven all night, arriving in Houston very early on Tuesday morning. Matt and I were sound asleep when the phone rang—I rolled over and picked it up. It was Shane Helms calling. "A plane just flew into a building," he said. "We could be under attack."

"What," I said groggily, "here, in Houston?"

"No, in New York."

"Then we're still safe," I said, hanging up the phone. I was still in that weird place halfway between being sleep and being awake—it could've been a dream.

"What was that about?" Matt said.

"I don't know. Something about a plane hitting a building."

"Maybe we ought to check it out," he said, getting up to turn on the TV.

As the picture came on, we saw the horrifying image of the second hijacked plane crashing into the World Trade Center. Needless to say, that woke me right up.

Neither Matt or I said a word for a good long while—we just sat there staring at the TV, watching and listening for any small piece of information that the media had at that point in time. It was just so hard to believe.

9/11 was such a weird and terrible day. I reacted much like everyone else in the world, with a combination of anger and sadness and shock. I think I felt exactly what the terrorists wanted us to feel—a blow to the heart of America. It didn't matter if you'd never been to New York, if you'd never been outside of the small town you lived in, it hit you right in the gut. It was a reminder that we're not the invincible nation that we thought we were.

At around ten-thirty that morning, we were told that Vince had decided to cancel the *SmackDown!* taping. Nobody was sure what we were going to do—Would we tape on Wednesday? Would we do it live on Thursday? Or would we cancel it altogether?—so we should just sit tight and see what happened.

I didn't care what we ended up doing. I felt something that I don't often feel—I felt helpless. I sat there, watching the news on TV, thinking, *Oh God, what's next?*

Matt and I started getting a little stir crazy, so we went down to the pool. Some of the other WWE people were there and we all hung out, talking and trying to express how we felt about what had happened.

By the end of the day, a lot of the WWE wrestlers and production crew were getting drunk in the hotel bar. I thought that was totally disrespectful and very inappropriate. I'm not saying that people needed to act miserable and sad if that wasn't what they were feeling. I just didn't think it was an occasion for getting loaded. Nobody was celebrating—they were just doing something other than sitting in their hotel room—but it still felt wrong.

I really didn't want to be there. It was a difficult,

It was such a raw, powerful moment. I couldn't stop the tears.

tragic day and I didn't want to be in that kind of atmosphere, so I went upstairs to bed.

When I woke up, I was still pretty shaken. I really needed something to distract me from the previous day's events, so I spent most of the day at the gym, doing cardio, watching the RPMs going by. It was a perfect way to temporarily forget about things, if only for a little while.

Vince decided that we would do a very special edition of *SmackDown!* live on Thursday night. It's usually pretty chaotic when we do TV, but that whole day was really calm. Everybody stood around backstage, talking about what they were doing when they found out, and what they'd been doing for the past two days.

It had only been two days since 9/11, so no one was sure what was going to happen—security was a real issue and there was no way to know if anyone would even show up. Sure enough, people were there. Twenty thousand people were ready to come out and go to a wrestling show.

The theme of the show that night was simply to entertain—there were no storyline driven matches, nobody did anything dirty. There was nothing especially violent, which sounds like an oxymoron for a wrestling show, but our goal was to provide an evening of good, clean entertainment.

The show started with Lillian Garcia's unforgettable performance of the National Anthem. As she sang, all the emotions that had been building inside me over the past two days, all the shock and sadness and fear, came to the surface. It was such a raw, powerful moment. I couldn't stop the tears.

When she was done, I wiped my eyes and gathered my thoughts—Matt and Jeff were in the first match of the night and I had to be at ringside. Then, later that night, I took on Ivory in a singles match.

All the Superstars were asked to say a few words about 9/11—how we felt, what we'd been thinking. "All I know to do when I have a problem is to take a deep breath and go from there," I said. "I hope that our show can be that deep breath. Hopefully the entertainment provided here tonight can help to get people's minds off what's been going on, even if it's only for a short time."

After the show, we were all itching to get the hell home. No one was sure what the deal was as far as the airports reopening, so Matt decided that the four of us—Matt, Jeff, Hurricane, and myself—should drive back to North Carolina as soon as *SmackDown!* ended.

Matt took the wheel for the first shift. I sat in the passenger seat and Shane and Jeff slept in the back. The plan was for Matt and I to each drive for four hours, then we'd switch with Jeff and Shane in the morning. But when the time came for Matt and I to switch, he had already made up his mind to drive the whole way home. He gets like that sometimes—he challenges himself to do an impossible task and refuses to give up. I tried arguing with him, even though I knew that there was no point. If Matt had made up his mind to drive twelve hundred miles all by himself, then that's what he was going to do.

I stayed up with him until about eight in the morning. I was exhausted—I was basically holding my eyes open with my fingers. The next time we took a rest stop, I switched with Shane. I crashed the second I hit the backseat, only to find out a few minutes later that Shane had fallen right back to sleep up front. I kicked him back to the back and stayed up with Matt the rest of the way.

We arrived back at Matt's house at around three in the afternoon on Friday—from Houston to Cameron in just over sixteen hours.

On Sunday night, Matt and I took a Southwest Airlines flight to *Raw* in Nashville—Jeff was scared to fly and drove there all by himself. I felt weird about getting on a plane so soon after 9/11, but flying is a huge part of our lives, and there was no way to avoid it for long. Things had to get back to some kind of normal.

A month or so later was the first time we went to New York after 9/11—we had a Sunday afternoon house show at Madison Square Garden. We got into the city on Saturday night, and Matt, Jeff, and I made a point of going down to Ground Zero. Even after seeing weeks and weeks of TV coverage, actually standing there in the rubble was just unbelievable. It was breathtaking and shocking and sad, all at the same time.

Chris Kanyon has a cousin on the NYPD and he arranged for the four of us to make a trip inside to the heart of Ground Zero. It was very casual—we signed a ton of autographs, took pictures with all the cops and firemen and construction workers down there.

It was a staggering experience—I was just totally blown away by how strong and resilient New Yorkers are. It was awesome how they were able to quickly get the situation under control, hold their chins up, and plow forward. Everybody we met had an amazing attitude, like, "This sucks, but we're going to pick up the pieces and keep going."

I admit, I'm not exactly a huge fan of New York City—it's expensive and crowded and difficult to get around in—but that gave me a whole new appreciation of the city. No matter what my feelings were, I had to give them props. *Man,* I thought, *this is one tough town.*

That weekend WWE held a brunch at the *World* for the families of New York City firefighters. I spent some time with this cute little boy who lost both his parents on 9/11—his mom worked in the Trade Center and his dad was a fireman. We were hanging out, joking around, and his uncle told me that it was the first time he'd seen him smile since the attacks. That was so touching! It means a lot to me that I'm able to do things like that.

It's a very powerful thing to be able to affect people the way we do. I'm not focused on being a celebrity, but the fact that I'm on TV every week sometimes affords me the opportunity to touch people's lives, or to drop some knowledge on them that they might not otherwise hear.

When I first started with the Hardy Boyz, we had a show in Springfield, Massachusetts, and WWE road agent Dave Hebner came to us and asked if we could pay a visit to a kid in a local hospital

His name was Nate Webster. He was fifteen years old and had a brain tumor. He was a huge WWE fan, so his family had planned to come see *SmackDown!* live, but before the show, Nate had to have emergency surgery. It was so sad—he was in a coma and it was pretty clear that he wasn't going to make it.

We spent some time talking to Nate's family, who were just the nicest people imaginable. I felt so awful for them. We gave Nate an autographed Hardy Boyz T-shirt, which his mom put on him. Then we sat there a while, holding his hands and talking to him. At one point, the monitor showed his heart rate going up, which made me think that he knew that we were there. It was very moving and really put things in perspective for me—it was right at the time that things were just beginning to get hectic for me and I was starting to get seriously stressed out. It reminded me to be thankful for everything I have.

About a month later, I received a letter from the Websters. Nate had passed away a few days after our visit, and his parents decided to bury him in the Hardy Boyz T-shirt that we had given him.

Since then I've kept in touch with Nate's younger brother Joel. I call him every couple of months, just to check in and see what's going on. He's a sophomore in high school now and has gotten involved in his school's amateur wrestling team. He's doing really great—he recently competed in a big tournament in Puerto Rico. I think it was because of Nate that Joel got into wrestling. It was kind of like a gift from his older brother, who he'd looked up to so much.

Meeting people like the Websters is the best part about the celebrity that comes from being a WWE Superstar. I've had a lot of unique chances to do some good in the world. I've read to underprivileged children, I've visited with kids from the Make-A-Wish Foundation, I've been active in WWE's *SmackDown!* Your Vote campaign. I'm particularly proud of the work I've done with WWE's "Get Real" program, visiting schools all over the country and talking about how important it is to get an education.

I can really help kids that want to drop out, because I've been there. I tell them how I knew dropping out wasn't a smart option, so I busted my ass to graduate early. I don't sugarcoat it—I tell kids to grit their teeth and graduate and then go find out what's really important to them. That honest approach really connects more than if I went in there and bullshitted them about how great school is.

Anytime I can convey a positive message to the fans—whether it's stay in school or your vote counts or spay and neuter your pets—I feel as if I've done something truly important. Hopefully people hear what I'm saying and take that positive message and pass it along to the next person.

CHAPTER 45

Matt and I were told that he was going to have a match with Stone Cold Steve Austin, whose troubled heel turn had led to his role as leader of the WCW/ECW Alliance. I was excited, because there were going to be a few pre-tapes leading up to it where I got to work with Steve's wife at the time, Debra. We were good friends, but had never had the opportunity to do anything together. I was also happy for Debra—her role as Mrs. Stone Cold had been so limited and this was a good chance for her do something fun.

Another career goal
I checked off my list.

The first vignette had me approaching Debra
backstage and telling her how impressed I was
with the way she didn't allow Stone Cold to dis
her on the previous week's *SmackDown!* "It must
be hard to live with a guy like Austin," I said.

"What do you mean by that?" Debra said.

"I didn't mean anything by it."

Debra stormed off and told Stone Cold that I
called him "trailer trash," and that Matt could
kick his ass. He immediately searched us out,
saying that Debra told him everything I'd said.

"But I didn't say those things," I insisted.

"Are you calling my wife a liar?" Stone Cold
replied, then challenged Matt to a nontitle match.

A little later, Stone Cold confronted me as I
was talking on my cell phone.

"Are you lying to the person you're talking to?"

"C'mon, Stone Cold," I said. "This is stupid. It's
all a big misunderstanding."

"We'll just see who looks stupid tonight,"
he said.

Stone Cold went and told Debra that I was
talking trash about her and that he stood up for
her like a good husband. "I'm going to whip
Matt Hardy's ass for you," Stone Cold said.

The pre-tapes were actually very similar to
the real-life Debra—she really does get her
wires crossed sometimes. Even though she
doesn't mean to, Deb will stir up shit by getting
important details of a story completely mixed

up. Debra and I clicked right from the very beginning. Our personalities are very compatible. She's got a real Southern vibe about her—she's very funny and easygoing, but underneath that easygoing exterior, she's tough as nails.

I got to know Steve because I was friendly with Debra. We're not close by any means, but I hung out with him a lot more than the other girls.

Even though he's one of the most successful wrestlers ever, Steve doesn't run the whole star trip in the locker room. He's always joking around with the boys, making wisecracks. When it comes to wrestling, he's all business, but overall he's really a very friendly guy. I've always felt comfortable going to him with questions or just to ask his opinion on things.

The best part of that night was at the end of the match—I went after Debra but Stone Cold caught me and gave me the Stunner. Unlike the last time, when I was supposed to be unconscious, I got to do the big bounce. It was a lot of fun. When I got to the back, I got a lot of compliments on how well I took it, which made it all the more exciting. Another career goal I checked off my list.

That little one-night-only story was a rare moment of clarity in the otherwise convoluted Alliance angle. The whole thing was so silly—everybody in WWE was a babyface and everybody in WCW and ECW were heels and it was just ridiculous. It was a very bad time in the locker room. A lot of talented people were neglected because so much energy was spent trying to salvage the Invasion.

At *WrestleMania* taking a 3-D.

I consider my mom to be an excellent gauge as far as angles are concerned—she never watched wrestling before I started on WWE, but since then she's become a big fan. If she doesn't understand something, then you can bet that the average fan doesn't understand it either. The reason I bring this up is because Mom was totally baffled by the whole WCW/ECW Alliance storyline.

"What's up with all the guys in black T-shirts running down the ramp?" she asked me. "I don't know who any of those guys are. I know that I'm not supposed to like them, because they're beating up the people that I do like, but I don't understand why!"

One of the big problems was that the Alliance story took precedence over everything else. There were so many titles floating around that they lost all meaning. The days when everyone from top to bottom had an interesting storyline were gone. Team Extreme spent a good portion of that time fighting with the Dudley Boyz over the WWE and WCW Tag Titles. The Dudleyz had been aligned with Stacy Keibler, which created some symmetry between the two teams and more importantly, added some heat to the rivalry.

Otherwise, creative didn't have a lot of ideas for Team Extreme besides trying to break us up. Stacy and I had a singles match on *Raw*—we were in Louisville, Kentucky—that was really just another attempt to create tension among the Hardyz and myself.

Stacy and I went back and forth until finally I went for a crossbody to the outside. Stacy avoided it and I smashed into the guard rail. Matt came running out to check on me, then helped me back into the ring. He started jawing at Stacy and she slapped him across the face. Matt got pissed—as he went to hit her, his elbow nailed me right in the eye. I managed to hook Stacy with a Twist of Fate for the win, but when Matt climbed into the ring to celebrate with me, I blew him off, holding my face where he hit me.

It was a classic example of how sometimes the line between reality and fiction can get all blurry. His worked elbow to my face really connected and I ended up with a nasty shiner. Matt and I went to England later that week to do promotion for the *Rebellion* Pay-Per-View, and everywhere we went, people tried to be funny by asking me about my big black eye—"Hey, did he give that to you?"

"Well, yes," I'd reply. "Actually, he did."

The story continued the next night on *SmackDown!* in Cincinnati. I came into the Hardyz' locker room to see if they were ready for our match against Stacy and the Dudleyz. Matt wasn't there, but Jeff saw my black eye and got all concerned. "That's a real bad bruise," he said.

"I'll be okay," I said as Jeff reached out and touched my face with his fingers.

Just then, Matt came walking in—"Oh hey, sorry to interrupt your little moment," he said, visibly angry. "C'mon, our match is next."

"At least Jeff cares about my eye," I said. "Unlike someone else."

I walked out in a huff. "It was an accident," Matt told Jeff. "I'm sick of apologizing and I'm not going to do it anymore."

We went out and had the match. The finish had Bubba shoving Matt into me, knocking me off the apron. Jeff came over to see if I was okay as Matt got 3Ded, giving the Dudleyz the win.

Although Team Extreme disagreed, creative felt that breaking us up was all that was left because we'd been around for such a long time. Well, so have the Rolling Stones and they still sell out concerts all over the world! We were still getting an amazing reaction every time we came out, so why mess with success?

They kept dancing around the breakup angle, to the point where we were like, "Just do it already!" Matt and I were hoping that the disintegration of Team Extreme would lead to our becoming a tag team, but nobody liked that idea except the two of us.

After *Survivor Series*—which put the nail in the coffin of the whole Alliance angle, thank God—we began working towards a brother vs. brother feud, with me stuck somewhere in the middle.

In a perverse way, there was a level of truth to the angle—Jeff had begun to lose interest in being a wrestler and was actively rebelling from Matt's influence. He didn't care if Team Extreme broke up, he didn't care if we stayed together. He didn't really care about even going to work.

It was hard for Matt and I to watch Jeff's behavior and not get frustrated, but at the same time, we both understood there was nothing we could've said or done that would've changed him.

Our storyline was pretty slight—it basically consisted of Matt and Jeff bickering all the time. One night on *Raw*, Jeff lost a match to Christian, and Matt started yelling about how he's always had to guide Jeff through life.

"You've always thought you were smarter and better," Jeff said.

"Well that's pretty obvious," Matt replied.

I tried to separate them, but Matt told me to shut up.

"It's obvious that you only care about yourself," I said, then walked out.

"Who feels stupid now?" asked Jeff.

Whether we liked it or not, the long-awaited Matt vs. Jeff match was booked for the upcoming *Vengeance* Pay-Per-View. A week before the show, the Hardyz got into another argument. I tried to stop them, but got shoved down for my efforts.

"You're always taking Jeff's side," Matt said.

"I'm not taking anyone's side," I said. "I love you."

"Oh yeah? How about you prove that you're not taking sides? How about you're the referee at *Vengeance*, and we'll see whose side you're on?"

"Fine!" I yelled as Matt walked away.

The weekend of *Vengeance* saw Matt coming down with a nasty stomach flu. He was puking his guts out before and after the match. I had the same bug the week before. Unless you're in the hospital, the boys always work. I've worked sick four or five times, either from flu or a little bit of food poisoning. One of the worst times was from a good old-fashioned hangover—it was the day after we all partied in Las Vegas and I pushed Stacy Keibler down to the floor.

After I had my little fight with Stacy, I kept knocking back the drinks—I did a few more tequila shots followed by a couple of Red Bull-and-vodkas. Needless to say, it wasn't long before I felt my stomach coming up. I ran towards the bar, my hand over my mouth in the universal sign of "I'm gonna puke!" and without hesitation, the guys from behind the bar handed me a big glass bowl. As I hurled my guts out, I remember thinking, *Wow, the bartenders are pretty thoughtful to have a big puke bowl behind the bar.*

Matt and Tommy Dreamer came over and carried me out of the club. They poured me into the backseat of our car and Matt, who was pretty drunk himself, got in front. He turned on the air conditioning and promptly passed out.

When I came to, the sun was up, the car was boiling hot, and there was no sign of Matt. No keys, nothing. I was about to suffocate from the lack of oxygen in there, so I just opened one of the doors and passed out again.

A couple of hours later, I heard Matt outside the car, talking to two girls. I was laying there, face down in the backseat, and I heard one of the girls getting all excited, "Oh my God! It's Lita!"

I pretended to still be asleep—I wasn't about to get up with dried puke all over my face and say, "Hi, nice to meet you."

I laid there and listened as Matt opened the hood and hooked up jumper cables to the battery—it had died sometime during the night from having the AC on the whole time. It turned out that Matt had woken up, realized the battery was dead, and went off in search of a jump. He was still kind of drunk, but he managed to hit two different gas stations. Unfortunately he got blown off both times, so he kept walking until these two girls spotted him. "Matt Hardy! Can we have an autograph? Can we get a picture?"

"No problem," Matt said, "but first I need you to drive me to Wal-Mart so I can get some jumper cables."

After he jumped the car, we drove back to the hotel where we were staying and slept for the rest of the day. My match that night—I vaguely recall teaming with Jacqueline against Torrie and Stacy—was rough, but I realized how much the fans can encourage and inspire you. I felt fine as soon as I got in the ring.

It's funny how stories tend to change after a little time passes. By the time I got to the building that day, the story had gone around that I'd taken Tom Jones' top hat off his head and puked in it. It seems Tommy Dreamer had told a number of people an elaborately embroidered version of the night's events. Among the people who'd heard the tale was WWE road agent Black Jack Lanza. One of his jobs is to to give the wrestlers cues, such as "go home" or "stretch it out." Jack came walking out during my match, just as was I getting ready to tag in. "Hold on," I told the girls, "Jack wants us to do something."

I watched as Jack held out his hands and stuck his head in between them. *I don't know this cue,* I thought. *I guess we should just continue the match as planned.*

When we got to the back, Jack was standing there laughing. "I'm sorry," I said. "Did you want us to do something?"

He started doing the same cue that he did during the match, holding his hands out and lowering his head between them. I just stood there, totally confused.

"You don't get it?" Jack said, cracking up. "It's Tom Jones' top hat!"

Thank you, Tommy Dreamer. Thanks a lot!

Getting back to *Vengeance*—Matt was really sick and Jeff was barely paying attention as we tried to put the match together. My job as Special Guest Referee turned out to be much more difficult than I'd thought. There's no training—you just put on the stripes and go out there. We did a little bit of work on my counts to make sure they were even, but other than that, the only advice I got was to just stay out of the way.

I spent the whole match calling it right down the middle—at one point I caught Matt using the ropes for leverage. In the end, Jeff countered a Twist of Fate off the top rope with a Swanton Bomb, then made the cover as I counted "one-two-three!" The only problem was that I didn't notice that Matt had his foot on the ropes.

The match was not very well received. To me, the only reason it got negative reviews is because the fans didn't want to see Matt and Jeff fighting. If they did, they wanted to see a *lucha* fest, but that wouldn't have made any sense—we were in the middle of a serious storyline and the match had everything to do with the story. A spectacular match that was filled with high spots would've negated everything we'd worked towards to that point. But the truth was, people simply didn't want to see them fight.

The next night at *Raw* was very stressful. No one had heard from Jeff all day. He didn't turn up until about the time the doors opened. He didn't have any excuse—he just didn't give a damn anymore.

On the show, Matt demanded a handicap match against me and Jeff. I went to the Hardyz' locker room and apologized profusely for not seeing his foot on the ropes. I tried to tell him that I didn't want to be the referee, but he put me there.

"I don't want to fight you," I said. "I love you!"

But Matt just ignored me and laced up his boots. He finally spoke as I turned to leave the locker room. "You're only saying that you love me to make me feel guilty," he said, "If you didn't want to be the referee, why didn't you just say so?"

He explained that he asked for this handicap match so that Jeff and I could try beating him face to face. "Just like the Hardy Boyz," he said, pushing me out the door, "we are breaking up!"

I stood there bawling in the hall as Matt slammed the door in my face. Then Jeff showed up and tried to comfort me—it was a totally misguided attempt at creating a romance between us, which the three of us agreed just wasn't happening.

The initial plan was for Jeff to kiss me. When Matt saw that on the monitor, he'd get angry and then that would give him more fight in the handicap match. We totally disagreed with that—what would've happened next? Jeff and I would skip off into the sunset as heels? I'm sorry, but if a guy's ex-girlfriend takes one step out the door and hooks up with his brother, then they're the heels. It wouldn't matter that Matt had been ornery lately. All people would care about was that Matt and I broke up and now I was with Jeff. Forget the fact that we were uncomfortable with the storyline— we also felt we'd be making definitive steps with our actions that there would be no turning back from.

They kept saying, "No, no. We think the crowd will pop for it," but Matt and I put our foot down. "Look," we said, "if we go ahead with this, then there's no turning back."

When Jeff finally got to the building, we told him what was going on. "I'm not doing that," he said. "I'm not kissing my brother's girlfriend."

They tried talking him into it, but he was adamant. "No way," he said. "I'm not doing it."

They eventually relented, and all Jeff and I did was hug. The whole experience was weird and awkward—we worked the match genuinely not knowing where our futures lay.

It turned out that no one else knew what to do with us. If we didn't want to split up, the only thing they could come up with was to give us a few weeks off of TV.

It all started—or ended, depending on how you look at it—a week after our handicap match. Matt was sent up to New York to host *Raw* from the

World, while Jeff got his ass kicked in a Hardcore title match against Undertaker.

'Taker started messing with me after I ran to the ring to check on Jeff. He tossed Jeff to the outside, then carried him up the ramp to the stage. He looked right at me and said, "This is on your conscience," as he gave Jeff the Last Ride off the stage through some tables!

As Matt watched in shock from the *World,* 'Taker grabbed me by the hair. I gave him a low blow, but he held on tight then threw me off the stage onto Jeff.

It was a good ten-foot drop. 'Taker was pretty cool—before we went out there, he said, "I'll just guide you over the edge. You take your own bump."

Right before I went off the side, it occurred to me that I really didn't know what was going to happen to me when I landed. Jeff was lucky—he went straight down and had some padding to land on under the tables. My only cushion was Jeff! I didn't want to crush him, but I really didn't have anywhere else to go.

As I landed, I skidded off Jeff and bounced onto the concrete. It hurt like hell—I bruised my hip bone and my thumb. When I got up from the floor, I thought, *Well, that didn't go too badly. Thumbs and hips, they're not that vital in the grand scheme of things.*

Matt tried to get revenge the next night on *SmackDown!*—even though he'd broken up with me just a week beforehand. 'Taker beat the hell out of him, then after the match ended, came back to the ring and beat him up some more. Matt took a nasty throat shot from the back of a chair and the EMTs came to carry him out of there.

After the show, Vince told us that he didn't know what to do with us at that point. The breakup angle might not have been the way to go, and he thought that the best thing would be for Team Extreme to take some time off from TV, then come back when there was a scenario that would suit us.

It was a little confusing, because giving people time away from TV is not the normal way of doing business. Matt and I were really unhappy with the decision. It was Jeff that was showing the signs of burnout. We were ready to go. We didn't want to disappear from TV, but we weren't given a choice. The decision was made and that was that.

As it turned out, our hiatus wasn't exactly the worst thing to ever happen to me—those few weeks were the first time that I actually had a chance to breathe since coming to WWE. Initially it was weird being out of the loop, but it ended up feeling quite good. I went to the gym everyday, I started painting and doing little crafts around the house. For the first time in forever, I felt peaceful—rested, relaxed, and ready to go.

We finally came back to TV at the *Royal Rumble* Pay-Per-View in Atlanta. In a classic example of WWE's "If we ignore it for a few weeks, maybe the audience will forget it ever happened" attitude, six weeks had gone by and Team Extreme was getting along just fine. I think the fans were supposed to assume that we had spent our hiatus working out our differences.

It was especially frustrating for Matt—he had spent weeks and weeks being painted as a heel, and now we were supposed to act like nothing had ever happened.

Even though Vince had promised us that there would be new opponents and new situations for us upon our return, there didn't seem to be anything for us to do. There wasn't a lot going on in the tag team division, there wasn't a lot going on in the women's division. Just as we'd been doing the previous months, Team Extreme was treading water.

CHAPTER 46

As someone who is always in search of new and interesting experiences, one of the best perks of being a WWE Superstar has been the opportunity to appear on all different kinds of nonwrestling TV programs. I've done awards ceremonies, I've done promotion on morning shows all over the world. In November 2001, I was asked to be one of the all-WWE contestants on the NBC game show, *The Stupidest Person In The Circle*—or, as some people like to call it, *The Weakest Link*.

Game shows may be fun to watch, but it wasn't much fun to do. The whole experience was very unpleasant. The contestants were myself, Trish,

Triple H and Stephanie, Kurt Angle, Booker T, William Regal, and Big Show. We arrived at the studio in the mid-afternoon and were there until ten o'clock that night.

The show was very popular at the time, so some of the Superstars were excited to do it. I'd never seen it before—all I knew was that they ask you questions and some mean lady insults you. She stands there in prayer position with her fingers crossed and her head down, throwing out these insults that seem to just come off the top of her head. Well, the truth is that there are a bunch of writers in the back, feeding her zingers. It sometimes took up to thirty seconds, and then they cut it together in postproduction to make it seem like she was firing off these one-liners on the spot. I stood there thinking, *God, what a rip off!*

So much of the show was done in post—the only things that were shot in real time were the segments where we introduced ourselves and said which charity we were playing for—mine was the Humane Society—and the actual rounds where we answered questions. Before we even started playing the game, they filmed us making ten different facial expressions—five as if we just answered a question correctly, and five as if we just got a wrong answer. I'm so used to working in a spontaneous environment, where you do your thing and they capture it on tape. Having to make these phony faces—"Darn it, I got it wrong!"—really threw me off. I was really surprised to discover that that was how a "reality" show was put together.

It was such a weird concept. The game show seemed to be all about the mean lady and her nasty remarks. She was really out for the jugular, which is not my style at all. Stephanie and Triple H love to bust people's chops, so they were cool about firing back, but I had a hard time coming up with responses to her insults—I didn't have Brian Gewirtz in my ear feeding me snappy comebacks.

"That's quite a tattoo," she said. "Do you really think that's attractive?

"Well, everyone's got their own thing," I replied. "I could probably get you a deal on one if you'd like one too."

"Oh no, I don't think so. That's the most atrocious thing I've seen in my life."

It was just brutal. Being insulted just isn't a lot of fun for me. I wanted it to end so badly, but I could not get voted off. It reached the point where I was about to vote myself off! It finally came down to me, Stephanie, Regal and Triple H. The three of them were being real serious about the competition. All I could think was, *Get me out of here!*

In the final round, I got two incorrect answers. The first one was, "What male vocal range is lower than a tenor, but higher than a bass?"

"Alto," I guessed. The correct answer is baritone.

My next question was, "What Canadian rock group recorded the singles 'Turn Me Loose' and 'Working for the Weekend'?"

Of course the answer is Loverboy, but for some reason, I answered, "Rick Springfield."

Game shows look easy when you're home, sitting on your couch with a big bowl of popcorn, but when you're on the spot in front of the camera it's a whole different thing. It's not so simple when the spotlight is on you and everybody is waiting for your answer.

At the end of the round, Regal and Triple H both voted for me as the Weakest Link—Steph thought she was being nice and picked Regal—and I was finally able to get out of there.

"Lita, you are the Weakest Link. Goodbye!"

Thank you! I thought, and got the hell out of there back to the green room.

Being on *The Weakest Link* was just awful—it was a long excruciating miserable day from beginning to end. The best part was that the losers still got to donate ten thousand dollars to their charities, which was very cool. I'm willing to go through a lot of crap to be able to help animals, so ultimately that made the whole thing kind of worthwhile

After my experience on *The Weakest Link,* you would think that I'd never consent to appear on another NBC prime-time show ever again. But you'd be wrong. It was mid-November—I was in the Bahamas doing the *Divas: Tropical Pleasure* shoot—when I was asked to be on some show called *Fear Factor.*

As I've said, I don't really watch a lot of TV, so I honestly had no idea what *Fear Factor* was all about. I called Matt and he explained that he'd heard it was a crazy game show where the contestants have to do a series of really wild dares and physical challenges. Both Matt and Jeff thought it sounded pretty cool, and had already agreed to do it. "Okay," I said, "I'm in."

For the next six weeks, whenever anybody heard that I'd agreed to be on *Fear Factor,* they'd look at me like I was nuts—"Oh my God, you're doing that? They do things like lock you into a car underwater and then you try to see if you can get out without drowning!"

What? I started getting nervous, like, "What in the world have I gotten myself into?"

It got even worse when I was told that it took three days to shoot the show—that's a whole week's off time gone. I was bumming out. I had to give up an entire week of my life to do this horrible show. Add in the unpleasant experience I had on *The Stupidest Person in the Circle,* and you can definitely say that I was not looking forward to *Fear Factor.*

"Oh my God, you're doing that? They do things like lock you into a car underwater and then you try to see if you can get out without drowning!"

The good news was that we'd be shooting *Fear Factor* the week after the *Vengeance* Pay-Per-View in San Jose, so at least we wouldn't have to fly back out to California. The night after *Vengeance*, Matt, Jeff, and I were backstage at *Raw* when Johnny "Ace" Lauraintis—one of the WWE agents—handed us each a thick-ass packet from NBC. "I need you to sign these things," he said. "I have to turn them in before you guys can do *Fear Factor*."

They were release forms—maybe thirty pages long, listing all kinds of legal mumbo jumbo that we had to agree to before filming started, as well as helpful information such as telling us to bring a bathing suit and a complete change of clothes to every day's stunt. I made a point of carefully reading through the whole document before turning mine in.

The next day, Matt and I were hanging out backstage, sitting on a road case, when Johnny walked by. "Oh, by the way," he said, "you guys need to stay in character when you're on *Fear Factor*."

"That's ridiculous," I said.

"That's what I've been told to tell you," he said.

"Sorry, Johnny, but that's bullshit."

"Well, that's straight from Vince and Stephanie, so I don't know what else to tell you."

I was so pissed! This was during the period where Team Extreme were ostensibly broken up, so now I had to give up my off time, do

"Well, you tell your producer that I think this is bullshit," I said, knowing full well that they could hear every word I was saying.

these crazy ass stunts where I might get killed, and act like I hated Matt. I was really starting to regret ever agreeing to be on the damn *Fear Factor* in the first place.

After we wrapped up the Pay-Per-View and TV, Team Extreme stayed on in L.A. to do *Fear Factor* with Test, Jacqueline, and Molly Holly.

We went out to a local pier to shoot the first stunt. Each day started with a slow-motion shot of everybody walking towards the stunt, kind of like the scene in *Reservoir Dogs*. I was walking next to Matt, but then Joe Rogan, the host of the show, got word through his earpiece that we needed to do a second take. "They want you two guys to switch places," he said to Matt and Test.

I didn't think too much of it. I thought it was about getting a cool visual and organizing us by height. The next thing we filmed was the six of us gathered around Joe as he explained the stunt to us. I was standing with Matt and Jeff on either side of me, and as we're filming, Joe stopped to listen to a producer on his earpiece. "They're telling me to have you stand over by your brother," he said to Matt.

Matt stepped in between me and Jeff, so that they were both standing to my left. Joe started telling us the object of the stunt, when, once again, they told him to stop.

"Matt, they want you on the other side of your brother."

I realized what was going on—they were trying to keep Matt and I apart on camera. "Who's telling you this?" I asked Joe, who, incidentally, is cool as hell.

"I don't know," he said apologetically. "I'm just getting a message from my producer."

"Well, you tell your producer that I think this is bullshit," I said, knowing full well that they could hear every word I was saying.

Matt moved to where they wanted him, but I was really angry about it. There we were, working on our day off, and they were doing everything possible to step on any good time we might be having.

Unlike *The Weakest Link*, there's a great deal of realism on *Fear Factor*. They try to keep you in as much suspense as possible to make sure that your actions and reactions are completely natural. The more freaked-out or amped-up you are, the better the segment will be.

"Are you guys ready to find out what your first stunt is?" Joe asked us. Just then, a helicopter swooped down and did a low flyby over us. As the helicopter hovered overhead, Joe explained that we would have to climb up a rope ladder as the copter did crazy eights over the water.

Oh man! We had already drawn names to decide who would be the first person to do the stunt and my name had come up. I was scared, but in a good way!

They gave me about five minutes to think about strategy or ask any questions that I might have. Well, I didn't have any strategy and I didn't have any questions—my only strategy was to climb up the ladder as fast as I could.

I grabbed onto the bottom rung as the helicopter took off. It wasn't until we got over the water that I thought, *Okay, I guess I'd better start climbing.*

As I reached for the next rung up, I was blown away by how hard it was—they had told us that the g-force of the helicopter more than doubled the body weight. "Holy crap," I thought, "they weren't kidding!"

I had the hardest time getting to the second rung. Looking up, I saw that I had at least fifteen more rungs to climb. "I don't know if I can do this," I thought. Then I looked down at the ocean and decided that given the choice between falling into the water or making the climb, I'd rather end up in the helicopter.

Eventually I made it to the third rung. I hung there a while, thinking, *I really can't do this I'm going to have to take the drop.*

As I hung there, I had an idea—if I swing my legs up, then I can be hooked onto the ladder in a way where I'm not hanging by my arms. It took me a little while—my strength was all about gone from all the time I'd been hanging there—but I managed to swing up there. Once I did it, I knew it wasn't going to a problem—I scurried straight up the ladder into the helicopter.

I was so psyched about finishing the stunt that when they let me off the helicopter, I ran over and jumped into Matt's arms. It wasn't that I was trying to say "Screw you" to the office—I just felt such a sense of accomplishment.

I was really proud of myself for finishing the stunt, but I knew that I had taken so long to do it—my final time was 1:55—that I had almost no chance of moving on to the next round. Plus, everybody else would know not to waste so much time hanging there—they would all swing up with their legs.

I was so bummed! It wasn't that I felt the need to go on and win the whole thing—my nature is more about being competitive with myself. It was that I had had such a fun experience and I wanted to keep on going and have more fun experiences.

Just as I'd expected, Molly and Jacqueline both beat my time and I was told that I had to leave. As I walked down the pier, I found myself getting so mad—it was a combination of being disappointed that I wasn't going to continue with the show, along with the fact that the WWE representatives had made Matt switch places so he wasn't standing near me. Just then, the two people from WWE came over to me, "Oh, you did great!"

I just stared daggers at them. Obviously I didn't do great, because I'm over here and they're over there! They asked me if I'd like a coat to wear—it was pretty freezing out there—but I behaved like a total baby. "No! I don't want a damn coat!"

"We got you a golf cart to take you back to the dressing room," they told me.

"No, I'm going to watch the guys," I said.

They got all nervous, "Um, we're not sure if you can stay and watch. Hold on and we'll ask the production people."

Of course, the production people had no problem with me watching. Why should they care as long as I wasn't on camera? I went and sat down on the railing at the end of the pier. It was a pretty precarious position—the WWE people were clearly nervous that I was going to fall into the water and kill myself, but I didn't even notice. I had my arms folded across my chest just like a little brat! I needed my alone time!

Eventually one of them got up the nerve to say, "Um, Amy, could you maybe not sit on the edge of the pier like that?"

I acted like I didn't hear a word they said. I didn't acknowledge them at all, but then I got off the edge and stood up against the railing.

I watched as Matt got on there—he swung his legs up and was up the ladder in just over a minute. Next was Jeff's turn. Of course, Jeff thinks he's Spider-Man, so he should make it up the ladder in no time.

Jeff grabbed hold, but instead of using his legs, he slowly started climbing using his upper body. I knew from experience that that wasn't going to work—sure enough, he finally ran out of strength two rungs from the top. I stood there smiling as Jeff let go of the ladder and did a perfect swanton dive into the water. It was just beautiful.

Of course, the WWE representatives started flipping out, "Oh my God! Oh my God! Ask if he's okay! Ask if he's okay!"

"He's fine," I said, a big grin on my face. "He's Jeff Hardy."

To this day, Jeff swears up and down that he thought he could do it quicker with just his arms. No matter what he says, part of me suspects that he was a little shocked at how fast Matt got up there. And if he couldn't beat Matt's time, then he had to do something spectacular. Falling from the ladder was just his way of making a big impression on *Fear Factor*. Jeff denies it completely, but that's my theory and I'm sticking to it.

Jeff came out of the water, soaking wet from head to toe, and of course, being Jeff, he didn't bring a change of clothes with him like he was supposed to. I gave him my spare T-shirt and Matt ended up giving him the surf shorts that he had brought for a bathing suit and the flip-flops that were his other pair of shoes. He looked silly as hell, but at least he wasn't freezing cold and soaking wet.

After we were done shooting for the day, the WWE people walked over to me and said, "Since you're off the show, we have to fly you home."

"No," I said. "I was told I was going to be out here for three days and so I'm staying out here for three days."

"Okay, but *Fear Factor* isn't going to pay for your hotel room anymore."

"That's fine. I'll just stay with Matt."

God only knows why, but I could tell that they weren't thrilled with the idea of my sticking around. I stood there, chatting to Jeff about doing some shopping on Melrose, watching out of the corner of my eye as they whispered back and forth conspiratorially. After a minute or two, they came back over to me and said, "Sorry, Lita, but *Fear Factor* doesn't want anybody hanging around the set after they've been eliminated from the show."

"Well, according to the thirty-page release I had to sign, guests are welcome as long as production knows they're coming," I replied. "I'll just be Matt's guest."

The office people were so nervous, "Oh, we're not sure. We'll have to find out." Two seconds later, one of the *Fear Factor* production team came by, a guy named Mike but known to everyone as The Chimp.

"Hey Chimp," I said, "do you mind if I come with Matt as his guest for the rest of the shoot?"

"Of course not," he said.

We all got in the limo to head back to the hotel and the WWE reps said, "Sorry Amy, we never actually got to speak to anyone about you hanging around the set, so I guess you won't be able to go with Matt."

"I took care of it," I said. "The Chimp said it wasn't a problem."

"Oh. Okay. Fine." I really don't know what the big deal was, but they were genuinely unhappy with the idea. All I cared about was staying with Matt and that was that.

At the next day's stunt, I decided that I was happy to be out of the competition. I definitely wouldn't have fared too well at the second challenge, which was drinking a margarita glass full of all kinds of disgusting ingredients like cow brains and Thai fish sauce.

When I saw that fish sauce was one of the ingredients, I thanked my lucky stars for being out of the competition. When I lived in DC, my friends and I used to get together for dinner and marathon games of Pictionary. One night I decided to cook *pad thai* for everyone—I found a recipe and one of the ingredients was fish sauce. I went to Chinatown and bought everything I needed, including the fish sauce.

I started cooking and when the time came to add the fish sauce, I opened the bottle and almost lost my lunch. No joke—it was the most ungodly smell I've ever smelled in my life! *You've got to be kidding,* I thought. *There is no way I would ever put even one drop of that in my food!*

The fish sauce actually became a bit of a running gag in my house. People would come to visit, I'd show them around and when we got to the kitchen, I'd say, "Hey, have you ever smelled fish sauce?"

Then I'd take them over to the refrigerator and open the bottle just under their nose to watch their reaction. It was always funny—they'd start gagging and freaking out. If you've never smelled fish sauce, there's really no way to describe it. You could take a huge pile of a dead fish, put them in a bathroom and shut the door for a month in the middle of the summer, and that wouldn't do justice to how horrible it smells.

Ugh! Just the thought of fish sauce makes my stomach churn—I can't even imagine what it must taste like! I was so glad that I didn't have to drink one of Joe's nasty concoctions.

It ended up that Matt and Jacqueline were the two people who were able to get the nasty pink goo down their throats—both Test and Molly didn't have the intestinal fortitude. I think the *Fear Factor* producers were a little disappointed about how the show turned out, with Matt facing Jacqueline. It would've been much more exciting if it ended up with four finalists or me and Matt or Matt and Jeff in the final stunt.

While I was glad that I didn't have to drink the gross slop, I would've loved to have tried the third stunt—we drove up to some nearby mountains where they'd set up a series of six tall wooden poles, each one a foot taller than the one before it. The object of the stunt was to climb up there, take a yellow flag from the first pole, and walk across the tops to the sixth pole.

"That's so cool," I said when I saw the gimmick. "I want to do it! Can I do it after we're done?"

Unfortunately, the day went really long and turned out to be pretty anticlimactic—Jacqueline basically chickened out and Matt ended up as WWE *Fear Factor* Champion. By the time they were done shooting, it was cold and dark and everyone wanted to get the hell out of there. Long

Ugh! Just the thought of fish sauce makes my stomach churn—I can't even imagine what it must taste like!

story short, I didn't get to try the poles challenge, but I still like to think that I could've given Matt a run for the money.

Just like when I did *The Weakest Link,* the money was the best thing about being a *Fear Factor* participant. Once again, the losers got to give ten thousand dollars to one of their favorite charities—this time I chose the Lange Foundation, which is a no-kill animal shelter in Los Angeles.

I picked the Lange Foundation because my old friend Bre works there. A month or so after *Fear Factor* aired, I was on the phone with Bre, shooting the shit, and she mentioned that they still hadn't received the money. "That's weird," I said. "Let me look into it."

I called Sue Aitchison at WWE—she's the liaison for all the company's charity activities. She was surprised—she'd actually heard from the Lange Foundation. "They sent you the most beautiful letter," she said. "They were very appreciative of your donation, but were curious as to how you found out about their charity."

"What do you mean how did I find out about their charity? My best friend works there."

There was a website on the letter, so I hit the Internet. It seemed that *Fear Factor* had mistakenly sent my ten thousand dollars to something called the Cornelia deLange Foundation—a charity for children with severe birth defects.

I was so upset! They had donated the money to the wrong Lange Foundation! Needless to say, I couldn't ask for the ten thousand dollars back—"Um, sorry kids, but some animals need dog food!"—but I didn't want to screw over the shelter.

I immediately called Sue. "This is horrible, Sue," I said. "I feel awful!"

"Oh my," she said. "Don't worry about a thing. NBC should take care of this, because it was their mistake, but if not, we'll handle it."

Fortunately, NBC dealt with it and made sure that the Lange Foundation also received a donation for ten thousand dollars. So it actually worked out pretty well—I might have been the first person eliminated from *Fear Factor*, but I got to help some animals and some really needy kids. All in all, doing *Fear Factor* was a pretty good day's work.

In addition to all the cool TV things I've done in the U.S., I've been lucky to travel all over the world to promote WWE. It seems Lita's popularity crossed all international boundaries.

One of my more interesting appearances was presenting an award at the MTV Asia Awards in Singapore. Even though my flight didn't leave JFK until ten the next night, I flew up to New York on Thursday evening. I spent Friday killing time in an airport hotel and finally got into Singapore at eight in the morning on Saturday.

When I got to my hotel, I was told that rehearsals were at eleven. I felt like I'd been on a plane for days, but I ate some breakfast, took a hot shower, and was driven over to the Singapore Indoor Stadium for rehearsal.

I was presenting the MTV Asia Award for "Best Breakthrough Artist" alongside a Malaysian rap group called Too Phat. We read off the list of nominees, then Too Phat passed me the envelope and I opened it—"And the winner is . . . Linkin Park!"

The MTV staff and producers started freaking out—I wasn't supposed to read the name of winner until the actual awards ceremony! Everybody looked at me like I was completely unprofessional. Hey, I'm not an awards show regular, I've never done something like this before. How should I know the proper etiquette?

After rehearsal wrapped up, I was driven back to the hotel—not to get some much needed sleep, but to do press interviews and promotion for the awards. Then it was time to get dressed and go to the show. When I got there, I was immediately herded into a holding area along with all the other presenters and performers.

There weren't that many Western artists there. The show was hosted by Mandy Moore and an Irish pop singer named Ronan Keating. Otherwise, the only people I recognized were Donatella Versace, Pink, and P.O.D.

I was hanging around the holding area and saw P.O.D. standing there so I decided to introduce myself and say hey. They weren't one of my favorite bands, but I definitely liked their sound and thought they had a really good vibe about them.

I walked over to them and said, "Hi guys, how's it going? I'm Amy. I'm a fan of your work, nice to meet you."

They turned and looked at me like I was just the rudest person ever. They totally iced me, leaving me hanging with my hand out. Finally, one of them shook my hand and then turned away and went back to their conversation, "So anyway, my breakfast this morning was cold. . . ."

For a band that sells themselves on their positivity, P.O.D. acted like total rock stars. Maybe they thought I was just some chick that was hitting on them, but that's still no excuse for being that unfriendly. *Wow,* I thought. *Fine. Cool. Whatever.*

The awards ceremony itself was pretty uneventful. I did my thing, but otherwise I found the whole thing to be fairly boring, mostly because I didn't really know most of the acts.

The highlight of the show was Pink doing "Get the Party Started." She was really entertaining, just totally energetic and full of life.

Even though I was totally exhausted by the time the show ended, I still felt the need to stop by the afterparty, just to check it out and see what it was like. I knew that I shouldn't hang out too long—I had a seven A.M. flight to Malaysia in the morning.

Being the biggest pop star in the room, Pink was naturally the center of attention at the party. I could tell she was digging it, she was having fun, joking around with her band. Despite my bad experience with P.O.D., I decided to say hello to her. I approached her and introduced myself—"Hi, I'm Amy"—and she was as cool as could be. We talked about what a pain in the ass it is traveling all the time, about what else each of us was doing while we were in Asia. She wasn't very familiar with wrestling, but asked me if I worked out a lot, and we chatted a bit about our various exercise routines.

What I liked most about Pink was that she seemed to be an honest, genuine person. She had no problem going from being the life of the party to just kicking back and having a nice one-on-one conversation. It's always nice to meet someone and discover that they're good people.

After the MTV Asia festivities had concluded, I went first to Malaysia and then to England for more promotional appearances. I've actually gone to England to do promotion so many times now that I've lost count. I don't know if it's because I'm especially popular over there, or if I've become like Mikey the Life cereal kid, "Ask Lita, she'll do anything."

Those trips are so physically and mentally draining. You go straight to the airport after two days of TV, fly all night, land in London at seven in the morning, hit the hotel for a quick freshen up, and get right to work selling the WWE product. God only knows why, the first day is always the busiest—I guess they want to cram as much in as possible in case something falls through and needs to be rescheduled.

I'm not the biggest TV viewer, but even I can tell that TV in England is just plain weird—there's a morning show called *The Big Breakfast* that is really aggravating to do. It's like a nutty version of *Live with Regis and Kelly*. The hosts—who are called "presenters" over there—are supposed to be all edgy and hip. They spend a lot of time trying to be funny and provocative, slinging sarcastic wisecracks loaded with incomprehensible British slang. They can be really mean, especially considering that I usually haven't the slightest idea of what they're talking about.

The only time I had fun on *The Big Breakfast* was when they made me play a game called "Guess the Litres, Lita." They showed me a bunch of items and I had to guess how much they weighed in litres. It was everything from a pail of water to a swimming pool to a horse.

One of the show's production assistants was a huge Lita fan, so they dressed him up in drag and put him on the show. Those Brits love doing drag, they think it's the funniest thing in the world. Anyway, I had a stack of cards with different amounts on them—10 litres, 20 litres, 100 litres— and I had to place them on each item. As I did that, the presenter was goofing around and suggested that I throw the drag guy into the pool.

"Okay," I said and tossed the guy into the water.

That turned out not to be the best idea. The presenter got reamed by his boss—the drag guy was miked and we ruined a bunch of sound equipment by throwing him into the water.

On the other side of the coin, they have a lot of very cool kids' shows in England, which are really fun to do. They do all kinds of skits and games, there are prefab pop groups that you've never heard of, there are endless fart jokes—they're just very lighthearted and high-spirited.

Even though I've had some good times, I've got to confess that those trips are really rough. Three days of press interviews and TV appearances in a foreign environment is really hard work. Usually I have to fly straight back to doing TV and by that time I'm just utterly exhausted and physically burnt out. People always think that traveling around the world must be just the greatest fun, but let me tell you, I think kicking it at home with Matt and Cody is even better.

CHAPTER 47

Team Extreme just kind of rolled along, fighting people like Billy and Chuck, but nothing was drawing the kind of excitement that had made us so popular in the first place. If there wasn't much going on for Team Extreme after coming back from our hiatus, there was even less happening for me as a singles wrestler. The Women's Division had grown pretty stagnant, with the exception of Jazz coming in.

She and I were good friends in ECW and from the time I started in WWE, I would always mention her as being someone who could add something to

the women's division mix. I was really psyched when she finally got the opportunity, but unfortunately she and I never got to have the awesome feud that I'd imagined.

We did work together in a Triple Threat match at *WrestleMania X8* in Toronto. It was my first real *WrestleMania* match—I was involved in TLC II, but not as an official wrestler. Trish, Jazz, and I put a lot of effort into setting it up and I was definitely happy with how it came off. I had thought up a lot of the spots and it's always exciting to see how ideas that looked good on paper play out in the ring.

The problem was that we were working in front of a crowd that had just totally blown its load for Hollywood Hulk Hogan vs. The Rock. They had just exploded in an unprecedented fashion and needed to catch their breath. Unfortunately, our match was put into that sacrifice slot. They needed something to break up the two main events, and so they decided that the women's match would make the ideal filler. It was frustrating— the audience didn't have any time to switch gears from the Match of the Century to us.

It didn't matter what we did out there—we got zero crowd reaction. It felt like we were in an empty arena at one in the morning, just like when we'd gone over the match three days earlier. As a result, it seemed like we were just going through the motions. The timing was just a bit off because there was no emotion from the crowd to feed off of.

When it finally ended and we got to the back, one of the writers from wwe.com pulled me aside to get a few quotes for the website's *WrestleMania* coverage. "How does it feel working your first-ever *WrestleMania* match?"

"It feels like shit," I said. "The crowd was horrible and I want to go home." Obviously that never quite made it to the website. They tried to ask Jazz the same question, and she was just as pissed off as I was. "I don't know, man!" was all she said before heading to the locker room.

Had our same match been in a different place on the card, I think it would've played out a hundred times better than it ended up. I'm glad to have been part of *WrestleMania X8*—better to be in a weak match than none at all—but it was still disappointing.

To be honest, *WrestleMania X8* wasn't nearly as good an experience as the previous year's. For one thing, it was in Toronto, and we Southerners tend to have an aversion to going to Canada. It just doesn't feel quite like home. Don't get me wrong—I have good friends that are Canadian—but I always feel slightly out of my element when I'm up there.

The highlight of that whole *WrestleMania* week was actually the night before the show. I'm pretty friendly with Chris Dibaldo, the guitarist in

Saliva—they played a couple of songs at *WrestleMania,* and after their soundcheck on Saturday night, a bunch of people went back to the hotel to hang out. It was Matt and me, Jeff and his girlfriend, Beth, our good friend Scott Matthews, who wrestled with Matt and Jeff in OMEGA, and Chris. We stayed up all night, running from room to room, jumping on the beds, just having a great time acting like silly little kids. To me, a simple pleasure like that— hanging out with people I like—was much more fun than the actual *WrestleMania* match itself.

It was frustrating—the audience didn't have any time to switch gears from the Match of the Century to us.

CHAPTER 48

Not long after *WrestleMania*, Vince revealed his latest master plan—the Brand Extension. The idea was to split *Raw* and *SmackDown!* into two separate and distinct shows. Needless to say, it caused everything in WWE to change once again.

The day of the Brand Extension Draft was absolutely chaotic. Vince called the entire roster into a meeting to tell us how it was going to work—he explained how the draft was all about entertainment and how the order in which we were picked didn't reflect our standing in the company. He explained

diner for something to eat. Matt called a friend of his on the cell phone to follow the draft on wwe.com. It took a while, but Matt's name finally came up—he was thirteenth, then Jeff was picked fifteenth. We were all like, "Ahhh!" We could breathe again! We weren't splitting up after all—everything was going to be okay.

The next night we were in Philadelphia for the final *SmackDown!* to feature both rosters. Matt had a match against Jericho—he ended up tapping to the Walls of Jericho, and then, after the bell, Chris put me in the Walls for good measure. It was always fun working with Jericho, but little did I know that that was going to be my last real appearance in a WWE ring for a long, long time. . . .

how the Brand Extension would create new opportunities for everybody, how having two separate rosters would make for a much more exciting product. At the end of the meeting he asked if anyone had any comments or questions.

I raised my hand, "Um, when are we going to find out which show we're on?"

Obviously, my main concern was being on the same show with Matt—it didn't matter if we were on *Raw* or *SmackDown!,* as long as we were together.

"Twenty of you will be drafted on the broadcast," Vince said. "Ten of you will go to *Raw,* ten to *SmackDown!* After *Raw* goes off the air, we'll have a 'lottery' on wwe.com—the rest of you can log on and find out what show you're on."

I thought he was kidding. We understood that they wanted to keep the draft picks a big surprise, but the only way we could find out our destinies was to call somebody with a computer?

After the meeting, I was called aside and informed that I was going to be the tenth and final draft pick for *Raw.* They only told me because they wanted to make sure that I reacted properly when my name got called. "Great," I said, "but what about Matt and Jeff?"

No one would tell me—I don't think anyone even knew where they were going yet.

"Okay, well, then what's my reaction when I get picked?"

"You're happy," I was told. "You're excited to be one of the ten draft picks."

"But I'm *not* happy," I said. "I'm very nervous that I'm going to be separated from my boyfriend, and that's the look you're going to get unless you tell me now, off the record."

"Sorry, but we really can't say."

I kept asking people—I went to the various writers, I went to the vari/ agents, but no one would tell me. I was pretty much freaking out all n/

The show started and I was in gorilla getting ready—Matt and I/ going out with Jeff, who had a match against Billy Gunn. Ric Fl/ storyline "owner" of *Raw* at that point, came over to me and sai/ you on my list, baby!"

"Can you put my boyfriend on that list too?"

Obviously there was nothing he could do about it, but Bru/ was standing there and he heard the stress in my voice. "I'r/ any promises," he whispered, pulling me aside, "but I b/ going to be on *Raw* with you."

I wasn't one hundred percent relieved, but at least I v/ down enough to go out to the ring. After the show, th/

CHAPTER 49

When an opportunity to do an appearance comes up, like acting or being on a game show, WWE will "ask" if you'd like to do it, even though in reality they're telling you to do it. A couple of weeks before the Brand Extension, I was "asked" if I wanted to be a guest star on the season finale of *Dark Angel.* "It's going to be directed by James Cameron," I was told, like that was a very big deal.

"Okay," I replied, "but I have no idea what *Dark Angel* is or who James Cameron is."

They explained that James Cameron was a very important Academy Award–winning director—he's made some amazing movies, from *Terminator* and *Aliens* to *Titanic. Dark Angel* was his Fox TV series, a sci-fi action show about a genetically enhanced superchick named Max who fights bad guys in a postapocalyptic future.

Wow, I thought. *I guess that is a big deal.*

I'd never really given much consideration to acting. I know there are some WWE Superstars who see wrestling as a way to branch out into other forms of entertainment, but for me, I've only ever cared about wrestling. Anything else is just gravy—it's fun to try other things and I'm always up for a new challenge, but it's not why I became a wrestler.

But if WWE wanted me to act, then that's what I was going to do. Mr. Cameron called me and we talked a bit about his ideas for the show. He explained the premise of the episode—my character was Thula, the leader of an elite group called The Phalanx. We were purebred warriors with all kinds of superhuman characteristics. Our mission was to kill Max, the show's heroine.

Mr. Cameron wanted my thoughts about how to incorporate wrestling moves into the story, how to work my signature spots into a street fight situation.

"Maybe Max could throw me towards a desk or something like that," I said, "then I can jump up onto it and do a moonsault or a hurricanrana."

"That's great," he said. "We can use boxes and crates to emulate the top rope!"

He also wanted to know if I needed a stunt double, explaining that there was one scene he'd written where my character would have to climb up a wall.

"Obviously you'd be in a harness," he said, "I just want to be sure you had no problem with heights."

"Well, I've never done anything like that before," I said, "but it sounds like a challenge."

I liked the concept of both the story and the character. Even though I was unfamiliar with *Dark Angel,* it sounded like something that would be pretty cool to be involved in.

The plan called for me to spend twelve days in Vancouver, Canada shooting the episode. Since Matt and I had been working and traveling together for two years, twelve days apart was going to be the longest we'd ever had to be away from each other. We were saying our goodbyes the night before I left for Vancouver and for some reason, I just lost it and started crying. I wasn't feeling especially sad—just seconds earlier, I had been thinking about all the packing I still had to do—but all of a

We were purebred warriors with all kinds of superhuman characteristics.

sudden, I got real emotional. In retrospect, it was as if I had some unconscious knowledge of what was going to happen.

The first week of shooting was pretty uneventful. Like on any new job, I spent a lot of time absorbing the atmosphere, listening to what other people were saying. The main thing I learned about acting was that I needed to be more subtle in my physical movements. Mr. Cameron explained that everything plays ten times bigger on screen, which is the exact opposite of what I'm used to. In wrestling, we're trained to exaggerate everything so that the person in the last row of the arena can see what we're doing.

The final weekend of the shoot we filmed the most elaborate fight scene they'd ever done on *Dark Angel*. Before shooting started, Mr. Cameron assembled the stunt team to go over the details. He explained the scenario—it was The Phalanx taking on Max and her Transgenics—then walked us all around the set, mapping out what would be happening where. After that, he told us to get with our partners to choreograph our individual fights. I got together with the woman who was Max's stunt double and we talked a bit about what we were going to do. It was all very informal—it was just the two of us and the stuntwoman's husband, who was one of the actors playing a member of my gang.

After a brief feeling-out process, we tried to work on the hurricanrana. I explained to her how she'd need to twist her body and roll with my motion.

"No problem," she said.

Because there was no safety harness, we opted to work with a crash pad—a stunt device used to cushion a fall. I explained that it might be hard to twist with the give of the pad, but I definitely didn't want to do it with just the concrete floor underneath us.

We decided to give it a go. I jumped off a desk, up onto her shoulders, and as I was swinging through, she lost her balance and buckled at the knees. As her legs collapsed under her, she dropped me and I landed square on my head and shoulders.

After I hit I was more frightened than I've ever been, especially being all by myself in such a foreign environment. The first thing I did as I laid there on the crash pad was wiggle my fingers and toes. The fact that I was able to do it calmed me down considerably.

If something like that had happened in the ring, it would still be scary, but at least I would know that I was in good hands and that someone would be there to take care of me.

Mitch, the guy they told me was *Dark Angel* stunt coordinator, came over and asked, "Can you get up?"

"Give me a few minutes," I said.

Wrestlers are a tough breed. When something happens that would have the average person screaming in pain, wrestlers go, "Nope, it doesn't hurt at all." Laying there, my thought process was that if I can move my fingers and toes and I haven't lost consciousness, then I should be okay.

I laid there a while longer, then swung my feet off of the crash pad to where they were on the ground. I tried to get up but couldn't. "If you push my back, I think I can stand up," I said, laying sideways with my feet on the ground. Finally, they got behind me and helped me to my feet.

I didn't know if I was hurt, but I was feeling very vulnerable. I needed someone to say, "Are you alright? Sit down, we'll take care of you," but nobody was doing anything for me. I got the feeling that no one was taking what had happened too seriously.

My head was going in a bunch of different directions—I was in Canada, and had no one to turn to. There was no physician, trainer or anyone else on the set that I could see to examine me.

Eventually, the stuntwoman who dropped me came over with a copy of the script in her hand, and said, "Do you want to go sit somewhere and talk stuff out instead of walking through it?"

"Sure," I said, "I guess so." I was following the wrestler's mantra: push on.

I honestly didn't know how to take control of the situation. I was pretty sure that I'd been badly hurt, but since no one else seemed to think so, maybe I was overreacting.

"I don't think you're really hurt," he said. All a doctor is going to do is pill you up.

Someone must have told Mr. Cameron what had happened because he came over to where the stuntwoman and I were sitting. "I guess you are human after all," he said, patting me on the shoulder. Then he walked away and went back about his business.

All I could do was sit there, nodding my head. After a while, I went and spoke to Mitch the stunt coordinator. "That was a pretty serious fall. I don't know if something is wrong with me," I said. "I'm going to need you to schedule me a doctor's appointment so that I can get checked out."

"I don't think you're really hurt," he said. "All a doctor is going to do is pill you up. We usually just deal with some local chiropractors and massage therapists. I can hook you up with a list of names, but we don't really have any regular doctors that we use."

"Well, I really don't think it's great to have anyone pushing and pulling on me until I know if something is wrong," I said. "I really think I'm going to need to see a doctor."

"I don't know what to tell you," he said. "Maybe the concierge at your hotel can set you up with somebody."

I was very lucky to have my mom waiting for me at the hotel. Since I knew there would be quite a bit of downtime on the shoot, she had

My mom.

come to Vancouver to hang out with me. I still didn't know if I was hurt, but didn't make a big deal out of it because I didn't want her worrying.

She helped me get my clothes off, which was a real struggle. I was wearing a sports bra and it felt tight—it hurt taking it off over my shoulders and head. Then I got into a hot bathtub and laid there for an hour, feeling strange.

Even though we were a few days away from finishing, the *Dark Angel* wrap party was that night. Although I was sore, I felt obligated to attend. My mom and I went—she was psyched because Mr. Cameron recognized her from my home video—but we didn't stay very long.

Sleep that night was difficult. I was getting increasingly sore, but then again, wrestlers deal with aches, pains, bumps, bruises, and strains all day, every day. Was this different? No one seemed to think so.

On Sunday, I didn't know what to do—I couldn't just bail on the shoot. I went to the set but the pain was getting worse. My neck was hurting me and my left arm was essentially dead—the two middle fingers on my left hand had actually curled up and turned blue.

Incredibly, no one treated me any differently or even asked how I was doing after what had happened on Saturday. It took me forever just to tie my shoes and put my costume on. The production assistant assigned to look after me kept telling me to hurry out to the set, until finally I yelled at him, "Don't knock on my trailer again!"

One of the scenes we had to film that day had someone handing me a gun so that I could shoot a photo of Max. I showed the other actor my messed-up hand, with the fingers all blue and curled up. "Do you think this is normal?" I asked.

"Um, no, I don't think so."

In order to hold the gun, I had to straighten the crooked fingers out with my other hand, pushing the blood back and shaking it out so that it looked relatively normal. We had to do the scene a few times, with the guy handing me the gun over and over again, and I needed to fix my hand for every take.

When we finished the scene, all I wanted was to go back to my trailer, but I couldn't get anyone to tell me what we were doing next. I was waiting for instructions, when one of the production assistants approached me. "We need your shoes to film a scene with your double," she said.

"Okay," I said, sitting down. "Can I go back to my trailer now?"

She just walked away without answering me. I was standing in the freezing cold, with no shoes and just a tank top on, my whole body was hurting, my fingers were numb and purple, and no one seemed to give a damn.

**My blood began to boil.
I stood there seething,
with nobody paying the slightest
bit of attention to me.**

My blood began to boil. I stood there seething, with nobody paying the slightest bit of attention to me. Finally I'd had enough—I was going to confront Mr. Cameron. I walked to the building where he was shooting. "I've got no coat, no shoes, and my fingers are curled and purple," I said. "Can somebody do something about this?"

All of a sudden, people came running at me. "Here's a coat!" "Here's a chair!" "Just go to your trailer and relax, we'll take care of everything!"

It wasn't until the next day that I got a visit from the production's "first aid" person. He was shocked at my condition—he was completely unaware that I'd injured myself, and was really worried that he was going to get blamed for not taking care of me right away.

Later that day, Jessica Alba, the actress who starred on the show as Max, told me how she'd hurt her neck once during a shoot and how her chiropractor totally fixed her up. "He's the best," she said. "He can do anything."

The production crew decided that they were going to bring Jessica's chiropractor to see me. My gut was telling me that it was the wrong thing to do, but I deferred to the professionals. At least someone was trying to do something.

I agreed to see the chiropractor. He came the next day and cracked my neck, which hurt so bad I almost blacked out. The level of pain was excruciating. "*Owww!* Get me up, Get me up!" I screamed.

The chiropractor just backed off—he was so scared to touch me that he didn't even try to help me up. I got so hot! I threw my feet down and pulled myself up. It hurt like hell, but I needed to get into a standing position.

"That's it, I'm done," I said and walked back to my trailer, crying in pain. Margaret the makeup lady came by with some aromatherapy spray she had—she jokingly sprayed it around like it was really going to help me. Margaret was super-nice and did her best to help me calm down.

Looking back, it's really incredible that I never stopped and said, "Get me to the hospital now!" But that's the wrestling mentality—if you're still conscious, then you keep on going. Plus, everyone was telling me it was no problem.

I continued working, doing my best to keep myself from falling apart. I was sitting on the set, stifling my pain, when the actor that was married to the woman who dropped me started acting like a total jerk. He kept making stupid jokes—belittling wrestling—and I simply didn't have the strength to acknowledge him. "Oh, come on," he said. "You're acting like you're not even having fun here."

I got so pissed. "You know what? I'm in a lot of pain right now, so shut up and leave me alone!"

He didn't even have the courtesy to say, "Sorry, I was out of line." He just didn't get it. His wife was the same way—she never even apologized for dropping me on my head. She just avoided me completely after it happened.

I shot my last scene five long days after getting dropped. After we finished, Mr. Cameron had the crew give me a hand for working hurt. Great, thanks a lot. A round of applause for working with an injury when I shouldn't have been working at all. At that point, I didn't care about anything other than going to the hotel, packing my stuff and getting the hell out of there. All I wanted was to get home and find out what was wrong.

CHAPTER 50

Perhaps the worst thing about my injury was that nobody seemed to believe or care that I was really hurt. From the second I crashed down onto my neck to when I was finally diagnosed correctly, it seemed that no one was taking me seriously. When the doctor eventually told me that my neck was broken in two places, my first reaction was, "See? Told you! I knew I wasn't just being a wimp!" Of course, a split second later, the reality sunk in and I felt my whole life come to a screeching halt.

Before that happened, I had to get out of Canada. I considered flying straight home, but I really needed to see Matt. I decided go straight to the WWE house shows in Texas.

The flight to Amarillo was really difficult. Every bump the plane took was excruciating. The person sitting next to me must've thought I was insane—I wasn't wearing a brace, so he had no way of knowing that I had a neck injury. I just sat there wincing from the pain shooting through my body.

I arrived in Amarillo and took a car to the hotel. Every little thing was such a chore, just trying to move and maneuver my body. My room was on the second floor and of course the hotel didn't have an elevator, so I had to find someone to help me carry my bags up.

Matt hadn't gotten in yet—he wasn't due to fly in until the next day. I spent that night laying on the bed with ice on my neck, just trying to numb the pain. *It's going to get better soon,* I thought hopefully.

When Matt finally got there, I felt the most profound sense of relief. Finally there was somebody that would care about what I was going though. I knew Matt would help take care of me.

We went to the arena and I found out that I was booked to be on the show. I didn't have a match—I was just going out to ringside with Matt and Jeff. There was no way I could've done anything physical. I had to hook my left hand into my belt loop for support and to keep my arm close into me.

The first people I saw when I got to the building were Steve Austin and Debra. She was all excited to see me, because we hadn't spoken since before I left for Vancouver. "How did your shoot go?" she asked, but before I could even answer, Steve said, "Is there something wrong with you?"

I told them an abridged version of the story, how I got hurt and nobody did anything to help me. Steve was totally sympathetic. "That's a load of horseshit," he said, which I thought was just so sweet.

As I walked to the locker room, everybody that saw me said, "Man, what happened to you?" Even though I was in pain, it felt so good—these people know me, they know I'm tough, and they could tell I was messed up just by seeing me walk down the hall. *These are my people,* I thought. *These are who I relate to, and this is why I don't like to leave very often.* I was glad to be home.

Arn Anderson, who's one of the WWE road agents, came over to Matt with a few suggestions about how to get me involved in the finish of the mat. "Are you crazy?" Matt said, but Arn didn't know that I was hurt. After he heard what had happened, he was very sympathetic—he could relate

to what I was going through, having had his neck operated on and then having nerve damage as a result of the surgery.

When it came time for the match, I went out there and held my hand in my belt the whole time. I had to walk up the steel stairs just to get in the ring. I was hurting, but I felt so much better being back with WWE.

After the two house shows in Amarillo and Odessa, we took a charter flight to Texas A&M University for *Raw*. The landing was rough—I had to bite my lip to keep from screaming because my neck hurt so bad.

Kane had torn a bicep lifting weights before the Odessa show, so WWE trainer Chris Brannan arranged for us both to see a local doctor. He took X-rays and had me move my head as much as I could, which wasn't very much.

"It doesn't appear that anything's broken," he said. "It's probably just swollen."

He prescribed a Medrol Dose pack, which I understand is an oral steroid anti-inflammatory. You take six pills the first day, then five the next day, four the next, and so forth. Steve Austin had actually told me that that was what the doctor would prescribe—"I'm no doctor, but I'm thinking one of those Medrol Dose packs will suck the inflammation right out of you."

That night on *Raw,* as The Coach interviewed me in the locker room about Matt's upcoming Pay-Per-View match with Brock Lesnar, Paul Heyman—who was Brock's "agent"—came barging in.

"Brock is either going to play nice or rough with Matt depending on how she plays with me," he said, sneaking a pair of my panties into his pocket. I slapped his face, which took every bit of strength that I had.

Even though I was a shell of my usual self, I went out with the Hardyz for their match with Booker T and Goldust. After it ended, Paul E. came out onto the stage with my suitcase. He opened it up and started tossing my stuff out into the crowd. When Matt ran up to stop him, Brock came out and gave him an F5.

It was actually my real suitcase and my real clothes that Paul E. was tossing out there. I was told that they were going to get a bag from the prop department, but it was such a hectic day that when the time came for the show to start, the production people said, "Oh, we'll just use yours."

Paul E. was pretty careful about throwing most of my things towards the area just off the stage before the seats start. During the break, I went to Nicky, the crew guy who usually brings back peoples' ring jackets or Stone Cold's vests or whatever. "That stuff that Paul E. was throwing around was my real clothes," I said. "If you could please try to get back as much as possible, I'd be really grateful."

I was having such a miserable time, the last thing I needed was to lose all my clothes. Fortunately, Nicky was able to get most of my stuff back to me.

The Medrol Dose pack cut the swelling around my spine, and over the next few days, I started to feel a bit better. On a scale of one to ten, the pain went down from an eleven to around six.

On Friday, we had a house show at Nassau Coliseum on Long Island. During the afternoon I went and got an MRI done. The intern who administered the test looked at it and told me that he didn't think it looked too bad—as far as he could tell, it was just a herniated disk. "I really don't think it's anything to be concerned about," he said.

He suggested that I see an orthopedist who could help me rehab my injury. Since I was feeling better from the Medrol, I took him at his word. That night at the show, Steve Austin asked me how my appointment went. "Did you get your MRIs?" he said. "Let me see 'em."

He held them up to the fluorescent lights and agreed that they looked alright, again noting that he wasn't a doctor—he was just someone with some experience in neck injuries. "Okay," Steve said, "that'll be a ten dollar co-pay and a case of beer."

The *Backlash* Pay-Per-View was in Kansas City on Sunday night. I had an eight A.M. appointment with an orthopedist in St. Louis the next morning, so rather than taking the charter flight with everybody else, Matt and I had to drive straight from the Pay-Per-View. It was a pretty long haul—we made it to the hospital just in time for the appointment.

Based on what the radiology intern had told me, I assumed the orthopedist was just going to give me some rehabilitation exercises and that would be that. But after looking at the MRI and speaking to the actual radiologist, he told me that the situation was very different than I'd been led to believe. "The radiologist thinks you might've left there thinking your injury isn't as severe as it actually is," the orthopedist said. "We're seeing some possible cracks in your neck, so we've made an appointment for you to get a CAT scan."

The appointment wasn't until late in the afternoon, and I had an autograph session scheduled for lunchtime. I called Ann Russo Gordon in Talent Relations and told her the situation. "If you didn't want to do the autograph session, it would be perfectly understandable," she said, but I hate blowing those things off—people often travel long distances to attend them—so Matt and I went and did it together.

From there we went to the arena to check in before my CAT scan. I told Steve and Debra what was going on and he apologized for his "misdiagnosis" the other day.

The CAT scan revealed the truth at last—I had three complete breaks

I had three complete breaks and a ruptured disc between my C6 and C7 vertebrae.

and a ruptured disc between my C6 and C7 vertebrae. We went back to the orthopedist, who suggested that I should go to the hospital and speak to a neurosurgeon—let's call him "Dr. Morriss."

"Dr. Morriss is an excellent doctor," I was told, "but he's in surgery and won't be able to see you until tonight."

Matt had to race back to the Savvis Center to face Brock in the opening *Raw* match, so I had dinner by myself at Chevy's, my favorite sit-down Mexican restaurant. I was so unhappy—I was all alone, totally exhausted, and starting to get nervous.

I went to the hospital and explained my situation, that the orthopedist wanted me to see

Dr. Morriss, but he was in surgery and that I should wait for him. The nurse went ahead and checked me into the hospital, which turned out not to be the best idea. But what did I know? Except for being born, I'd never even been in a hospital!

Matt showed up with Chris Brannan at around eight-thirty—he hurried over after his match and was still in his ring gear. After doing all kinds of paperwork, I was finally brought up to a room where we watched the rest of *Raw* on one of the hospital's pay channels.

Matt hadn't eaten anything all day, but was worried that if he went to the cafeteria, that would be when the surgeon would show up. "Go get something to eat," I said. "I'll just call you on your cell phone if he comes."

Matt and Chris left and I went to use the bathroom. Just as I put my hand on the door, Dr. Morriss came in with four residents in tow. "I'd like to talk to you," he said. "If you could please sit down."

"Alright, let me just go to the bathroom first."

"No, I need to talk to you now. Please have a seat."

I was turned off right away—I didn't care how good a doctor this guy was, he was just plain rude. I sat down and he began explaining the extent of my injury to me.

"Your neck is completely unstable," he said. "There's a very distinct chance that the slightest mishap—a sneeze or even walking into the bathroom—could cause you to become paralyzed."

Obviously, I was shocked and not a little bit scared. "Are you sure?" I asked.

"I'm recommending that you have emergency surgery as soon as possible," Dr. Morriss said. "The earliest I'm available is four tomorrow."

I was trembling as he explained the procedure to me—he would open me up from the front and the back, put a metal plate on both sides of my neck, throw some metal wiring in between the two and stitch me right back up.

"It's very simple procedure," he said, "with a recovery time of approximately three months."

As he was telling me all this, Matt came back from the cafeteria. Once he was brought up to speed, Matt asked if it was absolutely the only option. "We're WWE wrestlers," he said. "We have a regular neurosurgeon in San Antonio, Dr. Lloyd Youngblood, that has operated on a number of wrestlers' neck injuries. I'm not sure, but I think he has a very specific procedure that allows us to continue wrestling after getting this kind of surgery."

"I don't care if you're a professional wrestler or a schoolteacher," Dr. Morriss said. "The procedure is the same no matter what. My recommendation is for you to have surgery tomorrow. Until then, you should not leave this bed, not even to go to the bathroom—if you have to pee, use a bedpan. I don't want you to move anymore than using the call button to get the nurse."

I was just blown away—I'd been walking around in horrible pain for three long weeks and now, all of a sudden, it was a life-threatening emergency? Something just didn't feel right.

"I'll be honest," I said. "I'm not sure what I'm going to do."

"What do you mean you're not sure what you're going to do?" he said.

"I really think I need to get a second opinion from Dr. Youngblood."

"He is going to tell you the same thing I'm telling you. Your neck is broken. It's simply not stable, and any movement that you make is endangering you further."

"So you're telling me that all this time I've been walking around and doing stuff I've just been lucky?"

"That's right," he said. "You're extremely lucky. I don't know how you got up off the ground in the first place."

Dr. Morriss said that even if he did release me from the hospital, getting on a plane to see Dr. Youngblood in San Antonio would put me at extreme risk. The only way he could even imagine my leaving the hospital was if he put me in a surgical halo, which is a painful procedure in itself, and would leave horrible scars above my eyebrows. Plus, he pointed out that no plane would allow me to fly with a halo on because I'd be too much of a liability.

It was just the most awful feeling. This unbelievably abrasive doctor that I didn't know was basically telling me that I was trapped in his hospital until I allowed him to perform surgery on me. The other possibility was that I could end up paralyzed for the rest of my life. I was in a very vulnerable state and I needed somebody to help me make this decision. I turned to Matt and Chris—"I want to talk to Steve Austin."

Steve had been so supportive and he knew a lot about Dr. Youngblood's surgery, having gone through it himself. Matt called the arena and had someone find him. I got on the phone and started telling him what was going on—"This doctor says I'm going to have to have emergency surgery and I can't go to the bathroom and I have to use a bedpan . . ."

My voice began to crack. Steve could tell I was on the verge of losing it.

"Hey, hey. Hold on now," Steve said. "We're just two people here. Let's just talk like two people. Crying isn't going to solve anything."

Steve doesn't have much truck with any girly crying, but his attitude was really supportive. He really helped to calm me down and even make me smile a little bit.

"Let me talk to this doctor," he asked. "Let's get to the bottom of this."

I'd been walking around in horrible pain for three long weeks and now, all of a sudden, it was a life-threatening emergency? Something just didn't feel right.

Matt handed the phone to Dr. Morriss.

"Who is this I'm talking to?" he asked, thinking it was going to my mother or something.

"It's Stone Cold Steve Austin," I said.

Clearly that meant zero to this guy. He just made a weird face and said, "Hello."

Dr. Morriss explained the same thing to Steve that he'd explained to me. Then he handed the phone back and said, "Look, when are you going to know what you want to do? You need to make a decision as soon as possible."

"I don't know," I said, "but I'll let you know."

The doctor left and I got back on with Steve. "So, what do you think?"

"I'm not a doctor," Steve said, "but you've worn your pain on your belt loop this far. You've been walking around, you've been dragging your bags, you've been going from city to city. My instincts are telling me that one more day and one more flight is not going to paralyze you."

That was exactly what I needed to hear. Steve saying that to me made it all seem as clear as day. I'd probably taken ten flights in seventeen days—one more probably wasn't going to make a difference.

I decided that I wanted to get out of the hospital as soon as possible. At the same time, I was confused as to whether or not I could check myself out of there—the doctor made it sound like I was some kind of prisoner!

"You're a consenting adult of sound mind,"

"He's not going to bullshit you," Steve said. "He understands what you do for a living and he doesn't do surgery unnecessarily. Trust me on this, he's going to fix you up."

Matt said. "They can't stop you from leaving if that's what you want to do."

By this time, Dr. Morriss had gone home for the night, so Matt went and got the resident who had done the preliminary examination when I got there. I explained that I wanted to leave and he was good enough not to fight me on it.

"Just for the record, I don't agree with your decision," he said, "Are you planning to go elsewhere to get this problem taken care of?"

"Yes," I said. "I'm going to see another specialist in San Antonio."

"Good. I just needed to hear that so that I can sleep tonight."

He gave me the paperwork to fill out, making me repeat several times that I understood that I was leaving the hospital despite a surgeon's firm recommendation to stay, and that the possible consequences of my leaving were paralysis and death.

"Okay," he asked as I filled out the endless release forms, "so if you leave, what could the consequences be?

"Paralysis and death," I replied. It was just legal mumbo jumbo to protect the hospital from any potential malpractice suits.

Before I left, the resident gave me a Philadelphia collar to protect my neck—it's a hard rubber collar that restricts cervical spine flexion, extension and rotation. Not only was it uncomfortable, it came all the way up to my chin, which meant that I couldn't chew gum—and I'm a big gum chewer!

We finally left the hospital and went to the Marriott out by St. Louis International Airport. I was still pretty freaked out by everything that had been going on, but once I was settled into our room, I began to relax. I felt like I was home—the rooms may change appearance, but hotels are my home on the road.

Matt called Steve to tell him what we were doing, and Steve told us to go straight to San Antonio in the morning to see Dr. Youngblood. He was so cool—he said that if we couldn't get a flight, we could have his and Deb's seats and they'd just catch a later plane home.

"If you can get on our flight," Steve said, "we'll go over to the doctor's office with you."

He made Dr. Youngblood sound like a million dollars. "He's not going to bullshit you," Steve said. "He understands what you do for a living and he doesn't do surgery unnecessarily. Trust me on this, he's going to fix you up."

Listening to Steve put Dr. Youngblood over, I really felt sure that I'd made the right decision. "Screw that Dr. Morriss," I said to Matt. "That guy was an asshole! I'm going to go see Dr. Youngblood and everything's going to be okay!"

CHAPTER 51

I honestly don't know how I could've gotten through this whole experience without Matt by my side. He was everything I could have possibly wanted from a boyfriend in this set of circumstances. He was calmer and more levelheaded than most people would've been.

At the same time, I knew he was very affected by it. Matt knew he had to be supportive and be my rock, but I could see that he was upset and deeply concerned about me.

There are times when Matt's practical nature can be a pain in the ass. Sometimes, if I'm having a crappy day, I just want him to say, "You're right, Amy, that does suck." But he's so rational and reasonable—instead of showing sympathy, he'll offer advice on how to fix things, even if that's not I what I want to hear at that particular moment.

On the other hand, there's nobody I'd rather have as my support system when there's a legitimate crisis going on. Matt was there for me one hundred percent and then some.

We flew to San Antonio first thing in the morning—the WWE office was able to get us onto the same flight as Steve and Deb. I was a little nervous during takeoff and landing, because those were the two things the doctor had warned me about.

While we traveled, the office arranged for an afternoon appointment with Dr. Youngblood. Steve and Debra took Matt and I out to lunch at Luby's Cafeteria and then we went to the doctor's office.

Dr. Youngblood was exactly as Steve had described him—he talked to me like a person, not sparing any gruesome details, but with a much better bedside manner than Dr. Morriss.

"It's true that you could've been paralyzed," he said, "though the chances of that happening were much greater during the days after your accident. Since you've been walking around, the muscles in your neck have strengthened up to support you and to help compensate for what's happened."

He explained that paralysis wasn't entirely out of the question but that it would probably take a fall down a flight of stairs for that to happen. Then he told me about the surgery he was recommending—he would go in through the front, which meant that he wouldn't have to cut into any muscles. Once you cut the muscles away from the bone, they're never quite as strong again.

He would only put a metal plate on the front, so that when I wrestled again, I'd be able to bump on my neck and back. "Considering how unstable your neck is, most doctors would probably have put plates in front and back," he said. "My way might take a little longer to heal, but in the long run, it will be as healthy as if I'd done both."

Dr. Youngblood appreciated the fact that I wasn't even close to ending my career. He wanted to make sure that I was able to get back to where I wanted to be—in the wrestling ring, taking bumps and making the crowds pop. He was careful to explain that there were no guarantees, but the probability of my wrestling again was pretty good.

The next available surgery time was a week later. He gave me a prescription for a more comfortable cervical collar and gave me a rundown

I was pretty emotional throughout all of it. I did a lot of crying that day.

of things to do, which was basically nothing—no lifting anything more than five pounds, no driving, no working out, and so forth.

"If you're uncomfortable with waiting a week and want to get this done immediately, I'll squeeze you in tomorrow," he said.

I told him that the next week would be fine. He seemed so calm about it, that I figured I could trust him. It's not like he was asking me to wait a month. What was another week at that point?

Before I left San Antonio, Dr. Youngblood had me do all kinds of presurgery things, like chest X-rays and EKGs, not to mention filling out tons of paperwork. I was pretty emotional throughout all of it. I did a lot of crying that day.

We had to travel from office to office, floor to floor, giving blood and taking various tests. At one point, the elevator opened onto the main lobby area of the medical center and there were a ton of fans hanging around waiting for me. I guess the buzz had spread that Matt and I were there. As I was walked slowly through the crowd, the people yelled, "Lita! Hey Lita!"

I turned to Matt and said, "I really can't deal with this right now."

He signed some autographs, saying, "I don't think Lita feels really good right now, sorry."

This woman came over to me and said, "I'm so sorry, do you want anything? Can I get you a chair? Would you like any water?"

"No thanks," I said quietly, "I'm fine."

"Okay," she said. "I don't mean to impose, but my daughter is just such a big fan . . ."

"No. Sorry."

I was in no mood to sign autographs. The nerve of some people really blows me away. I always try to go out of my way to do the right thing by the fans, but there are times when they're not equally considerate about my feelings.

As luck would have it, this woman kept showing up in every office I had to go to. She kept trying to chat and make friends, so I gave her the autograph just to shut her up. I hate to be rude, but I just wanted nothing to do with anybody.

Matt and I finally flew home to North Carolina that night. The rest of the week was rough—I had to come to grips with the reality of my situation. I was going to be having major surgery and I was going to be out of work for a year at the very minimum.

When I flew back to San Antonio, I was feeling pretty positive. My state of mind was very gung ho, like, "Okay, let's do this thing."

I wasn't thinking about the long term—I just wanted to get through the surgery. I knew there were risks involved and I just wanted to wake up after the operation and find out that everything had gone okay. I wasn't thinking about wrestling whatsoever. Obviously my goal was to get back in there, but I also know that there are a lot more important things in life than wrestling.

Matt was supposed to go to England for house shows, but WWE was nice enough to allow him to go a day later so that he could be with me for the surgery. Dr. Youngblood's office hooked us up with a special hospital suite. It's just like a hotel suite, only there's a hospital bed in one room, then a separate family room with a pull-out couch. It's nice, because your loved one can actually spend their time there with you.

My mom flew in to be there for the surgery, so she stayed in a hotel for the two nights that Matt was there. Then she joined me at the hospital for the next couple of nights.

My surgery was first thing in the morning—I had to wake up and scrub down with an antibacterial solution called Betadyne, concentrating on the areas where Dr. Youngblood would be cutting. The nurses came for me at around six-thirty and wheeled my bed to the waiting area outside the operating room. My mom and Matt sat there with me, but we didn't really talk much at all. I was certainly in no mood to chitchat or make small talk.

Dr. Youngblood came in and said, "Good morning. How are you doing?"

"Ready to go," I replied.

They hooked my IV tube with an anesthetic they called the "Methodist

Obviously my goal was to get back in there, but I also know that there are a lot more important things in life than wrestling.

margarita"— the name of the hospital was Methodist Hospital. After a few minutes, the nurse asked, "Do you feel it yet?"

"Not really," I said. "I feel like I just did two shots of tequila back to back but that's all."

Of course, as soon the words left my mouth, I got pretty loopy. They began wheeling me to the operating room—my mom and Matt walked alongside me as far as they would allow.

As they brought me into the operating room, one single tear ran down my cheek. They put me onto the table and the last thing I remember seeing was the bright lights overhead.

The surgery consisted of Dr. Youngblood cutting open my neck and moving everything aside to get to my spine. Then he pulled out the ruptured disc and replaced it with some bone that he extracted from my hip. After that, he slapped on a metal plate to reinforce everything, put a couple of screws in, and sewed me back up.

They actually taped the whole procedure to show on WWE TV. I was given the raw footage and what freaked me out most was seeing Dr. Youngblood turning this two-foot-long screwdriver, twisting those screws into my vertebrae——they looked just like regular screws that you could buy at any old hardware store! It amazed me to think that they were actually inside my neck, holding the plate in place!

The surgery took a little over three hours

and as far as anyone could tell at the time, it was a resounding success. There was no way to tell if my neck was going to actually be strong enough for me to wrestle again, but as far as Dr. Youngblood was concerned, the surgery went absolutely as planned.

When I came to, I was in the recovery room. As I woke up, I heard the nurse saying, "Okay, you're all done."

I wiggled my fingers and toes to see if everything was cool, then went right back to sleep. They wheeled me back to my room where I snoozed a while longer. I woke up and heard Matt talking on his cell to Scotty 2 Hotty—he was having neck surgery with Dr. Youngblood the following week and called to see how I was doing.

"Give me the phone," I said. I was still a little loopy, but I wanted to say hi. "You're going to be just fine, kid," I told him.

I also spoke to Steve and Debra that night. "Are you doing your breathing exercises?" Steve asked, referring to these exercises that the nurses make you do in order to be sure that there are no side effects from the anesthesia. It's just one of those things that you would never know about unless you've had the surgery. It was like Steve and I were part of a little club. We'd shared an experience that only a few people can understand.

In addition to the breathing exercises, one of the most important things I had to do after the surgery was get out of bed and walk around as

I wiggled my fingers and toes to see if everything was cool, then went right back to sleep.

much as I could in order to keep from getting blood clots in my legs. I had to wear these elasticized support tights which compress the muscles and increase the circulation. I cruised around the floor with my IV attached to my arm—you have to have a constant flow of antibiotics after any serious operation.

I hated having the IV attached to me. I had to drag it around the floor as I took my laps around the hall. It was at a snail's pace, but I tried to get as many laps in as possible.

Amazingly, I wasn't in all that much pain. There was a button that I could push for Demerol, but the anti-inflammatory they were giving me—Toradol—has analgesic properties, and that cut a good chunk of pain I was feeling.

The nurse took my IV out sometime in the middle of that first night. The next day Matt and I took a walk around the hospital grounds. We didn't go very far and we couldn't go very fast, but it was nice just going outside and getting some fresh air.

Dr. Youngblood told me that Chris Benoit walked fifty stairs the day after his neck surgery. I told Matt and my mom that I had to do the same thing—in fact, I was determined to break his record. That afternoon, when my mom took Matt to the airport to go to England, I went to the stairwell and very slowly walked fifty-two stairs. It felt great—it gave me a real sense of accomplishment.

Three days later, Dr. Youngblood said that I was allowed to leave the hospital. For some reason, hospitals make you sit in a wheelchair when you check out—I hated that! I can't stand feeling like a cripple, especially considering the fact that I was walking just fine.

I was sitting in the wheelchair, waiting for my mom to bring the car around, when my cell phone rang—it was Vince McMahon, calling to check up on me.

"How you doing, pal?" he said.

"I'm okay, Vince," I said. "I'm in a wheelchair, getting ready to check out of this place. I'll tell you one thing, though—Benoit did fifty stairs the second day, but I did fifty-two."

That cracked Vince up. "Atta girl," he laughed. "I'll have to rib him about that one!"

My mom and I went from the hospital to the Hampton Inn out by the airport, where we stayed until our flight back to North Carolina the next day. That night I started feeling pretty lousy—the bed wasn't very comfortable, I had pillows piled up behind me to support my neck. Then my mom started snoring real bad, so I took an extra pain pill, which gave me a

nasty stomach ache. I laid there, thinking, *I screwed up. I should've stayed in the hospital one more day.*

At the same time, I was determined to be just as tough as any of the people who've had Dr. Youngblood's neck surgery—Stone Cold, Benoit, Rhyno. They're a bunch of tough S.O.B.s and I was going to hang with them.

Before my flight the next morning, I was visited by Funaki and his new baby—he lives in San Antonio, but couldn't make it to see me while I was in the hospital.

"I have two problem," he told me over the phone. "One is the dryer—pow pow pow."

"It's broken?"

"Yes, dryer broken," Funaki agreed. "And my wife dance classes."

"Okay, Funaki," I said. "Just come see me at the hotel on Friday then."

He was very cute—he brought me a box of cookies and I took pictures with his little baby before I left for my flight. My mom and I didn't get home to Sanford until ten-thirty that night. Her flight home to Atlanta was early the next morning, and by Saturday afternoon, I was all alone.

It was right about then that my tough façade finally cracked and I lost it altogether.

It was right about then that my tough façade finally cracked and I lost it altogether.

CHAPTER 52

My first day at home was incredibly difficult — my mom had left, Matt was still in England. I'm not the kind of person who can't handle being on my own, but that day, I felt lonelier than I've ever been in my life.

Matt called that evening to see how I was hanging in. "What did you do today?" he asked.

"I watched TV," I said, "and I washed the padding in my neck brace . . ."

I barely got the sentence out before I broke down and started bawling. I think that was the moment where I first digested what had happened to me, what the next year ahead of me was going to entail.

Up to that point, I had maintained a very positive mindset, saying, "No problem. This is just something I have to get through." Matt was pretty taken aback by my crying—he was five thousand miles away and there was nothing he could do to help me.

That phone call marked the beginning of my dark period. For the next few months, I felt helpless and depressed in a way that I'd never experienced before. Nothing had ever happened to me before that had completely stopped me dead in my tracks.

I felt very out of my body emotionally as well as physically. I'm an incredibly self-reliant person and when I had that self-reliance taken away, I had to become somebody new.

I was in a deep emotional funk for a good three months after the surgery. I basically just wanted to be left alone. I kept my phone unplugged most of the time, because I really didn't want to talk to anyone. There were a lot of people that sincerely wanted to wish me well, but I wasn't ready to make surface-level small talk—"Hey, thanks for calling!"

I just wanted time to pass. It was very hard to sleep with the collar on, so I would stay up most of the night watching bad television, just to get myself as tired as possible. I'd finally fall asleep at six in the morning, then wake up in the late afternoon.

That was actually the best time of the day for me, because *Trading Spaces* was on TV. Before I got hurt, I barely watched any TV because I was on the road so much. I'd always heard how house moms have their "shows"—well, this was the first time I ever had my shows. Even though they aggravated me, I'd find myself watching all the stupid dating shows, like *Blind Date* and *The 5th Wheel* and *Change of Heart*. I also would watch MTV and VH1 shows like *Behind the Music* and *I Love the '80s*, but my absolute favorite show was *Trading Spaces*.

For those of you who've never seen it, the concept of *Trading Spaces* is simple—two neighbors get to decorate a room in each other's house with the help of a decorator and a carpenter. The first time I watched was late one night—there was a family who needed a comfortable space where the kids could play. Their neighbors put together this very cool ultra-contemporary family room and as I watched, I thought, *Oh my God, they're going to hate it!*

I couldn't help myself—I had to stay up to see what happened. I had to see the looks on the family's faces when they saw their new room. From that point on, I was hooked. I watched it as often as possible. After getting injured and being trapped in my house, *Trading Spaces* became one of the few bright spots in my daily routine.

It turned out that I wasn't alone—*Trading Spaces* is a major cult show with a really broad audience. There have been times where it's come up in

Me and my angel.

conversation and people that I never would've expected to watch it are big fans. *Trading Spaces* devotees have an instant bond—you can discuss your favorite designer on the show or how much you both like Ty Pennington, the show's cute carpenter. It's like the wrestling of home décor!

I've also found *Trading Spaces* to be inspiring—I've gotten ideas for my own house from watching the show. Sometimes they work, sometimes they don't. I've got a number of half-finished projects going. There's one wall that I started to paint but have only gotten as high as my arm can reach, because I'm hesitant about standing on a ladder. I'm still nervous about falling from things, so the paint only goes up about six-and-a-half feet. It's funny—it doesn't bother me at all. I've actually grown used to the unfinished way it looks!

In addition to *Trading Spaces*, there are two shows on Animal Planet that I try not to ever miss—*Animal Cops* and *Animal Precinct*. Of the two, *Animal Precinct* is the better show—it's about the ASPCA's Humane Law Enforcement Department, the law enforcement group in New York City devoted to investigating crimes against the city's animal population. They work together with the NYPD to bust people for animal cruelty. It's great—they kick down people's doors then take the abused animals back to the shelter and adopt them out.

It's a great show because it shows people what's really going on out there as far as the kind of tough job animal control officers are doing every day. It's also created real interest in the ASPCA—I was in New York recently and had a day off so I decided to see if I could maybe volunteer for the afternoon. When I called, the ASPCA volunteer line said, "If you've seen *Animal Precinct* on Animal Planet, please press five."

Since I was stuck in the house with not much to do, my diet went all to hell. I'd always taken good care of myself as far as eating right and exercising regularly, but I was so blue sitting on the couch, one of my only comforts was eating junk food. I was able to go back to things that I hadn't eaten in years.

Some junk food junkies get into fried things or bags of chips, but for me it's all about my sweet tooth. I love cakes and cookies and sweetened cereals—I can eat Little Debbie snack cakes for days! Suffice to say, my carb intake went up considerably in the months following my surgery.

The highlight of my week was when Matt would come home for his two days off. He still had his life to deal with, so I'd drive around with him as he went about his various errands.

After two months, I began to drive again, which at least gave me some freedom as far as things like going and getting my own groceries. I was still wearing my hard collar, which made driving pretty dangerous—I

I'm still not entirely out of the darkness—it's not so much depression as it is resentment and anger towards the circumstances of my injury.

couldn't turn my head to see what was coming from my left or my right. I had a few choice locations that were easily navigable, like Matt's house or the gym.

I had to wear the hard collar for a longer time than most people—four of the longest months ever. The reason I had to wear it for so long was because in addition to the disc damage, I had three broken bones. It takes at least six months for bones to set properly. The collar effectively served as a cast to keep my neck still and straight as much as possible so that the cracks in my neck could heal.

I wasn't allowed to do much of anything except for walking. If the weather was nice, I'd walk around the length of my neighborhood. When Matt was around, I'd go with him to the gym and walk on the treadmill for however long it took him to do his workout.

I actually hated going to the gym, because everyone would stare at me in my hard collar. It wasn't because they recognized me as Lita—it was more like they pitied me. Plus, the little amount of working out that I could do—walking on the treadmill, lifting two-pound weights—started to depress me almost as much as not doing anything at all. All it would do was remind me that I was hurt and couldn't do anything else.

Arn Anderson—who knew a thing or two about neck surgery—asked me how I was doing and I told him how frustrated I was. "I just can't do a whole lot," I said. "All I can do is walk and use five-pound weights. I know I should look at the bright side and be thankful to even be able to lift that much, but it's pretty aggravating."

"I hear you," he said. "The thrill of walking wears off after a while."

That summed up my mindset exactly. I didn't want to hear about how lucky I was. I was feeling very fragile and very broken.

I found myself getting angrier and angrier with people. It never ceases to amaze me how rude people can be. I'd be out to dinner with Matt and strangers would come over and say, "Hey, do you want me to beat him up for you?"

It made me so mad—they're joking as if Matt had done this to me, when the truth was that he was the only person in my life that was there when I needed him. I know that no one could know that, and that they were just trying to be friendly, but I couldn't find anything even remotely funny about my condition.

I'm still not entirely out of the darkness—it's not so much depression as it is resentment and anger towards the circumstances of my injury. What happened, happened. There's nothing I can do to change that. As for my future, I'm not worried—I'm going to get back in the ring.

The problem is that I retain a lot of bitterness about the fact that so many people avoided responsibility when it came to dealing with what happened to me. I'm not sure if I'll ever be able to entirely let go of those feelings. It's a grudge I might hold onto for the rest of my life.

A few months after my surgery, one of the WWE lawyers asked me how I felt.

"To be honest with you," I said, "I'm pretty pissed off."

"Have you spoken to anybody about this?" he asked, meaning, "Have you talked to a shrink?"

"I don't need a psychologist to tell me why I'm pissed off," I replied. "I got dropped on my head, it shouldn't have happened, and now I'm pissed off. I'm pretty sure that's a natural reaction."

I got really mad when he said that. It was just so patronizing.

I don't want to be bitter and I don't want to be resentful—I don't want to be a negative person. The more time passes, the better I feel about it. But that's only because I've got other things to deal with. I haven't come close to forgiving the people who've done me wrong.

I would never wish injury or harm on anyone but at the same time, I wish the people involved could experience just one day of what I've been going through. It's especially frustrating to me knowing that the person directly responsible, the girl that actually dropped me on my head, is continuing her life just as she did before she dropped me on my head. She didn't lose any sleep over what happened. Her life is exactly the same, whereas my life has been forever changed.

I hate to think this way, but that gets me really, really mad. Just saying it makes me feel like a whiny bitch and I don't think that's the type of person I am. But I also have to be flat-out honest with my feelings.

It might've been different if I had been treated nice, if everybody had gone out of their way to make sure things didn't happen the way they did. Then I could think, *Well, this is an unfortunate circumstance, but what are you going to do?*

But instead, I got screwed all the way around, on every possible level.

But instead, I got screwed all the way around, on every possible level.

CHAPTER 53

I began going stir crazy from spending so much time in my house, so I started going out on the road with Matt. Hanging around backstage at the house shows and TV made me feel so much better. I needed to be out of bed and back around the business again.

One month after my surgery, WWE had me out doing personal appearances—ticket on-sales, autograph sessions, and so forth. It was a way for WWE to keep me in the public eye.

Autograph sessions were especially difficult—they were just torture on my neck. Sitting there, looking up and looking down for two hours straight made my head feel like it was going to fall off my shoulders.

I started doing the appearances so soon after my surgery that my brain never fully switched off from the autopilot mode that I had to be in to survive life on the road. *Even though I'm injured,* I thought, *I still work for WWE, and part of my job is promotion for the company.*

Even though I was depressed and miserable, I agreed to every appearance they wanted me to make. Anytime I got the call, I just said, "Where and when do you need me?" I felt like the only break that I'd had was the four hours I spent on the operating table.

But the fact of the matter was that I was bored out of my mind. Doing appearances was grueling and ultimately unsatisfying, despite the fact that I know how much those things mean to the fans. I needed to come up with a way of occupying my time that would make me feel useful and productive in some way.

The problem was that I'd spent so long being immersed in wrestling that I had no clue what else I was capable of doing. I sat there on my couch thinking, *What the hell did I do before I wrestled?*

I realized there were two things that I did before I got into wrestling—working at a kennel and hanging out with musicians. Seeing how Sanford, North Carolina, is not exactly the punk rock capital of America, I decided to look into working with animals again.

The next morning, I set my alarm for the first time in weeks. I dragged myself down to the San-Lee Humane Society, a privately run, no-kill shelter located just three miles from my house. I walked in there and asked if I could help out in some way.

"Sure," the girl at the counter said. "Go ahead."

It was just that simple. San-Lee wasn't a very big facility, just twenty dogs and ten cats. I fed and watered the animals, I cleaned the cages out—anything that a kennel employee would do, I did.

The people that worked there were shocked. No volunteer ever came in and did those things. Most people just wanted to hang out with the animals, maybe walk a few dogs. But I wanted more than that. I needed to get my hands dirty.

I was just scooping dogshit out of cages, but it felt more satisfying than walking on a treadmill for forty-five minutes. Although I was still majorly depressed, I started feeling like I was doing something beneficial—for the animals and for myself.

It also felt nice to just be Amy Dumas for a change. Nobody recognized me as Lita, and if they did, they didn't say anything about it. That was great—I wasn't volunteering so that I could talk about what a cool guy The Rock is behind the scenes.

Unfortunately, within a month of my signing on, San-Lee was forced to shut down due to lack of funding. There simply wasn't enough money or local interest for them to stay in business. I tried to help them raise funds

I felt like the only break that I'd had was the four hours I spent on the operating table.

Julie.

by doing my first-ever charity autograph session in the Sanford area. We had two tents—one with animals for adoption and another where I signed autographs and took pictures with fans. It was scheduled for two hours, but the turnout was so huge that it went on for closer to four.

It was incredible, really—it rained all day, but people had no problem standing on line. Everybody was drenched, people's glasses were all fogged up. Everyone got so wet that they just said, "Oh well," and had a good time with it. Even in the tent, the ground got so flooded that my shoes got completely trashed.

Despite the weather, the day was a big success—we got five animals adopted and raised over five thousand dollars. Regrettably, that wasn't enough to keep San-Lee afloat. All the animals were trucked up to the Boston Rescue League, a long-established animal shelter with a very high adoption rate. Then we cleaned the place out and shut the doors. (The good news is that eight months later, after more fund-raising and tons of community awareness, the shelter reopened under a new name—Carolina Animal Rescue and Adoption, or CARA for short.)

Working at the shelter helped bring me out of my dark place by making me feel like I was of use again. I felt good about the work I'd done at San-Lee that I wanted to keep doing it. I was told about a new animal facility that had just opened on Highway 15-501, the Moore County Animal Center.

I wanted to get a sense of what went on there before I committed to volunteering, so I drove over there and said I was looking to adopt a dog. It looked great, clean, and well-organized, with hard-working caring people.

I decided to go for it. Because it's a county-run facility, I had to go to the local court house to register for volunteer work. A few days after I filled out the paperwork, I got a phone call from the manager, Julie Bryant, saying "Come on down."

I think they were pretty psyched about my coming to work there—not because I was Lita, but because they thought I was a great volunteer. I had so much experience from working at kennels and volunteering at other shelters, they didn't have to waste time teaching me what to do. Plus, I'd already had my rabies shots, so I could pretty much handle any animal in the place.

Working at the shelter was such an escape. When I was there, I wasn't thinking about my neck or how much time I was going to miss from my wrestling career. I was busy and I was around people that couldn't care less if and when I got back in the ring. They liked me for who I am, not because I'm on TV. That really helped me relax and come out of the dark place that I'd gotten myself into.

The staff at the shelter are a diverse and dedicated bunch of people. They remind me a lot of the motley crew I worked with at the Montrose Animal Shelter all those years ago. Animal people tend to be a little nutty—it's not glamorous and there's not a lot of money. You don't find a lot of snotty, prissy people working in kennels, which is why this kind of work is totally up my alley.

Julie has become one of my best friends—no matter where we go, people ask us if we're sisters. She always gets a big kick out of that. "No," Julie says. "I wish!"

She's an incredibly nice person, warm and outgoing. Even though her work at the shelter is so overwhelming, Julie manages to find time to have a family life as well—she's married and has a ten-year-old daughter.

Apart from the satisfaction that I get from working with the shelter, apart from the fact that it got me out of my house, it's great that I was able to make such a good, strong, personal connection.

Having such a kickass staff is the reason the shelter runs so well. The budgets for animal centers are so small. When the county delegates what money goes where, animals are always going to be at the bottom of the list. It takes motivated people to make the most of the funds they have, and to raise as much awareness as possible in order to get charitable donations from the community.

The Moore County Animal Center does very important work—they provide a wide variety of community services, from putting dogs and cats up for adoption, to doing low-cost rabies vaccinations and spaying and neutering. They also provide pet owners with AVID microchips, which stands for American Veterinary Identification Device. It's injected under the animal's skin and allows us to track lost pets and identify found ones.

Our animal control unit picks up dangerous strays and abused pets. We've won several cruelty cases in court—we've helped send people to jail for starving and mistreating their animals. We've also got a very high success rate for adopting out the cruelty cases. That's such a good feeling, finding good homes for animals who've been horribly mistreated.

Unfortunately, the pet overpopulation problem is such that we have to euthanize animals. Sad as it is, there are so many animals without homes that euthanizing has to be done, simply due to the numbers.

A private shelter can avoid euthanizing because they get to pick and choose which animals they accept. The Moore County Animal Center is county-run, so they can't refuse any animals.

Of course euthanizing is a last resort—it's usually done to the least adoptable animals. When the animal control officers bring in a stray dog or cat, there's a mandatory hold period of seventy-two hours. Unfortunately that's not always a long enough period to find an animal a home. The springtime is especially horrible—that's when so many animals are having their litters and it's just impossible to find homes for that many puppies and kittens.

The sad truth is that, regardless of the amount of animals that find good homes, there are still too many out there to make a serious dent in the population. Every person in America would have to have fourteen pets, a combination of dogs and cats, in order to get the overpopulation under control. Then the next generation would have to have seven pets each. And that's adding into consideration the idea that every one of those dogs and cats will be spayed and neutered so not to have any more litters. Let's face it—that's just not going to happen It's completely unrealistic to think of every person having fourteen animals. Therefore, we have to euthanize. It sucks, but that's how it's got to be for now.

Together, Julie and I can be very effective in increasing the public's awareness of the animal overpopulation problem. She's so smart and knowledgeable, and because of my WWE celebrity, I can be very valuable in terms of doing fund-raising and community outreach work, helping to increase public awareness of animal issues. The long-term goal is to increase both the adoption rate and the awareness of the pet overpopulation problem so that the Moore County Animal Center can become one of the few county-run no-kills.

It's very satisfying that I can take advantage of my celebrity status to benefit the animals. When I did a segment about the shelter on *WWE Confidential,* it was not only good publicity, it helped educate a lot of people about what we do. More importantly, it showed the county commissioners that there are people that care a great deal about the shelter.

If, God forbid, I was never able to wrestle again, I'd definitely want to work in the animal field. When my wrestling career does come to an end, I'm sure that's exactly what I'll do. It could be a shelter, it could be a grooming shop, it could be a boarding facility.

I have a vision of something social, where people and their pets could spend time together, like a café where you can buy dogs biscuits and have a little cup of coffee. There could be group activities for people and their pets. I used to do art projects with Cody, using his paws for paintings or making plaster moldings. I think it'd be so much fun to have a business where people and animals could do those sorts of things.

I've also thought that I could do something on Animal Planet. I've got skills as both a communicator and as an entertainer. If Slater from *Saved by the Bell* can host a show, then why not me?

In the meantime, I've begun work on my own foundation devoted to animal issues, called ADORE—Amy Dumas Operations Rescue and Education. I feel that because of my ability to reach people—including the WWE fans that share my love of animals—I'm in a unique position to raise awareness of the many pet-related issues out there. If you would like information or even to make a donation the address is: ADORE, P.O. Box 4483, Sanford, NC 27331, or log onto adoreyourpets.org.

I'd like for ADORE to be able to help provide medical care for needy animals, and help promote pet adoption. ADORE could also help shelters across America that are in need of funds or volunteers to find people who are willing to give a hand or donate money. Most importantly, I want to use ADORE to educate people on how they can do their part in the quest for there to be no more homeless pets.

Being able to do these things is unquestionably one of the best parts about being a WWE Superstar. If there has been one positive thing to come out of my injury it's that I've gotten involved with animals again. I think being an animal activist is one of the best things I've ever done with my life.

CHAPTER 54

In August, I was asked if I'd like to try doing commentary on *Velocity*. It went pretty well— I enjoyed doing it and WWE Executive Producer Kevin Dunn seemed very happy with the job I did.

When Kevin asked me how I'd feel about becoming one of the regular announcers on *Sunday Night Heat,* I was definitely interested. It made perfect sense for me to become an announcer. It was an ideal way for me to be involved in the WWE product without requiring any physicality on my part.

I liked the idea of adding another skill to my resume, the ability to do commentary. Plus, doing commentary was an opportunity to do more talking in front of the cameras—I never really got to do a whole lot of speaking as Lita, either in the ring or in pre-tapes.

I was scheduled to make my *Sunday Night Heat* debut in Houston, but the day before I left, I began regretting my decision to go back to work. I was so not ready to be around people. I didn't want to get back in the loop. I needed to relax and get better, not add stress to my life. I just felt gross about the whole thing.

When I walked into the Compaq Center, the first person I ran into was Christ Jericho. "What's up Y?" I said—I always call him "Y" for Y2J, and he always calls me "A" for Amy.

"Not much, A," he replied. "I see you're opening the show tonight."

"I am?" I said. "I thought I was just here to do commentary on *Heat.*"

"Well, that's what I saw written down in Vince's office."

I had what I think must've been a full-blown panic attack—it was hard to breathe, my stomach felt all queasy. *I'm not ready for this,* I thought.

Later, writer Brian Gewirtz explained the segment to me—I'd exchange words with *Raw* General Manager Eric Bischoff, who would then give me one of his patented Three Minute Warnings. Before Rosey and Jamal could touch me, Jeff Hardy would come down the ramp, do a quick spot, then get taken out by Rosey and Jamal. I was supposed to stay in the ring until Booker T and Goldust came down—that was my chance to escape.

I wasn't even close to comfortable with that. I was still very panicky and insecure about my neck—I didn't like being in crowds, I kept imagining someone coming up behind me, hitting me from behind and breaking my neck again.

In my head I was seeing big bodies flying everywhere, with me bouncing around in the ring. I was scared that I was going to get hurt again and for what? A silly little segment?

"I don't feel comfortable with this, Brian," I said. "There's too many people in the ring at once. I could fall, someone could inadvertently hit me getting thrown out over the top rope. I'm just real apprehensive about this whole thing."

"Don't worry," he said. "We'll go over it before the show and make sure that everybody's positioned so that there's no danger of you getting hurt."

Of course, we never did go over it—I had to tape two *Heats* at once, because I was booked for an appearance the following Monday and couldn't be at *Raw.* I came out, filmed my first *Heat,* ran back and changed my shirt, then came out again to film my second week's *Heat.* After that I had to go right back out to the ring to kick off *Raw.*

"If you had some respect for the wrestlers," I said, "then they might respect you."

The show opened with me standing in the ring with Bischoff. He reamed me out for an interview I'd given to wwe.com where I said that *SmackDown!* was a better show than *Raw,* and it sure as hell wasn't because of the talent.

Ratings had been going down and there were a lot of people laying the blame on the talent, like they weren't working hard enough or giving it their all out there in the ring. The truth is, the wrestlers bust their asses night after night after night—I couldn't say for sure who was to blame for the problems *Raw* was having, but it really bothered me that anyone would point the finger at the boys in the locker room.

I think what ended up happening was that the writing team took legitimate offence to my statement and turned it into a worked segment.

"You little bitch," Bischoff snarled. "You think you're a big star. You went to Hollywood and got yourself a broken neck. Now you've got a cushy announce job on *Heat* but otherwise you're basically worthless."

"If you had some respect for the wrestlers," I said, "then they might respect you."

Rosey and Jamal snuck into the ring and were ready to kick my ass when Jeff ran in to make the save. They beat him down pretty quickly, but then Booker and Goldie came down and they had themselves a tag match as I snuck out of there.

When I got back to gorilla, nobody said anything to me. It turned out that they weren't happy with my facials or how I interacted with

Bischoff. I'm the first to admit that I wasn't thrilled to be out there. I must've looked scared and nervous, like "Please God, I just want this segment to end without me getting hurt."

I went to Brian afterwards and told him that I wasn't interested in being interjected into storylines. I was happy to be working on *Heat,* but that was as far as I was willing to go. If they wanted me involved in wrestling angles, then I'd rather just stay home. He was pretty understanding and we agreed that that would be my final in-ring appearance for the time being.

Doing commentary was a real challenge at first, because there's no training or anything—I was just thrown in there behind the microphone. In a way, being an announcer has nothing to do with being a wrestler—it's a completely different job. It didn't matter how much wrestling I've watched over the years. I had to learn a whole new set of skills.

The commentary for *Sunday Night Heat* isn't done live—we do a couple of live head shots when the matches are taped before *Raw* goes on the air, but the actual commentary is recorded on Fridays at WWE's Stamford studios.

I had to travel to *Raw* tapings every week knowing that all I'd be doing was two ten-second on-cameras. The rest of my time was spent sitting around and observing. Being at *Raw* really broke my heart—I had to watch my friends doing something I wanted to be doing.

On Friday mornings, I'd fly up to LaGuardia and get driven to the studio. Everything would be laid out for me and The Coach—the bumpers, the graphics, the sponsor billboards. We would take a quick look at the outline, then go into in a sound booth and watch the show on little monitors, getting direction through our headsets.

That required some getting used to. Early on, I was calling a match and I heard, "Okay, fifteen seconds to bumper. Ten, nine, eight . . ."

I sat there, listening to the voice in my ear, thinking, *Okay, stop counting, I'm trying to talk.*

There were so many things I had to learn, like how to recite prewritten lines in a very precise amount of time—"You've got seventeen seconds to announce the card for the Pay-Per-View."

I also had to refrain from speaking in the backstage terminology I was used to. We were recapping the previous week's *Raw* and I made the mistake of referring to 'Taker instead of Undertaker. The producer explained the difference to me. " 'Taker hangs out backstage in the locker room," he said. "Undertaker beats people's asses."

There were usually a couple of points that we were supposed to touch on during the matches. During the first match, we'd sell the *Heat* main event. Then during the second match, we'd talk about one of the many exciting things that was scheduled for *Raw* the next night.

It was hard for me to put over things that I didn't really believe in. Enthusiastic bullshit is not one of my specialties. There were so many times when I've had to talk about "What a great match that was last Monday!" when the truth was, I didn't think it was all that. Even worse is when I had to fake interest in storylines like the Katie Vick necrophilia angle.

We had to recap the funeral parlor segment and there was some extremely silly dialogue I had read, "What a disturbing ploy, Coach! Triple H sure is a sicko!" It was close to impossible to make those lines sound convincing, but that's what the job called for, so that's what I did. They certainly didn't want me saying what I really thought, *This is the stupidest storyline I've ever seen, Coach!*

Also, I hated having to talk about *Raw* at the expense of calling the match that's going on during *Heat.* I feel that does a disservice to the hard work the wrestlers are doing in the ring. For instance, there was a match between Jeff Hardy and The Hurricane—two of my best friends—and a minute into it, Coach started saying something about what Eric Bischoff did on *Raw.*

"Forget Eric Bischoff, Coach," I said. "Check out Jeff Hardy and The Hurricane!"

Working alongside Jonathan Coachman was one of the things I enjoyed most about doing commentary. He was a big help to me every step of the way, even if there were times when I couldn't get a word in edgewise.

In the beginning, I didn't have a whole lot of confidence so I was glad that Coach would talk up a storm. At the same time, I felt very on the spot when I had to interrupt him—I felt like if I was going to say something, it had better be really good. There were any number of times when I held back, thinking, *I'm going to keep quiet. I don't want to sound stupid.*

But the longer we worked together, the more natural our rapport became. Over the eight months that I announced on *Heat,* I grew increasingly comfortable with being behind the microphone. I can definitely see myself returning to commentary in the next stage of my career. But I never really got past the idea that it was just a way of passing the time until I got back to what I really wanted to be doing—wrestling. It was frustrating as hell sometimes. I didn't want to be talking about it. I wanted to be out there in the ring doing it.

CHAPTER 55

On my twenty-eighth birthday we did *Raw* in Richmond, Virginia. Since it was within driving distance, I asked Julie if she'd like to come with me.

She had a great time. When I introduced her around, maybe thirty people said we looked like sisters. Bubba Dudley said that there's an old saying about how everybody has a twin somewhere out there in the world and that Julie and I had found ours.

Julie's not really a huge wrestling fan. She's really only watched because of Matt and me. Nevertheless, we were in catering and she got a

big kick out of seeing Ric Flair, which just goes to show how famous he is even with people who don't watch a whole lot of wrestling.

After the show, we drove back to Sanford. We were on the road when Renee called to see when I was going to be home—she needed to go back to her place and do some homework on her computer. Normally she'd spend the night with Cody, but since I was headed home, she figured that he'd only have to be alone for an hour or two.

"No problem," I told her. "Go on home and do your homework."

But fifteen minutes later, Renee called back sounding very panicky and worried. "Cody's not looking too good," she said. "He fell over trying to come in from outside. He can barely stand up, his gums are all white, and his breathing is really irregular."

I took a deep breath—I knew in my heart that this was it. It was Cody's time. He'd been diagnosed with cancer at the end of December, just after Matt and I celebrated our first Christmas in Matt's new house.

I'd actually gotten the sense that it was coming a couple of days earlier. Spring was just starting to break, so we went for a walk in the woods behind my neighborhood. I brought my digital camera with me and took a bunch of pictures of him, playing in the creek and rolling around in the field.

The next day he was in the backyard and I noticed that he was moving kind of slow. I was getting ready to go out, but when I opened the door for Cody to come into the house, he just laid there in the sun. *Oh God,* I thought. *I think this is it.*

As much as I didn't want to think about it, I knew Cody was getting ready to go. I had done some reading about losing a pet, and it said that sometimes pets will hold on longer than they really want to because they can sense that their owner is not ready for them to leave. I went out there and laid down next to Cody, petting him, saying "It's okay, Co. It's okay."

I didn't want to try and coax him up. I didn't want him to do anything he didn't want to do. I just wanted him to know that I loved him and that he didn't have to fight anymore.

We laid there for a half hour or so. Finally I got up and said, "Do you want to go inside, Cody?"

He stood up and followed me inside. He seemed a lot better than he had just a short while ago. He even ate some of his food.

Obviously, I was pretty relieved. The next day was *Raw*—before we left, Julie called to say she was running a little bit late. Since I had the extra time, I decided to take Cody on a walk. One thing about Cody—no matter how he was feeling, he always wanted to go on his walk. I grabbed the leash and said, "C'mon Cody, you want to go outside for a walk?"

He just looked at me. He didn't come over, he just stood there looking at me. I knew right then that it was going to be soon. I didn't know if it was going to be that day or even that week, but I could feel that Cody wasn't going to be with me much longer.

It tore me up, knowing that there was nothing I could do for him. I couldn't even be sure that I'd be there with him when it happened—every time I left town, I'd have bad anxiety about Cody needing me and not being able to get to him. I laid down next to him and stroked his head, telling him that I loved him and that everything was going to be alright.

So when Renee called, I wasn't shocked or surprised. I put the gas pedal down and drove home extra fast—I was so scared that he was going to go before I got back to say goodbye.

When I walked into the house, Cody didn't look good. Renee was sitting with him, saying, "See, I told you she'd be back."

Cody tried to get up and walk towards me, but he only made two or three steps before he started to wobble. I got underneath him before he collapsed and he laid there in my lap. His breathing was very labored—it sounded almost like his lungs were filled with fluid. His tongue just hung out of his mouth, his gums were as white as a ghost.

In actual fact, my Cody was already gone—he was just a shell of the dog that I loved. *This isn't what my dog looks like,* I thought. *My dog runs around and plays outside with me—he doesn't have his tongue hanging out of his mouth and can't stand up.*

I didn't want him to have to fight any more. I looked up at Julie and said, "He's ready. Can you please help him out?"

"If you're sure," Julie said.

"I'm sure,' I said, so Renee drove Julie to the shelter for the sodium phenobarbital and ketomine to put Cody to sleep.

I spent the next hour with Cody on my lap. He kept trying to get up, but I just held him and told him everything was going to be okay.

Julie called me when she got to the shelter. "I just wanted to make sure you haven't changed your mind."

"Nope," I said. "He's ready."

When Julie and Renee came back to my house, they had Ira, the head animal control officer at the Moore County shelter, with them. He's a really nice guy—unless you're someone that mistreats animals, in which case you'd better watch out.

By this time Matt had also come over. He drove straight to my place from a *SmackDown!* house show in Fayetteville. I was worried about Cody freaking out from so many people being around, but at the same time, I was glad to have my friends there with me.

It tore me up, knowing that there was nothing I could do for him.

I stroked his head as Julie gave him a little shot of ketomine to calm him down. I kept saying, "It's okay, boy. You're okay."

"Tell me whenever you're ready," Julie said.

"I don't need any more time with him," I told her. "We've had ten great years. It's his time."

I was so sad, but I tried not to cry—I wanted to be strong for him. I remember my mom telling me about when her mother was dying from cancer. Mom stayed with her for the last two weeks before she died, and while she was there, she would take my grandmother's things and say, "Look how nice this outfit looks on me, I've got a nice purse that'll match this" or "This little end table is so cute, it'll go with my furniture in the living room." My grandmother was happy because she knew her favorite items would still be around.

When Mom told me that story, I was amazed that she was able to do that. "I'd be too devastated to be that strong," I said.

"The good times I've had with my mother were already over," Mom explained. "All that was left was for me to be responsible and take care of her. No matter how hard it was for me, my obligation was to be strong for her at the end."

That's how I felt about Cody—I was determined to be brave for him. It was the least I could do after everything he'd given to me.

My body ached from crying. It was hard to breathe, I was so tense.

Finally Julie injected him with the sodium phenobarbital and within five seconds, I could see the life come out of him. His heart stopped beating and my Cody was gone.

I got a blanket and wrapped him up. Then Ira, Matt, and I carried him to the car and drove him to the shelter where someone from the Good Shepherd Pet Crematory could pick him up.

Matt and I went back home and got into bed. That's when it finally hit me. Hard. It was so quiet—I had to get my head around the idea that Cody wasn't there. I used to always hear his ID tags during the night as he adjusted himself in his bed. When I'd roll over, he'd lean his head into me for a rub on his ears. But now it was just pitch black, dead silence.

I've been very lucky—I've never really experienced the loss of a loved one. When my grandma died, I mourned for her, but because she wasn't part of my everyday life, it wasn't so painful for me to get over. It was very sad and then I found a place for her in my heart.

Whereas every single thing I did for ten years involved Cody in one way or another. He was the one constant through all the various life changes I'd had, all the places I'd lived, all the jobs I'd had. He was my best friend.

As I lay there, thinking about Cody, I started crying harder than I've ever cried in my entire life, just full-bodied hysterical sobbing and crying, I couldn't have stopped if I tried. My crying kept waking Matt up, so after a while I just crawled into Renee's bed in the guest room. Eventually, I ran out of tears—I'd cried so hard, there was nothing left in me. My whole body hurt, and somewhere around eight, I managed to fall asleep.

The alarm clock went off two hours later—Matt had to be at *SmackDown!* in Virginia Beach that night. My body ached from crying. It was hard to breathe, I was so tense. I decided the best thing would be to go with Matt to Virginia. I didn't want to be around the house by myself. Before we left, I put Cody's ID tag around my wrist, just to remind me of him.

Backstage at *SmackDown!* I stood there watching the show on the monitor. It was an odd feeling, but for the first time since becoming a wrestler, I found myself watching the show just like the fans at home. It wasn't a conscious moment, but at a certain point during the show I started breathing again. I was being entertained and stopped thinking about Cody. In other words, it did its job. I thought that was so cool—just like when we did the show after 9/11, I was reminded of what WWE is there for.

A few days after Cody passed, I made a little shrine around his urn. I gathered all my favorite pictures, including a Christmas photo I took of him wearing a cute little angel outfit, with wings and a halo. I also laid out some of the art projects we made together, like the little plaster heart with his footprint in.

I take a lot of comfort in know that when Cody passed, he was surrounded by his loved ones. That made me consider the fact that so many animals have to be euthanized because nobody loves them at all. The only people that have any compassion for them are the ones who are taking their lives from them.

Cody hung on when I needed him most—he was there for me through my injury and my surgery and my recuperation. It's almost as if he knew that I was ready to make a fresh start. He knew his job of taking care of me was done and he was giving me a clean slate to start anew.

CHAPTER 56

After *WrestleMania XIX* and *Raw* in Seattle, I flew down to San Antonio to see Dr. Youngblood. He told me that everything looked good—he didn't want me taking any major bumps, but I could begin working out in the ring again.

We scheduled another appointment for July, by which time he suggested I try taking a few full force bumps. That way he could see if they had any effect on my neck or if I needed a bit more time to heal. But as near as he could tell, I was on my way to one hundred percent medical clearance. If everything went according to plan, I could be ready to come back in time for *SummerSlam* in August.

When I told Vince what Dr. Youngblood had said, we agreed that the best course of action would be to take me off of TV altogether. Even though I'd been out of the storylines and off of *Raw* for more than a year, doing commentary on *Heat* kept me in the public consciousness. I was gone, but not really gone—for an hour every week I was there on *Heat,* telling stupid jokes and laughing with The Coach.

Vince and I both wanted my comeback to be a big deal, but how could the fans miss me if I never really left? The writers came up with the perfect solution—General Manager Eric Bischoff had been on a bit of a tear lately, firing Stone Cold Steve Austin and J.R. Why not have him fire Lita?

The following week's *Raw* was in Atlanta—what better place could there be to get fired in front of twenty thousand people than my hometown? The initial plan was for me to give the fans an update on my neck, only to have Eric Bischoff interrupt. He'd pull a clip from my *Heat* commentary where I said something about how he abuses his power and then say, "You think I abuse my power? Well, how about this—you're fired!"

Instead, they decided to work in a plug for Torrie Wilson's appearance in *Playboy* by having Eric sexually harass me and then fire me just like he'd fired Stone Cold.

Stephanie was very adamant about Eric and I rehearsing the bit before the show. I'm not known for my promo skills, so I had no problem going over the scene in advance. I think it helped me to feel a lot more comfortable out there than previous times.

Eric was really great. He was actually very shy about doing the whole perverted boss scenario. When we were rehearsing, Stephanie said, "Okay, Eric, now stroke her hair."

"No, not now," he said. "I'll do it out there."

The Coach introduced me and called me to the ring. It was especially nice to come out to the ring and be engulfed by the crowd again. I came out every week for *Heat,* but the commentary table is up by the ramp, which is very different.

I'd forgotten about how you can hear single voices in the midst of the pop. There's always some asshole shouting "You suck!" at the top of his lungs. When Eric came down, one guy yelled, "Slap him! Kick his ass!" As the segment progressed, I distinctly heard another fan screaming, "Boring! C'mon already, this is going on too long!"

That always cracks me up. *Okay Eric, let's wrap it up,* I thought, laughing to myself. *There's a guy in the second row that's bored.*

All in all, it was kind of an awkward little segment, but at the same time, I don't think anyone will remember the details when I come back—the only thing that will matter is that I haven't been around for a long period of time.

The best part of the angle is that my being fired leaves my return very open-ended—there's no way to know how, where, or when I'm coming back. Will I come back to *Raw?* Will Stephanie try to sign me to the *SmackDown!* roster? The storyline has suspense built right in, which is always a plus.

Ideally, I'd like to come back and be paired up in some way with Matt. Maybe we could be the King and Queen of Mattitude, with all the MFers doing our bidding. Shannon Moore can do my laundry, things like that.

Not that I'd mind coming back to *Raw* as a singles wrestler, fighting for the Women's Championship. Trish and Jazz and Victoria have spent the past year busting their asses in the ring. My only problem is that their characters are kind of one-dimensional. They all have their eye on the title and that's about it.

As much as I enjoy the physicality and excitement of a full-on wrestling match, I also believe that character and storylines are what keeps the fans interested and involved. No matter what happens, my goal is to come back and find the right blend of in-ring action and entertaining angles.

Of course I have a lot of work to do in order to physically prepare for my return. I need to spend an enormous amount of time in the gym, getting my body back into the condition that it was in before my injury.

I'm determined to become a better wrestler than I was before my injury. I want to take Lita to a new level, I want to see the character grow and evolve as much as I have in my real life.

Some wrestlers create characters that are complete products of their imagination, while others—like myself—are more like an exaggerated version of their true selves. It's only natural that Lita would evolve, because Amy has grown so much over the last few years.

⊰ EPILOGUE ⊱

This book came together as I worked through the most difficult year of my life—as a result, I've sometimes cast my experiences in a somewhat more negative light than I might have if I'd been happy and healthy and wrestling every night. Nevertheless, I've tried my best to be as open and honest as possible.

I've tried to live my life being as blunt and truthful as a person can be. A friend of mine and I were once talking about how that aspect of my nature has affected me. "Welcome to the consequences of honesty," he said.

He was right—being so honest definitely has had consequences in my life, sometimes positive, sometimes negative. But I don't know how to be anything else—it's my nature to be direct and candid and straight-forward, no matter what the cost.

I also wouldn't mind coming back to *Raw* as a singles wrestler, involving myself in the fight for the Women's Championship. The Women's Division has grown considerably in my absence, and it looks like I'll have a pretty long list of names to cross off, the women have really been busting their asses this past year. My only problem is that I feel women in wrestling can have multiple facets, as opposed to having tunnel vision in their fight for the title. Watching the show while I have been out, it seems the Women's Division has been fairly one-dimensional, not a whole lot of character development, just match after match, all for the title.

In one of my first interviews under WWE contract, I stated a few goals I wanted to accomplish in my career—to be the Womens Champion, be featured in a video game, and have my own action figure. Once I achieved those goals, people often asked me what I hoped to achieve next. But at that time, everything was moving so fast, I never really had a chance to stop and think about it—I just knew I wanted to keep going.

Well, being injured gave me plenty of time to consider my goals for the future. I want to:

1. *Continue to innovate the role of women in wrestling*
2. *Be featured in a comic book*
3. *Put out a new book, unrelated to wrestling, about . . . you'll just have to wait and see!*
4. *Utilize my free time by working with motivated individuals on pet overpopulation education and responsible pet ownership, with a focus on raising funds for ADORE*
5. *Keep on having fun with the gift of life!*

One thing I'm determined to do is be the best that I can be without letting myself get too overwhelmed. The experience of being injured and having everything taken away from me has made me appreciate the little things in life, so I'm resolved to not get stressed out about things that are out of my control—having to change my schedule to accommodate last-minute appearances, flight delays, luggage getting lost.

I've had an amazing journey up to this point and I look forward to continuing it. My time in WWE is still just beginning—I'm not even close to discovering how far I can go in the wrestling business.

At the same time, I want to make sure that wrestling isn't the only thing in my life. I really thought my life would be over without wrestling, but I was wrong. Being injured affirmed to me that no matter what happens, I'm strong enough to face life and come out fine. I'm not worried about the future—there are so many more things other than wrestling that I want to do. There are a lot of paths for me to take before I reach my final destination.

I remember when I first got my shoulder tattoo, people would say, "What is such a pretty girl doing with that big, ugly thing on her arm?"

As soon as I became Lita, everything changed—"That tattoo is so beautiful! Where did you get that?"

Before I was just this skater chick with this gross thing on my arm, but since I was in WWE, my tattoo was okay. I was the exact same person, but people's perceptions of who I am changed the second I started appearing on TV.

The truth is, from high school to working at the strip club to becoming a WWE Superstar, I'm still the same skater tomboy punk that I always was, only I wear more makeup now. Everything that I've experienced, everything I've done, just goes to prove one simple truth—a little attitude can take you a long way.

❧ ACKNOWLEDGMENTS ❧

I would like to thank the following people who have inspired or affected me in some way, shape, or form.

My mom and dad for bringing me into this life. Mom, I have never stopped learning and growing from you. Cody—your pride, loyalty, strength, affection, and spirit inspire me every day. Matt—thanx for coming along for the ride—it wouldn't be the same without you around. You and Jeff have given me more amazing moments—both personally and professionally—than I could have ever hoped for.

WWE and the McMahons, thank you all so much for the once in a lifetime opportunities—past, present, and future! The boys and girls on the road for busting their asses, everyone behind the scenes making the WWE the kickass company that it is. All of the wrestlers past, present, and future, who inspire me to be the best I can be. Maryland Championship Wrestling (RIP), Music City Wrestling, 7 Seconds—who positively affected me at a very impressionable time in my life. Lookout! Records, East Bay Punx, Fifteen, Atlanta Str8 Edge/HC scene, Moore County Animal Center staff, and Carolina Animal Rescue and Adoption for helping me make the most of a bad time in my life and helping me to remember my passion for animal welfare. Renee Moore, Bre Johnson, and Lauren Rungee . . . basically anyone who's path I have crossed providing me with both positive and negative life experiences, as we learn from them all. Lastly a big thank you to Margaret Clark of Pocket Books, Stacey Pascarella of WWE, and Michael Krugman—your presence and help with this project have produced a work I will always be proud of—thank you so much!

—Amy

First off, my thanks to Amy Dumas. Her openness and honesty made it a pleasure to assist her in the writing of this book.

My gratitude and respect go to Margaret Clark and all at Pocket Books, along with WWE's Stacey Pascarella.

This book would not have been possible without the invaluable assistance of Abby Royle. There aren't enough words to express my thanks.

As ever, my heartfelt appreciation goes to superagent Dave Dunton at Harvey Klinger, Inc. Much love to my family, David, Cynthia, and Michele Krugman. And of course, big ups to my usual collection of cohorts and compadres—Ken Weinstein, Keith Lyle, Jonathan Gordon, Mike Flaherty, Jason Cohen, Nevin Martell, Nick Stern, and Deb Bernardini—for putting up with me through the writing of this book. Respect!

Finally, none of this would have been worth doing were it not for the endless love and patience of my beautiful and talented tag team partner, Carrie Hamilton.

—Michael